UNDERSTANDING PROPHETIC DREAMS & VISIONS

FREQUENCY REVELATOR

Global Destiny Publishing
House (Pty) Ltd

Copyright © 2019 Frequency Revelator.

All rights reserved. No part of this book may be reproduced, stored in a retrieval system or transmitted in any form or by any means, electronic or mechanical, photographic (photocopying), recording or otherwise, without the written permission of the copyright holder.

The author has made every effort to trace and acknowledge sources, resources and individuals. In the event that any images or information has been incorrectly attributed or credited, the author will be pleased to rectify these omissions at the earliest opportunity.

Scripture quotations are all taken from the Holy Bible, the New King James Version (Authorized Version). First published in 1611. Quoted from the KJV Classic Reference Bible, Copyright © 1983 by The Zondervan Corporation

Published by the Author © Global Destiny Publishing House,

Sandton, South Africa

Website: www.globaldestinypublishers.com

Email: frequency.revelator@gmail.com

Phone: 0027622436745/ 0027785416006/0027797921646

Book layout and cover designed by Frequency Revelator

for Global Destiny Publishing House

OTHER 50 ANOINTED BOOKS PUBLISHED BY APOSTLE FREQUENCY REVELATOR:

How to Become a Kingdom Millionaire

Deeper Revelations of the Anointing

The Realm of Power to Raise the Dead

How to Operate in the Realm of the Miraculous

The Realm of Glory

New Revelations of Faith

Unveiling the Mystery of Miracle Money

The Prophetic Dimension

The Realm of the Spirit: A Divine Revelation of the Supernatural Realm

The Prophetic Move of the Holy Spirit

The Ministry of Angels in the World Today

Throne Room Prayers: The Power of Praying in the Throne Room

7 Dimensions of the Supernatural Realm

Divine Rights and Privileges of a Believer

Keys to Unlocking the Supernatural

The Dynamics of God's Word

7 Supernatural Dimensions of Financial Prosperity

Spiritual Laws and Principles of the Kingdom

Rain of Revelations Daily Devotional Concordance

Practical Demonstrations of the Anointing

Understanding Times And Seasons In God's Calendar

How To Defeat The Spirit Of Witchcraft

The Practice Of God's Presence

21 Ways Of How To Hear God's Voice Clearly

How To Activate And Fully Exercise The Gifts Of The Spirit

The Prophetic Significance Of Gold Dust Silver Stones, Diamonds And Other Precious Stones

Deeper Revelations Of The Five-Fold Ministry

The Anatomy And Physiology Of The Anointing

Understanding Prophetic Dreams And Visions

Deeper Revelations Of The Glory Realm

The Power Of The Apostolic Anointing

The Anointing, The Mantle & The Glory

The Power of Speaking In Tongues

Miracles, Signs And Wonders

The Essence of Worship

Rain of Fire

Healing Rains

The Realm Of Love

The Revelation Of Jesus Christ

The Second Coming Of Jesus Christ

CONTENT

Acknowledgements

Chapter One: Understanding The Realm Of Dreams And Visions

Chapter Two: The Prophetic Significance Of Dreams And Visions

Chapter Three: The Seven Different Types And Categories Of Dreams

Chapter Four: Understanding The Anatomy And Physiology Of Dreams And Visions

Chapter Five: The Four Dimensions Of Prophetic Dreams And Visions

Chapter Six: Interpretation Of Dreams And Visions

Chapter Seven: Dream Interpretation Practicals

Chapter Eight: Dream Activation: How To Activate Your Dreams

Chapter Nine: Deeper Revelations Of Prophetic Dreams And Visions

Chapter Ten: The Four Realms Of Dreams

Chapter Eleven: Understanding Prophetic Visions

Chapter Twelve: The Prophetic Dream Dictionary

Author's Profile

ACKNOWLEDGEMENTS

This publication is primarily dedicated to the Holy Ghost, who is the author and the finisher of the deep revelations encapsulated therein. This insightful, refreshing, profound and biblically sound revelation awakens the believer to the reality of the times and seasons in God. It is chiefly the Holy Ghost who trained me in matters of operating in the deeper realms of the Spirit, hence it is my passion that the reader will see Him throughout the pages of this book and not any man.

I would like to express my deep and unparalleled gratitude to Prophet Alph Lukau for global forensic prophecy; Prophet Maphosa for a higher dimension in the prophetic, Dr. Peter Tan of Eagle Vision Ministry for his anointed teachings on the supernatural; Pastor Chris the President of the Believers' Love World International Ministry for his deep revelations on the ministry of the Holy Spirit and Pastor Benny Hinn of the World Healing Centre Church, who have immensely coached me in the direction of moving and operating in the deeper realms of the Holy Spirit. I would like to express my deepest and most heartfelt gratitude to my most beautiful and adorable wife Delight Nokuthaba Mpofu who is the love of my life, my life coach and business partner, for having supported me in every way in my ministry as a renowned global author. She is indeed such an amazing blessing that I will forever be grateful to have received from God. I owe a special gratitude specifically to one of my best spiritual sons, Paramjeet Singh Makani and his wife Preeti Makani from the nation of India, who inspires me a lot through the demonstration of undefinable, uncharted and unrecorded miracles, signs and wonders in this very hour.

I would like to extend my gratitude to my ministry partners for creating such a conducive platform and spiritual climate for me to move in greater depths, higher realms and deeper dimensions of the anointing to shake the nations and touch multitudes around the globe. It is for such a reason that I have been used by God as a vehicle to propagate the new waves of God's anointing to the furthest territories across the globe, to accomplish God's divine plans at such a time as this. My thanks also goes to Global Destiny Publishing House Pty Ltd, for making my dream of writing a reality and for enabling me to fulfil God's dream for propagating the world with the revelations of God's word.

Allow me to extend a hand of appreciation to Great men and women of God all around the world who have been an inspiration to me: Dr Yana Johnson (London), Prophetess Nomsa M. Maida of New Breed ministry, Apostle Chris Lord Hills of the Supernatural Church, Dr Franklin Ndhlovu (South Africa), Prophet Mathew B. Nuek (Malaysia), and Prophet Samuel Njagi (Kenya), for being instrumental in creating a conducive spiritual climate for the birthing forth of the revelations which God has laid in my spirit. Words fail to capture the gratitude I have for my own staff at *Global Destiny Publishing House* (GDP House), who have typified a new type of man coming forth on the earth, rising beyond the confines and dictates of the realm of time, to access higher realms of the Spirit: Further thanks goes to my ministry partners all over the world who have supported me tremendously by demonstrating an unquestionable thirst, perennial hunger and an insatiable appetite to read my books. I command the blessings of the Lord to abundantly marinate every sphere of your life with the rain of the anointing in Jesus Name! Further thanks goes to my siblings namely, Nothani Ndebele, Zenzo Nkomo, Caspa Nkomo, Innocent Nkomo, Kaizer Nkomo, Sithembiso Nkomo, Samukele Nkomo, Target Nkomo, Keeper Nkomo, Sanelisiwe Nkomo, Presence Nkomo and Anastacia Nkomo for their love and support in every way.

- **Apostle Frequency Revelator**

CHAPTER ONE

UNDERSTANDING THE REALM OF DREAMS AND VISIONS

It is of paramount significance to unveil from the onset the divine truth that dreams are an essential tool by which humanity can connect, communicate and hear the voice of God. Throughout the entire Bible, God as always been known to communicate to His people through dreams and visions. Dreams are a very powerful connection with the spirit realm which every believer should be acquainted to. Dreaming is also a mechanism to connect with God and receive messages from him regarding your life or your future. Dreams are an important part of our lives in the sense that real life is lived in dreams and our waking hours are a replay of what one would have seen or experienced in the dream. There is a necessity to be one who dream dreams if you want to reach into the height and greatness of God's plan for your life. And this divine truth is evident in the life of Joseph the dreamer The truth is that dreams are the fertile ground for the Holy Spirit to work and move in our lives. Throughout the history of the Bible, turning points for individuals and the church came through dreams and visions. All the great men of God who have done great things are dreamer of dreams. Dreams are so powerful that they can change your life and your destiny. In fact, if you really allow them to minister to you your whole life and destiny can change. The more powerful you are in a dream, the more powerful you will be in the physical. That is why if you want to defeat Satan and his demonic cohorts, you must defeat them in the dream life. If you can master the art of how to control or change things in your dream life, then you can change your life in the natural realm. If you want to gauge your spirit level and have a self-introspection about your spiritual life in general, simply look at how your dreams life and you will have all the answers you need. This is because your dream life is a movie or pictorial representation of what you are in the natural realm.

Frequency Revelator

Colloquially speaking, it is interesting to know that all of us do dream. The truth is that no one can say he or she does not dream. Every one of us dream to a certain extent, every night or at multiple times a night. In fact, you may be dreaming as many as three dozen dreams each night. Those who claim not to dream are not realistic. The only real issue to address is not the dreaming per se, but the trouble remembering those dreams. Even though some of you say you don't dream at all you do dream except that you forgot your dreams. Sometimes we remember the dreams when we wake up but then they slowly evaporate from the figment of our imagination as we get preoccupied with our daily duties and assignments. God commonly uses dreams to either instruct, warn and direct us and for that reason alone, it is a good idea to pay attention. People who say they don't dream or don't remember their dreams are missing out and should develop a way to key into their dreams because God speaks in dreams and visions. That is why it is important that we develop the quality of our spirit so that it catches the significant meaning of our dreams even when our minds do not remember. To further demonstrate in practical terms how impactful dreams are, did you know that an average human being spend *one third* of their life dreaming? That means by the time you are *60* years old, you would have spent *20* years of your life in "dreamland".

Dozens of folks are entrapped in a morass of debilitating circumstances of poverty, lack and limitation in progress because they have not learnt the art of how to receive things from the spirit realm through dreams. Did you know that dreams are a channel or pipeline through which spiritual substances are transacted from the spirit realm into visible and tangible manifestation in the physical realm?Dreams are a mechanism by which wealth is transferred or transacted to those God has positioned to receive a landslide of wealth in these end times. To substantiate this divine truth with reference to a quintessential example, have you not heard of how Solomon became the world's richest man through a dream? God visited him in a dream and asked him what he wanted and upon asking for wisdom, wealth was supernaturally transacted to him. In a similar vein, divine instructions were heralded to Jacob in a dream, outlining how he was to acquire Laban's wealth (Genesis 31). This tells me that the dreamland is a realm of great achievements, a realm that catapults one to dimensions beyond the faculties of human comprehension. Did you know that there are great musicians who composed songs which became a world-wide hit because they received them in a dream? Did you know that there are many prophets who received great prophesies touching the destiny of the masses across the globe because they received them in a dream? Did you also know that there are many great scholars and prolific authors who wrote books after receiving divinely inspired messages in a dream? Only if you could cultivate and nature your dream life, you will be thrilled at how great doors, breakthroughs and opportunities will stream in your direction, catapulting your spirit to higher realms of the supernatural realm.

However, it is disheartening to note that outside of the four walls of the local church there are thousands of people who are have a hunger in their heart for supernatural encounters – they want to know what their dreams mean, and sadly because of lack of emphasis of dreams in church, they gravitate towards the supernatural movies, occultic books, and psychic experiences for answers and solutions to explain their dream encounters. The problem is that even dozens of Christians have encounters in dreams yet when they wake up, they are completely lost at sea as to what their dreams meant. It is for this reason that the Bible says in Job 33:14: "*For God may speak in one way, or in another, yet man does not perceive it*". This means that dreams are one of the means God uses to communicate even though mankind doesn't fully comprehend the meaning or rationale. This scripture alludes to the unfortunate reality that God does speak and give prophetic direction through dreams and visions, but many people do not perceive it. Owing to lack of revelation, there are dozens of believers who are praying Heaven down and going for elongated periods of fasting to the extent of even begging and cajoling God to answer their prayers concerning their debilitating life circumstances of poverty, debt, sickness and limitation in progress yet God has already answered them in dreams and they did not even know that they already received the answer.

The greatest challenge is that in our modern world, dreams have been pushed aside where we don't give them much emphasis. The problem may be that many of us are dismissing our dreams, relegating them to nothing but a figment of human imagination. From the modern psychotherapy view, scholars attribute dreams to unresolved and emotional issues, deepest longings, and anxieties an individual is not willing to admit about themselves. They contend that to accept the ability to receive knowledge by way of extra-sensory perception in visions and dreams is simply psychotic or neurotic. In the process, they are missing out a lot of the things which God wants to unveil to humanity in the depths of their sleep through dreams. The truth is that dreaming is one of the ways through which God speaks to us, hence if we do not take heed to our dream life, we might find ourselves missing a lot of the things God wants to give us from the spirit realm. Sadly, its only modern men through their misconstrued intellect, logical and worldly wisdom who doesn't believe that dreams can mean anything more. Do you realize that in the Old Testament, dreams were considered very significant in shaping the prophetic direction and destiny of nations yet in our modern society, we relegate them to something insignificant and unimportant. The truth is that God wants us to be dreamers because He Himself is a dreamer. To attest the reality of this divine truth, consider how he fashioned the world into being by first incubating in the depths of his imagination the exact prototype of the world he wanted and when that vision had fully conceived, he spoke the world into existence. It is for this reason that we must always develop a quality to be a dreamer of dreams so that we can also learn the spiritual art of creating things from the spirit realm.

Owing to lack of revelation, many of God's people are missing what he is telling them because they have no regard for their dreams. The regard dreams as mere psychological illusions which are part of human nature. For example, the great scholars and philosophers Aristotle and Plato, have affected the educational system of the whole world, through their concepts of *philosophy* and *humanism* thereby drifting the masses further from the reality of their dreams. Plato taught that you could receive knowledge through three areas: the physical world, the intellect and through what he called divine activity. To us, we understand it to be the activities of the spirit realm but when Aristotle came, he only accepted that knowledge could come only through the intellect. Consequently, in today's world system, education is based on the fact that knowledge can only come through sense knowledge and the intellect. In the process, they completely discarded the spirit realm. That is why education is the elimination of spiritual knowledge. It is for this reason that the average educated person regards dreams as something wishy-washy that is nothing significant. They totally ignored the aspect of the spiritual, which is unknown as far as the intellectual man is concerned. This is a grave mistake especially taking into account the fact that a lot of the leadings that we tend to miss in our conscious lives come through our dreams. Therefore, if you would pay attention to the messages that are coming in your dreams, you will not go astray of God's perfect will.

This book is an activation tool that will usher you into the realm of operating in prophetic dreams and visions. It will activate you into a place of hearing from God in a clearer way when it comes to dreams and visions. It will catapult you to a prophetic realm, dimension and level where your dreams become solid material that communicates spiritual realities and transforms things in your world. As you inundate your spirit with Throne Room Revelations that are encapsulated in this book, God will activate your dreams and visions such that you will supernaturally connect with him and receive messages that will transform you and the destiny of those around you and the world. Strikingly, while you are still reading this book, you will experience a torrent of overflowing prophetic dreams concerning your life, family, region, city or nation that will revolutionise the destiny of the masses across the globe. The reading of this book will cause you to delve into the realm of God's metaphorical language to download spiritual solutions to interpret dreams and visions for both yourself and others. Imagine someone in your family, workplace or circle of friends sharing a dream that has impacted them deeply and they are completely lost at sea as to what it means. Imbued with an understanding of the spiritual knowledge of dreams shared in this book, you will be able to unlock the mysteries, clarify the dream and share with them the God-given solution to the dilemma they are facing. Through the reading of this book, you will emerge as a new breed prophetic voice that God will raise up in this generation with a calling to raise up seers and carry a strong prophetic anointing as well as an awesome ability to teach and activate people in the realm of understanding dreams and visions. For this reason, I would like to strongly encourage you to write down your dreams even the most insignificant ones. You will be surprised that many of your dreams tell you about your job, your career, your business decision, your ministry and all the important things that are usually missed in your sphere of contact.

DEFINITION OF DREAMS AND VISIONS

What Is A Dream And A Vision?

> *This is what was spoken by the prophet Joel: And in the last days it shall be God declares, that I will pour out my Spirit upon all flesh, and your sons and your daughters shall prophesy, and your young men shall see visions and your old men shall dream dreams: yea, and on my manservants and my maidservants in those days I will pour out my Spirit; and they shall prophesy. And I will show wonders in the heaven above and signs on the earth beneath, blood, and fire, and vapor of smoke; the sun shall be turned into darkness and the moon into blood before the day of the Lord comes, the great and manifest day. And it shall be that whoever calls on the name of the Lord shall be saved* (Acts 2:16).

In the context of the above scripture, Peter quotes and echoes the prophecy of Joel for the last days as a way to explain the tongue-speaking phenomenon that the people who came to Jerusalem for Pentecost were witnessing. It was a prophecy of the outpouring of the Spirit of God. It is important that we define *Dreams* and *Visions* with reference to their original context in Greek, so that we can secure a deeper understanding of these significant divine concepts. There are two Greek words for dreams. One is the word *onar,* which is the ordinary word for dreams which is only used three times in the Bible in the New Testament. The other Greek word is *enupnion* which is not the normal word for dream and has only been used once in a negative sense in the New Testament. This is the same word that is used here Acts chapter 2 where it says old man shall dream dreams. This word is so special that it refers to a message, a vision or a spiritual conscious experience of a direction and leading of God in the subconscious stage. Note that in this context, when it says old men shall *dream dreams,* Paul is talking about those who are spiritually mature in the Lord and not those of age. He is using analogy to speak about spiritual matters in a figurative sense.

From the usage of the negative sense you could see the fullness and the meaning in the positive. The negative sense is used in Jude verse 8 when Jude talks about those who were like Sodom and Gomorrah who are being given over to sensuous *"dreamings"* and so defiling the flesh and going about in their own ways. In this context, Peter here is not referring to people who are sleeping but he is talking about people just moving along not knowing what they are doing but just driven along by their flesh. In other words, they are moving subconsciously and drawing on their own lust. In Jude verse 8, this group of people who were led by the flesh, were led not only consciously but they have reached a point where they were led sub-consciously. Sadly, many people do things subconsciously that is why both our conscious and our subconscious mind need renewal. Our subconscious mind is not the human spirit but a part of our soul that needs renewal by the Word of God. For this reason, we need the Word not only in the conscious mind but we need to get it into our subconscious and get it further down into our spirit.

In Order For Us To Secure A Clear Understanding Of What A Dream Is, It Is Imperative That We First Define What A Vision Is Because A Vision Is What Translates Into A Dream When It Gets Into Our Subconscious Realm.

Definition of A Vision

A vision is like a supernatural flash, picture or image that is revealed to an individual right in front of his very own eyes as God communicates a message concerning the things that are happening in the supernatural realm. A vision is a very plain, straight forward visual experience and spiritual perception of supernatural realities that is communicated to a person in the natural realm. It is a supernatural picture or snapshot of what God wants you to see, do or become. Metaphorically speaking, a vision is like camera that flashes images about things that you see ahead of you while a dream is like a television that plays a movie or a film where you see yourself participating in events and activities taking place in the spirit world.

Seeing visions is an integral part of the end time move of the Spirit. The last-days' movement is mainly characterized by an aspect of seeing, hence Joel prophetically declared, "Young man shall see visions and prophesy." The Greek word for *vision* in the New Testament is the word *optasia*, which means a sight or vision (Luke 1:22; 24:23; Acts 26:19; 2 Corinthians 12:1). Another word for vision is *Horama* which connotes to something gazed at, a sight, a thing seen, vision (Matthew 17:9; Acts 9:10,12; 10:3; 18:9). Lastly, another key word for vision is *Horasis* which refers to a sight, an appearance, seeing (Acts 2:17; Revelation 9:17). In terms of the character of its manifestation, a vision can be manifested through a picture that flashes in our minds, in a cartoon fashion or symbolic representation to covey a figurative or metaphorical message, through a video or movie-like images in the mind's eye, and through a sense of actually seeing with our natural eyes while fully conscious. A distinctive feature of a vision in comparison to dreams is that a vision comes as a flash or picture during our conscious state. In a vision, one sees into the spirit ream or has perception of the supernatural things. In other words, the natural senses are allowed to experience the invisible realm of the spirit. A vision can be received during times of payer, worship, contemplation and meditation and some other times when we least expect it. They can occur while awake (Daniel 10:7; Acts 9:7) during daylight hours ((Acts 10:3), or in the night while asleep (Genesis 46:2; Numbers 12:6; Job 4:13, Daniel 4). Visions are more literal while dreams are more symbolic in their composition, yet their still require clear and profound interpretation (Acts 10:17). Visions are imprinted on our memory and spirit and at times visons can become so tangible that at times it becomes difficult to distinguish them from real life (Acts 12:9-10).

There are two main ways through which visions are seen and these are *internally* and *externally*. *Internal visions* are seen with the mind's eye such that we often think of these visions as dreams (Daniel 7:1). *External visions* on the other hand are experienced while one is fully awake. These can be seen in three possible ways , which are; through an *open heaven experience* (Ezekiel 1:1-3; Isaiah 6:1-3; Genesis 26:10; John 1:50-51; Acts 7:55-57). The other ways is through *coexisting spiritual realm,* in the case of Elisha's servant, a young prophetic in training whose eyes were opened to the spirit realm so that he could see the army of God. (2 Kings 6:17). The other ways is through *the realm of the future*, in the case of Daniel and John the Revelator who saw visions of the future with open eyes (Daniel 10:7; Revelations 1:1). The apostle John was given a visual perception of the future such that he compiled and recorded what he saw in the form of a book we call Revelation. God can give you a vision right now but that vision only touches your conscious mind. As that vision grows in you, it becomes a part of your subconscious too. That vision usually is a part of your spirit since it comes from your spirit but what our spirit has does not come out unless it can flow through the soul that is renewed. So, the first time we begin to understand and receive a leading in vision, it is our conscious mind that receives. Spiritually young men who have overcome the devil now receive visions. As they continue walking with God for long, they become spiritually old men whose visions have now sunken into their subconscious so that they now dream dreams. Therefore, when the scripture talks about young men seeing vision and old men dreaming dreams, it alludes to the same vision that is now sunk into the subconscious realm.

When The Depths Of God's Leading And Spirit In You Being Received To The Extent That It Comes To The Level Of Your Sub-Conscious, It Translates From A Vision Into A Dream

Definition of A Dream

A dream refers to a message, vision or a spiritual conscious experience of a direction and leading of God in the subconscious stage. It speaks about the depths of God's leading and spirit in you being received to the extent that it comes to the level of your sub-conscious. It is a supernatural suggestion or impression received during sleep or a subconscious state.

Apply this meaning positively to the scripture of old men dreaming dreams, it speaks about the depths of God's leading and spirit in you being received to the extent that it comes to the level of your sub-conscious. Note that in our opening scripture above, when he says *your sons and your daughters shall prophesy, and your young men shall see visions and your old men shall dream dreams,* the Apostle Peter is specially speaking about the three dimensions of the supernatural which is, *prophesying, visions and dreams.* That they begin manifestations of prophesying, visions and dreams. This scripture reveals to us the three main dimensions of the Prophetic Stream - prophets, seers and dreamers of dreams.

Frequency Revelator

The Prophecy talks about 'sons and daughters prophesying' denoting the Prophet, 'young men seeing visions' denoting the Seer and 'old men dreaming dreams' denoting the Dreamer of dreams.

The actual Greek definition of the word *shall dream dreams* is *enupniazo enupnion*. It's derived from the word two words combined *"en"* and *"upniazo"* which means simply something being presented during your subconscious state, which is usually your sleep. So, when we combine these two words together, they have the word *enupnion* which is a supernatural suggestion or impression received during sleep or a subconscious state. Let me put that statement *"Old men dream dreams"* into that and see how it sounds. It will read as, "Old men shall receive supernatural suggestions and impressions during sleep or a sub-conscious state". The whole context talks about the outpouring of the Holy Spirit.

The word translated as dream here is not the ordinary Greek word for dream. The ordinary Greek word for dream as used in Matthew chapter one and chapter two in the life of Joseph and in the wise men life is the word *onar*, which is the official Greek word for the word dream. Notice that *onar* has been used for the first dimension and second dimension. The word *onar* in Matthew one and two refers to Joseph having a dream about this angel coming to him and talking to him. *Onar* is used even in the second dimension of dreams. But in Acts 2, the word *dream* is not the word *onar* but is the word *enupnion* which talks about receiving a leading, an impression, a direction, a vision, a spiritual encounter, while in the state of rest. Moreover, the word *prophesy* is not talking about the office of the prophet but the *gift of prophecy* which God has freely made available to every believer in Christ. The phrase *last days* does not speak on a specific day when the Lord will judge the world but rather represent the time from the birth of Jesus Christ until his second coming. The use of the words, *"sons and daughters"* and *"young men"* and *"old men"* is a Hebrew parallelism used to show that all people from every demographic, young and old, male and female, will all have access to the outpouring of the spirit, unlike in the old days when only the chosen prophets could hear from God.

Understanding Prophetic Dreams & Visions

I will pour out my Spirit upon all flesh, and your sons and your daughters shall prophesy, and your young men shall see visions and your old men shall dream dreams: yea, and on my manservants and my maidservants in those days I will pour out my Spirit; and they shall prophesy. (Acts 2:16).

The above reference scripture is not just talking about merely having a vision, as we know it, because in the days of Joel and prior days, many young men were having visions and prophesying. So, for it to be prophesied and be said to be possible after God pours out His Spirit upon all flesh in the last days, then it is deeper than it looks. Throughout history, the Holy Spirit has guided God's people through dreams, visions and prophecy. But according to Acts 2—where Peter quoted the prophet Joel—we are on the verge of a major intensification of this type of activity. In fact, it has already begun. But if God says He is going to increase this form of communication with us as Jesus' Second Coming nears, then there is nothing wrong with positioning yourself to be a recipient. In fact, in these last days, we are going to hear and see more people operating in the realm of visions, dreams and prophesying. As we experience the outpouring of the Holy Spirit, this grace is going to be executed to higher degree and alarming magnitude. That's what God is going to do in these last days. What is prophesied is that God will pour His Spirit upon His people.

I will pour out my Spirit upon all flesh, and your sons and your daughters shall prophesy, and your young men shall see visions and your old men shall dream dreams: yea, and on my manservants and my maidservants in those days I will pour out my Spirit; and they shall prophesy. (Acts 2:16).

Note that the above scripture specially and *categorically* mentions *sons and daughters, young men* and *old men*. That scripture has always puzzled me until God began to give more light. It cannot be that God is talking about physical age alone but a level of spiritual maturity. This is because we know that old men also can prophesy and that young men can also dream dreams too and old men can see vision. Therefore, this is not just something to do with physical age but something more than that. It is referring to the spiritual age of children, young men and fathers and old men. Moreover, this has nothing to do with physical age because not all fathers are spiritual fathers since some are old when they are born again and they are spiritual babies as far as God is concerned. The best way to understand this scripture is by cross referencing to another scripture in I John which talks about spiritual age and not natural age.

I am writing to you, young men, because you have overcome the evil one. I write to you, children, because you know the Father. I write to you, fathers, because you know him who is from the beginning. I write to you, young men, because you are strong, and the word of God abides in you, and you have overcome the evil one (1 John 2:12).

Taking the leadings from the epistle of John, in 1 John 2:12, the writer uses the words *children, young men* and *fathers* to illustrate the different levels of spiritual growth and spiritual maturity. In view of the above passage of scripture, it is apparent that it talks about spiritual age. *Little children* are those who have just been born again while *young men* implies those who are mature in the things of God to a level whereby they are strong in the revelations of God's Word and have overcome the enemy. *Young men* speaks of Christians who are operating at the peak of their spiritual life, moving in the supernatural realm, walking in the depths of revelations of God's word, overcoming spiritual battles and living in the reality of the promises of God. *Spiritual fathers* are those who are now mature in the things of the spirit. *Knowing God* from the beginning implies the depth of revelation of God. It means that their knowledge of God covers a vast expanse. He has to write from the beginning saying: *I am writing to you, young men, because you have overcome the evil one.* In this case, he is talking about the middle part of nurturing, and overcoming the devil, the lust of the eyes, the lust of the flesh and the pride of life. That is how we spiritually grow into the depths of God. As we grow in our spiritual life we graduate from the stage of being children through the level of being young men to the level where we become spiritual fathers in the Lord. The other reason why our opening scripture does not refer to physical age is because we all know that its not only old men who dream dreams but young men also dream.

And I will show wonders in the heaven above and signs on the earth beneath, blood, and fire, and vapor of smoke; the sun shall be turned into darkness and the moon into blood before the great and dreadful day of the Lord And it shall be that whoever calls on the name of the Lord shall be saved. (Acts 2:16).

Understanding Prophetic Dreams & Visions

If you analyse the exegesis of this scripture, you will notice that immediately Peter talks about people operating in prophesy, dreams and visions, he mentions the issue of signs and wonders. Why? Because it is prophesy, visions and dreams that will catapult the masses to the realm of signs and wonders. These supernatural manifestations or occurrences will enable people to move and function in the realm of the miraculous. There will be massive demonstrations of God's power and divine exploits that will shake the nations of this world and we are witnessing this happening already in the church. Do you also notice that immediately after signs and wonders, he talks of *the great and dreadful day of the Lord*. This means that the signs and wonders is what will usher the second coming of the Lord. That means chronologically speaking, the greatest revival that shall usher the second coming of Jesus Christ will begin with people operating in prophecy, visions and dreams, followed by signs and wonders then the second coming of Christ. In this prophecy the last thing that's mentioned after dreams, visions, prophecies, miracles, signs and wonders is that *all who call on the name of the Lord will be saved*. This implies that what's going to get people saved in these last days will be a tangible release of dreams, visions, and God's prophetic power. These experiences will reveal a tangible evidence of the Kingdom of God being released in our midst, glory to Jesus! (Acts 2:19-21).

Do you notice that the second coming of Jesus will be preceded by the shaking of celestial bodies such as the moon and the sun? Not only will there be demonstration of power but there will be a shaking of celestial bodies as well. Why signs on the sun and moon? Because scientifically speaking, the moon and sun controls the earth and any slight movement of the moon or sun can cause destruction to the earth. So, the controlling force emanates from there. The Bible says *God created the greater light (sun) to rule the day and the lesser light (moon) to rule the night* (Genesis 1:5). What we call day is when the earth rotates and faces direction of the sun and what we call night is when the earth rotates and faces the direction of the moon. Scientifically speaking, the moon controls whatever happens in the sea while the sun controls activities of the earth. Any slight movement or shift of the moon releases a gravitational force that causes heavy tidal waves which can destroy life in the sea. By the same token, any slight shift or movement of the sun can cause the release of ultraviolet radiation to earth which depletes the ozone layer, causes global warning and gross damage to all forms of life.

It is for this reason that the Bible says there is a great star that will fall from Heaven and cause great damage and devastation to the earth and mankind (Revelations 8:10-12). It is for this reason that there will be blood, and fire, and vapor of smoke; the sun shall be turned into darkness and the moon into blood. This is what will happen on the dreadful day of the Lord, as the curtain of this age is eternally closed.

Why Does God Choose To Speak To Us Through Dreams And Visions?

There are many reasons as to why God at times chooses to speak to us in dreams and visions and not through other direct means such as prophecy and audible voice. Firstly, the most obvious one is that many people get to be so busy during the day such that it would be practically impossible for them to hear God speak. During the day, you might not hear God due to the distractions of your busy schedule such as work meetings, school deadlines, children's needs, home chores, parents' needs and even relationships can eat up your time and leave none for God. So, sometimes, God waits until we are knocked out, and snoring, before He speaks to us. It may be the only time you are actively listening! Because you don't listen during the daytime, you don't have a choice but to watch and hear the dream that plays through your mind when you're asleep. It's hard to turn it off! Therefore, through prophetic dreaming, God can communicate direction to you that perhaps you would not be able to hear while awake in your distracting environment.

Secondly, the other reason why God communicates to us through dreams and visions is that the dream language uses symbols, codes and pictures which are at times parabolic and not easily understandable to the senses. God uses this parabolic language so that men would search for Him. If God were always to speak to us in a straight forward and direct manner, man would not see any need to search diligently for him. Thus, the enigmatic communication that comes through dreams in a way forces man to search for the meaning and in the process also search for God, his ways and methods. It is for this reason that the Bible says, " *It is the glory of the Lord to conceal a matter and it is the honour of Kings to search for the matter*". God loves it when men embarks on a spiritual journey of searching, unveiling and investigating his ways and spiritual operations. It pleases the father as he is also a rewarder of those who diligently seek him .

Thirdly, God speaks to us in dreams and visions because pictures, symbols and codes are the language of communication in the spirit realm. God speaks in metaphorical language. He speaks in language of codes, symbols, and signs that at times can appear strange to us. It is divinely coded and spiritually discerned. That's basically how the communication is effected in the spirit realm. Most of the time, we don't understand what He's saying, because we haven't developed the ability to understand the language of the Spirit. The reasons why angels at times uses man's language when communicating with us is because they would have gravitated to your level so that you can easily understand them, otherwise, that is not their language of communication. The spirit realm operates on codes, symbols and pictures and it is your responsibility to join the pieces of the puzzle to make sense out of it. God is looking for a people of maturity, and a people who will begin to develop a dream language or a metaphorical language, or understanding with him. Since the dream language is one of the key ways that God connects with you, and you can connect with God on a deeper level, it is therefore important that we master the language of communication of that realm if ever we want to be effective in the spirit world.

Prophetic Action Prayer:

Heavenly Father in the name of Jesus Christ, I pray that you would help me to recognize your voice when you speak to me in my dreams. Open my eyes, and my ears, to your metaphorical language. Help me to develop a dream language with you that's personal. Give me dreams and visions that activate my metaphorical understanding, in Jesus' name. Amen.

THE TWO DIMENSIONS OF DREAMS

There are two categories of dreaming dreams, namely; dreams that we experience while awake and the other connotes to dreams that transpire while we are asleep. The Greek word *enupnion* as used in the book of Jude speaks about a dream like state while conscious and it can be also in total deep sleep like in Job 33. In dreams there is no limitation to the physical areas of our life. You can ether dream in your sleep or dream when you are awake. It's important for us to allow our dreams to soar to the heights ordained by God because there is no limit when it comes to dreaming. So, the ability to dream is an important one. It does occur even in your waking moment and as well as in your deep sleep. What we encourage you to do is to dream dreams and go beyond those areas that have limited you. If you could dream of things that are impossible to you, you can move into that realm.

Dreams That Transpire In A Deep Sleep (When We Are Asleep)

The first dimension of dreams are those that transpire in our subconscious, when we are in deep sleep. Let's make reference to Job 33:14-18, a statement made by Elihu. If you remember there were three friends who came and then the fourth was mentioned later in the book of Job. Towards the end of the book of Job, God rebukes the first three friends but not the fourth, implying that the statements made by the fourth (who happened to be Elihu) were acceptable to God and were prophetic. In Job 33 is a statement made by Elihu, which carries a lot of truth.

For God speaks in one way, and in two, though man does not perceive it. In a dream, in a vision of the night, when deep sleep falls upon men, while they slumber on their beds, then He opens the ears of men, and terrifies them with warnings that He may turn man aside from his deed, and cut off pride from man. he keeps back his soul from the Pit, his life from perishing by the sword (Job 33:15).

In our opening scripture above, it tells when those dreams occur, in a deep sleep. It's even called the *vision of the night* meaning it transpires during night time when men fall asleep. These are dreams that only occur when you enter into very deep sleep. According to modern dream research, our night sleeping hours are in cycles. As you fall into sleep in the first phase of your sleep there is no dream. Then in the second phase of your sleep dreams occur. They know when dreams occur because of your REM sleep or rapid eye movement sleep. The first part there is no REM. The first part possibly has to do with the physical body resting. This is a typical ways in which God communicates to most people. We need to understand what God is doing in our conscious and thought life. But in order to be full-fledged Christians for God and let God live in our lives twenty-four hours, we have to understand what God is doing while we are asleep. To cement this divine truth with reference to further scriptural evidence, lets consider the words spoken by Peter below:

> *This is what was spoken by the prophet Joel; And in the last days it shall be, God declares, that I will pour out my Spirit upon all flesh, and your sons and your daughters shall prophesy, and young men shall see visions, and your old men shall dream dreams* (Acts 2:17; Joel 2:28).

Do you realise in the context of the above scripture that when the Bible talks about old men dreaming dreams, it is not alluding to a *dream* in an ordinary sense. It's not the ordinary word for dream like *onar* which is implied here. Rather, it is a special word *enupnion* that is implied which talks about something received from the Lord supernaturally in the subconscious state. This is the impartation that comes from God when we are sleeping. Here it says that God speaks to people in dreams, meaning while they are in their deep sleep. This is the first area with regards to our dreams and the dreams that God gives us in our life. Let's look at the book of Daniel 7: 1;

> *In the first year of Belshazzar king of Babylon, Daniel had a dream and visions of his head as he lay in his bed. Then he wrote down the dream, and told the sum of the matter.* Then verse 15 *As for me, Daniel, my spirit within me was anxious and the visions of my head alarmed me.*

The question you are probably asking yourself here is: In the context of the above scripture, was Daniel still in a dream or has he woken up? He says in verse one that he had a dream, visions in his head while on his bed and he wrote down all the main facts. Yet in verse 15, he suddenly says *I Daniel was grieved in my spirit within my body and the visions of my head troubled me.* It is very obvious that in verse 15, he was already outside of his dream. Because he says in verse 15, the dream or vision of his head disturbed him like the way Pharaoh and Nebuchadnezzar were disturbed in their dreams. Apparently there was a continuation to the dream but it came to him possibly in a vision or another dream. Let me show you how his dream experience is corroborated by Pharaoh's dream.

After two whole years, Pharaoh dreamed that he was standing by the Nile, and behold, there came up out of the Nile seven cows sleek and fat, and they fed in the reed grass. And behold, seven other cows, gaunt and thin, came up out of the Nile after them. And stood by the other cows on the bank of the Nile. And the gaunt and thin cows ate up the seven sleek and fat cows. And Pharaoh awoke (Genesis 41:1).

This implies that Pharoah must have wakened up in the middle of the night. Then in verse 5, it says *then he fell asleep and dreamed a second time.* This means that in between the two dreams, he woke up and he slept again. In the case of Daniel, in Chapter 7, he had a dream and in verse one, he was writing about the dream. That tells us that there must be some time that has taken place. And by verse 15 he was still disturbed about the dream. So, we know one thing. Either his second part after verse 15 was in a vision or in a second dream. But definitely there was a break point between verse 1 and verse 15 onwards. This tells us that dreams can be continued or repeated in a person's life. And even if you were woken up halfway in your dream and when you get to sleep again you will get the same contact. Here we are talking about dreams as if it's a real spiritual contact. If you contacted the spirit realm and something was broken in the contact, there will be a continuation.

Dreams That Transpire In A Conscious State (When We Are Awake)

This is what was spoken by the prophet Joel; And in the last days it shall be, God declares, that I will pour out my Spirit upon all flesh, and your sons and your daughters shall prophesy, and young men shall see visions, and your old men shall dream dreams (Acts 2:17; Joel 2:28).

In retrospect to dreams that occur during the night as expounded in the preceding section, there are also dreams that occur when people are awake or in a conscious state. This is evidenced by our opening scripture above in book of Acts 2:17 or Joel 2:28 where it says *your old men shall dream dreams..* Unknown to casual readers of the Word, this does not necessarily speak about a dream that occurs when we are asleep but to dreams that occur while we are awake. The Greek word for *dream dreams* is the word *enupnizo-*

mai enupnion. The normal Greek word for dream is the word *onar*, which is used in the book of Matthew when Joseph had a dream. Here in Acts 2:17, he is talking about a dream state and not necessary a sleep state dream. The word *enupnion* speaks about a kind of dreaminess whereby one sees or receive spiritual communication in a subconscious state. It is almost like what we use in the English word *dreamy*, like someone sitting quietly in a corner and they are like in a world of themselves dreaming. This is from the special Greek word for dreams *enupnion* and not from the ordinary Greek word for dreams *onar*. And this word *enupnion* has been used to refer to people who are dreamers in their waking state. Let's cross reference to another scripture in Job 33 which refers to those in their sleeping state, although it has been used in the negative sense in the book of Jude verse 8, *Yet in like manner these men in their dreamings defile the flesh, reject authority, and revile the glorious ones.* Here, he is talking about those who in a negative sense dream of the wrong things. They are not asleep but are awake. We immediately see that there is such a thing as a dreamlike state while conscious and a full dream state while in deep sleep.

UNDERSTANDING THE DIFFERENCES AND SIMILARITIES BETWEEN DREAMS AND VISIONS

Highlighting The Similarities Between A Dream And A Vision

"For God may speak in one way, or in another, Yet man does not perceive it. In a dream, in a vision of the night, When deep sleep falls upon men, While slumbering on their beds, Then He opens the ears of men, And seals their instruction." (Job 33:14–16).

In retrospect to understanding dreams and visions, it is important that we first look at their similarities before we can delve into their differences. This is because in many instances in the Bible, the words *dreams* and *visions* has been used interchangeably. This is what leaves many casual readers of the word wondering what exactly are the differences between the two important divine concepts. If you are trying to turn to scripture to secure a solid definition of a night vision, you might find that it implies the same thing as a dream. That's why in some context, the word *Vision of the night* is used to refer to Dreams. In fact, you could even ask two different Old Testament prophets and get two different answers. To substantiate this view with reference to scriptural evidence, let's look at 2 Samuel 7, whereby the Prophet Nathan recounts this extremely long word God gave him for King David. At the end he tacks on the phrase, *"In accordance with all these words and all this vision, so Nathan spoke to David"* (2 Samuel 7:17 NASB). But the same scripture begins with the words *"In the same night the word of the LORD came to Nathan"* (2 Samuel 7:4 NASB). This leaves many wondering whether a dream implies the same thing as a vision since both terms are contextually used to refer to the same thing. It also leads you to couple those together and classify it as a night vision since the Hebrew word used is *chizzayown*, which can mean *"vision in the night."*

Now, the question you could be asking yourself is: What the Prophet Nathan experienced, was it a Dream or a Vision? Some Biblical scholars contend that it was not a dream because nowhere does it mention anything about him being asleep. But only the King James Version, New American Standard Version and New Living Translation of the Bible use the word *vision*, whereas the others Bible translations chose an alternate English words such as *"oracle, prophecy, divine communication"* Nathan's choice of words is vague. It is doubtful that Samuel actually wrote 2 Samuel because he dies in 1 Samuel 25, so many think either Nathan wrote it or a scribe with access to his notes did. But the bottom line is, the prophecy still proves true till this day. On the other hand, some Biblical scholars says that the Prophet Nathan actually had a dream. This is because we see the same phrase *"night vision"* used again in Daniel 2:19–45 (depending on your translation; some say *"vision of the night"*), and yet the word used is an Aramaic one that has no connection whatsoever with night visions. It is *chezev*, which means *"vision, appearance."* That is why it is a bit tricky to concretely ascertain with a level of precision what a night vision is or is not, or if it is merely a dream. To cement this fact with reference to further scriptural evidence, let's cross reference to another scripture in the Book of Job where it says: *"In a dream, in a vision of the night, When deep sleep falls upon men, While slumbering on their beds, Then He opens the ears of men, And seals their instruction."* (Job 33:14–16). This makes it sound as though a vision of the night is a dream and that both occur while slumbering on the bed. However, we must be careful not to lose revelation because of conflict of words.

Highlighting The Differences Between A Dream And A Vision

In the last days it shall be, God declares, that I will pour out my Spirit upon all flesh, and your sons and your daughters shall prophesy, and young men shall see visions, and your old men shall dream dreams (Acts 2:17; Joel 2:28).

While dozens of Christians uses the words *dreams* and *visions* interchangeably, it is important that we distinguish between these terms as the distinction carries a greater revelation. We need to make reference to scripture and understand the usage of words in their original context in Greek and Hebrew so as to secure a solid distinction between a *vison* and a *dream*. A vision is a very plain, straight forward visual experience of supernatural realities that is not restricted to time. It is a supernatural picture or snapshot of what God wants you to see, do or become. It can occur either during the day or night time while dreams are typical of night times. Although one can dream during the day (*fiesta*), in most cases those dreams are not apparent or significant. At an experiential level, I have had plenty of visions, and I know that they are different from dreams. I have had visions while sleeping in bed, while praying in my closet, while writing a book, while meditating on God's word, or while at an event or a friend's house for supper, at such times when I was not even expecting a vision at all. A dream on the other hand is merely a regular type of vision that occurs during sleeping time.

Secondly, another difference between dreams and visions is that visions are *literal in nature* and less complex, whether it's an inner vision, a trance or an open vision while dreams are symbolic in nature. This is evident in the experience of Cornelius in Acts 10:1. Immediately after he saw a vision of a man from Macedonia, he quickly understood what it meant and responded with ease. The interpretation of a vision does not require much scrutiny as it doesn't contain a lot of hidden metaphors in most cases. To substantiate this truth, let me make reference to a practical example, when you have a vision, it's usually pretty simple and straight forward. For example, you might say "I had a vision of me preaching in front of a crusade full of thousands of people. I preached and people got saved". That's it." It's interpretation is very simple and need no dictionary to elaborate, elucidate or disentangle its meaning. Dreams on the other hand are metaphorical, enigmatic and symbolic, coupled with divinely coded mysteries which makes it harder to understand. This is evident in the experiences of Pharaoh and Nebcardnezer who were left puzzled for life after experiencing dreams. To prove how complicated their dreams were, they even went to the extent of consulting Magicians to try and interpret the dream and even going to the extremes of giving ridiculous rewards amounting to half of the kingdom to whoever would interpret the dream. This is to show you how complex dreams are. Let's cement this truth with reference to an experiential example. Let's say you dream of a harvest field. While you are still looking, all of a sudden scene changes and the next thing you know you're on a big platform and there are people everywhere. Then the scene changes again and you're seven years older in this experience. Then it's over. That is how complex dreams are in comparison to visions. In some instances you might encounter numbers in a dream, for example "7" which might also need its own interpretation, making it a double task for you to secure the interpretation of the meaning of both *words* and *numbers*. Did you know that both the dream and the vision say the same thing, but one is metaphorical and one is not? The dream contains different imagery yet it implies the same thing as a vision.

There's a reason why God chooses to speak to us in a dream, rather than a vision. It's what I would call the *"paying the cost of clarity"* factor. Dreams and visions sometimes come with spiritual warfare. I would prefer to have God speak to me in a dream rather than in a vision, most of the time when it comes to major revelation. In the co-existing spiritual arena, there are times where the enemy can see what God shows you. If you have a vision of a crusade, and you are preaching in it, and it's thousands of people, what happens sometimes, is that all hell breaks loose against that dream because the devil says, "All right! We know who he is! He's got the call to be the next Reinhard Bonnke, get him." But if the devil watches a dream, he sees this other obscure imagery, and says, "I don't even know what that means. Then, in the still small voice of God, when you're with Him alone, He says, "Son, you're called to have a platform to preach to millions of people. You're called to bring souls into the Kingdom." This is because you actually got a vision for what God's calling you to do, without the warfare!

Lastly, a dream is *internal* while in most cases a vision is *external*. In other words, in a dream, you see yourself being part of the events that are taking place but in a vision, you are outside the events as you watch them unfolding before you. A vision is like a flash or picture that is shown right in front of your very own eyes as God communicates to you a message concerning the things that are happening in the supernatural realm. A dream on the other hand comes like a film where you see yourself participating in events and activities in the spirit world. Metaphorically speaking, a vision is like camera that flashes images about things that you see ahead of you while a dream is like a television that plays a movie of which you are a apart.

What Is The Purpose Of Dreams And Visions?

For God speaks in one way, and in two, though man does not perceive it. In a dream, in a vision of the night, when deep sleep falls upon men, while they slumber on their beds, then He opens the ears of men, and <u>terrifies them with warnings that He may turn man aside from his deed</u>, and <u>cut off pride from man,</u> he <u>keeps back his soul from the Pit,</u> his <u>life from perishing by the sword</u> (Job 33:14-18).

Consider the highly evocative language Job uses to describe his understanding of the purpose of dreams and visions from God. He says God opens the ears of men, and terrifies them with warnings that He may turn man aside from his deed, and cut off pride from man and keeps back his soul from the pit, and his life from perishing by the sword. In view of this reality, it is imperative for you to understand that dreams and visions are given for a specific purpose. That is why they should never be taken lightly as their occurrence might impact the destinies of individuals, families and even nations. In our opening scripture above, the purpose of dreams and visions is therefore revealed:

- **To turn man aside from his deed.**
- **To cut off pride from man.**
- **To keep back man's soul from the pit.**
- **To keep back man's life from perishing by the sword.**

Categorically speaking, dreams from God are infused with His power and purpose, and they can lead us, show us the error of our ways, warn us, and reveal areas of our lives that have not taken on Christ-likeness, be prophetic in nature, or convey spiritual insights. Dreams are of the same creative essence as the arts, they illuminate the same spiritual process, of which arts have a revelatory distinction. Imbued with this understanding, when you receive dreams and visions from God, you will take them seriously and document them, knowing that your life might be grossly dependent on those spiritual experiences.

CHAPTER TWO

THE PROPHETIC SIGNIFICANCE OF DREAMS AND VISIONS

It is worth exploring the truth that dreams are part of the means of the leadings of God in our lives today as they give direction and seal important instructions in our lives. Sometimes we cannot hear God clearly in our working hours hence He tries to emphasize it again in our dream life so that you don't miss Him. For this reason, it is highly advisable that any child of God who desires to walk closely with God cannot afford to leave the area of dream life out. They must learn to consecrate their dream life to God. Do you know that a normal human being spends one third of his life sleeping and the remaining two thirds of life is spent doing all kind of things. Sadly, greater emphasis is spent on training Christians to hear God's voice and move in the Spirit of God when they are conscious. Unless we touch the other one third and tell you how to make use of that part of your life, you missed out a lot of your life. Since we spend one third of our life sleeping, it is imperative that we know how we can be sensitive to God during those times. This is what will help us gain a full understanding of dreams and visions and the things that happen in our subconscious life when we are sleeping.

Why Is It Significant To Experience Dreams And Visions?

Dreams Are A Means By Which God Communicates With All Humanity

Frequency Revelator

For God speaks in one way, and in two, though man does not perceive it. In a dream, in a vision of the night, when deep sleep falls upon men, while they slumber on their beds, then he opens the ears of men, and terrifies them with warnings, that He may turn man aside from his deed, and cut off pride from man; He keeps back his soul from the Pit, his life from perishing by the sword. (John 33:14).

A dream is God's second means of communication to us. It is the language or medium of communication in the spirit realm. Dreams are a means by which pertinent spiritual information is communicated to us from the spirit realm. God's greatest way of communication is not English. God can speak something to you with just a picture in a dream that can reveal way more than you realize. In our opening scripture above, verse 14 says *for God speaks in one way, and in two, though man does not perceive it.* This implies that God will always consider speaking to us in other audible and direct ways before He resorts to speaking to us in a dream. As expounded in one of my books titled, *"21 Ways Of How To Hear The Voice Of God Clearly"*, there are numerous ways by which God speaks to us. These include, dreams and visions, prophecy, audible voice, sensations/promptings, written word (logos), spoken word, divinely orchestrated situations and circumstances, conviction, revelation, prophetic actions, prophetic presbytery, manifestations, the inner witness – the inner knowing, leadings, check in your spirit, thoughts, anointing, quickenings, gifts and signs, leadership of the church, wise counsel and conscience. All these are special leadings of the Holy Spirit of which the Bible says that God has spoken in some ways to all men. There is no exception to the modus operandi of God's communication because even for other people who are not believers, God still speaks to them through conscience which figuratively speaking is a roadblock that prevents you from going out of the way. However, if then man does not hearken to God's voice through the above mentioned methods, God then resorts to speaking to them through dreams. That is why the second major method in which God directs our lives is through dreams. However, this does not mean that dreams are of less spiritual significance. Everyone who is born into this planet earth has dreams whether they know God or not.. Are you not surprised that God spoke to uncultured personalities in the Bible such as King Pharaoh and Nebcudnezer? Why? Because dream is the last resort available for God to communicate with every human being whether born again or not born again.

Dreams Come During The Most Critical Time When Humanity Requires Divine Intervention In Critical Matters

You notice in the bible that dreams had come at critical points in people's life and at critical points of a nation. Joseph received a dream when he was very young because he would need that dream to keep him for the rest of his life. And that was the dream that kept him alive through those years of rejection. When he went through all those sufferings, persecutions, trials and tribulations, he held on to that dream. That is why hypothetically speaking, if you stop dreaming, you also stop living because we all live to fulfil a particular dream, which is connected to our destiny. He may have dreamt many other dreams but these two stand up above the others. And they came just before he was to go through the hardest time in his life: to be sold by his own brothers. What did God give to Pharaoh at the most critical point of his nation? After all they were just at the edge of a great harvest of seven years of plenty. But after that came the seven years of famine. They were at the edge of something great happening and God gave a dream for them to act on that dream. In the book of Matthew, dreams came at the most critical point in Joseph's life. If he had not listened to his dreams he would have made mistakes and perhaps disrupted the course of destiny of the Messiah. If Pharaoh and Joseph did not hearken to those dreams that were given in Genesis, millions would have died. This is to tell you how significant dreams are to humanity.

Dreams Are A Means By Which God Warns Us Of Dangerous Or Precarious Situations

A dream can signifies a warning to your life. In fact, dreams are a secondary warning. When we are awake, our primary warning comes from our conscience and the voice of our human spirit teaching us and telling us what is right and wrong. If we obey it, then our dreams won't have to warn us in that area. The fact that God warns you in a dream, it means that he tried other methods of communication first and you did not listen or hear him speak. But when His voice is ignored the urgency increases, hence the dream is the second line of defence for us that God has implanted for us.

A dream carries a warning whereby God is bringing alive the secondary line of defence for their life in their dreams before they go outside His will. You can be sure that if they ignore the secondary line defence, they will move out of God's will completely. Then they will taste the consequences of the sword or the Pit or the pride of life that brings sorrows before the attention comes to them. Not all sicknesses are caused by sins or disobedience; there are natural causes too. But we do realize that sometimes a person falls sick because they are going on the wrong direction. And they have open doors to devils and natural circumstances and their sickness brings them to the attention that they have to re-examine what they are doing. But they don't have to go to that stage. You don't have to go to that stage where you lose something paramount before you say, "What am I doing with my life?" We don't have to reach that stage. But it is sad that some will allow that. See, evil doesn't come from God, it comes from the devil. God places roadblocks; of His inward voice, in the conscience and dream. We have to pay attention to the dream.

Dreams are picture communication hence we have to understand what they represent. The purpose for dreams is to turn us from pride, and eventual destruction. There are several things mentioned here in Job 33: 14 which God can warns us against. These are pride, destruction and perishing from the sword or from circumstances that will destroy you. A sword symbolizes war or circumstances that destroy people's life. The phrase, "from going to the pit" means eternal condemnation. So, God directs men in dreams to prevent them from being destroyed or destroying themselves. There are several people in the Bible who were saved from their circumstances because they took heed of God's voice when he warned them in a dream. Joseph was warned to escape with Jesus to Egypt when Pharaoh wanted to kill all baby boys, He was also warned not to send his wife Marry away after she was found to be pregnant with Jesus. Matthew 27 verse 19 records a dream received by the most unlikely person, Pontius Pilate's wife.

> *While he was sitting on the judgment seat, his wife sent word to him, "Have nothing to do with that righteous man, for I have suffered much over him today in a dream."*

Understanding Prophetic Dreams & Visions

Do you notice that Pontius Pilate's wife received a warning from God through a dream. Its a pity that his husband did not take heed to the dream otherwise he would not have proceeded with executing judgement against the Lord Jesus Christ.. Another quintessential example of someone who received a warning through a dream is Laban. Jacob was running away from his father-in-law Laban, who was seething with anger. Now in that state of mind, there is no telling what Laban was planning to do against Jacob as he was determined to give Jacob a piece of his mind. That was the reason behind the pursuit. But that very night before he met Jacob, God visited Laban in a dream. By character, Laban is a crafty sly shrewd man and who knows, if God did not intervened through a dream to warn him, he could have harmed Jacob. But God warned him not to speak evil against Jacob. He took heed to the message in the dream such that the very next day when he saw Jacob, he didn't do anything stupid because he had been warned in the dream.

But God came to Laban the Aramaean in a dream by night, and said to him, "Take heed that you say not a word to Jacob, either good or bad."(Genesis 31:24).

In a similar vein, Abimelech was warned by God in a dream not to touch Abraham's wife after he lied that she was his sister. God said to Abimelech, "You will die" but fortunately after hearkening to the warning of God in a dream and releasing Abraham's wife Sarah, his life was spared. It is always in a dream that you receive warnings to give you direction in life. That is why you must never take your dreams lightly.

Dreams Are A Divine Source Of Divine Inspiration As They Are Not Limited By The Natural Realm.

What makes dreams so paramount to us is that they are not limited by the natural realm. The natural realm, especially after the fall of man has inherent limitations or obstructions that hinders humanity from fulfilling their destinies in God. For example in the natural realm, your income may be say about seven hundred dollars a month and you are just struggling to live by yet in your dream, you are not limited by your income. Do you know that all you have to do is just close your eyes and dream? In your dream or imagination, you could see yourself living in a mansion with lots of hills to meditate. You could be going by a hill and suddenly the hill turns to a diamond hill. You could be driving a car and suddenly your car turns into an aeroplane. Some of you could never play any musical instrument. All you have to do is close your eyes and dream. And you could see yourself playing the musical instrument. Don't you think that's a powerful tool that God has given to us? There are no limits in your dreams. Whether by your financial standing, level of education or by anything at all, in your dream there is a fertile ground for anything to happen. That is why the realm of dreams is the realm of possibilities. There are no limitations, as we know it in this natural world. For this reason, what you want to stir in your life in the natural realm, you can start in your dream life and it will manifest in the natural realm. Is your mind limited by only what you think is possible? You refuse to think of things that are impossible. You dare not even think of such things. You need to think of things that you never thought before.

This is how important dreams are in our lives. That is why we need to cultivate ourselves so that we become dreamers of dreams. That's where our faith begins to take hold of some of the things you dream about. Perhaps you are in the business world and you are struggling. You are living by your rational intellectual mind. You are always seeing what can be done that is not impossible. You are not a dreamer of dreams. You dare not even think of things that are impossible. For a moment of time put aside those little things that are limiting you. Take time to go aside and just dream dreams. See your business grow. See yourself owning your own business premises. And dream dreams of the day that you own your own premises and your business going nation-wide and worldwide. You could dream dreams of things nobody dream about. Some of the things you dream about may not be God's will for you but you need to stretch your spiritual muscles. Then after you dream of dreams you come back into reality and you find yourself refreshed. Then you began to look at some of your problems about planning to own your own business premises and you will be thrilled to find out that they don't look so impossible any more. You have been weight lifting with 45 pounds and you come back and you take the 25 pounds, no sweat. It becomes easier for your muscles have been stretched. And we need the stretching of our imagination of our dreams, especially in this year because this is a year of great possibility, a year where your dreams can be fulfilled and your destiny secured, glory to Jesus!.

Dreams Bring About Hope In The Lives Of People In The Face Of Adversity And Debilitating Circumstances

Have you ever heard of the saying, *"If you stop dreaming, you stop living"*. Unknown to many people, this cliché alludes to the reality of how impactful dreams and visions are in fostering hope in the lives of the masses who are swarmed by vicissitudes of life and entangled in a morass of debilitating life circumstances such as poverty, debt, sickness or disease. It is for this reason that the Bible says *where there is no vision, people perish* because the absence of a *vision* produces an unhealthy atmosphere of hopelessness, that breeds lack of sense of purpose, and derails human dignity. The only thing that keeps some people going in the face of adversity is the fact that they still can dream their way into the future. That is why *dreams* and *hope* are almost synonymous. If you lose your dreams you lose your hope. Hope is different from faith yet faith is built on hope. In Hebrews 11:1 it says *faith is the substance of things hoped for and the evidence of things not seen*. This alludes to the fact that where there is no hope, then there is no conducive environment and ripe atmosphere for faith to grow and for hope to develop. Faith comes by hearing and hearing by the Word of God. By the same token, hope comes by dreaming and dreaming the things of God. When we dream our hope increases. No matter how depressed you are, if you have a good dream, it encourages and inspires you to face the unknown future. On the contrary, when your dreams die, your courage also dies. That is why we need a conducive environment and an atmosphere where we can dream and project our future based on what we see in our dreams.

In the epistles, Paul enumerates *three* significant elements needed to build a powerful Christian life. He mentions *faith, hope* and *love* and says love is the greatest. But do you know that although he just enumerates these elements in passing, there is an interlinking relationship between these *three* concepts in that *faith* produces *hope* and *hope* demonstrates *love*. Faith is what produces hope because it is a *substance* of things *hoped* for. In other words, it causes those things that we *hope* to achieve to crystallise into a solid material and tangible reality in the natural realm. Figuratively speaking, faith is the *condensation of hope* into solid, crude and raw material called *love*. Likewise, hope is what demonstrates *love* because when we achieve those things we have been hoping to, *love* which is an intrinsic quality of the human spirit, is manifested. However, although *faith* produces *hope*, the energy needed to set those things we *hope* for into motion, comes through *dreaming*. Dreaming is a catalyst that speeds up the rate at which our *hopes* are realised in the natural realm. Dreams can go beyond your ability and touch those areas which you would never be able to reach under normal circumstances. For example, you might not have money in your pocket but if you dream having lots of money, your dream will produce a spiritual energy that will magnetise, attract and cause money to speedily manifest and stream in your direction in the natural realm. That is why I mentioned earlier that your dreams are *creative tools*; they will create money for you if you need it. As you keep dreaming, what you see in the dream will turn into a reality if you dream it often enough and long enough. For this reason, never make a mistake and limit your dreams.

Dreams Are The Fertile Ground Of Faith To Take Root.

Despite the fact that not that all your dreams may come true, they are the fertile ground by which faith can take root. Dreams are the spices in which faith builds up. That is why we need to dream dreams to keep our faith healthy. If you stop dreaming dreams your faith has very little catalyst to work with. As aforementioned, faith is the substance of things hoped for. Who knows one day you could be a multi time millionaire and build the largest church that covers a million people before Jesus comes. Could you dream it? In a dream all things are possible. These kind of dreams cause our faith muscles to stretch all the time. That is why dreams are important for our faith as they are the right recipe and much needed diet for our faith to build up. Faith takes from your dreams. Faith takes from your hope and builds it into reality. And we need to dream because in dream we contact the great things and the wonderful things of God. We all know the scripture Isaiah 64:4 corroborated by I Corinthians 2 that *eyes have not seen nor ears heard the things that God has in store for those who love Him and for those who wait on Him.* But in our dreams we contact those realms. When the scriptures says *faith is the substance of things hoped for*, a dream is one of the spiritual substances of faith. For your faith to take root or have a grip, you need to have something to work on and a dream is that spiritual substance or material available to cause those things you hope and want to see in your life to materialise in the natural realm.

For example, you could dream of owning numerous Christian hotels and you could use them for conventions. You could dream owning private jets and using them to transport ministers of the gospel to various parts of the world. You could dream owning multinational food chains and using them to feed millions of poor people in orphanages. It is these dreams that will catapult your faith to higher realms of the supernatural and cause those things you believe God for to materialise speedily in the natural realm. If you keep dreaming, it won't be long before God sets your faith in motion and *substantiates* your faith into tangible realities in the natural realm. Figuratively speaking, Show me a man with great dreams and I will show you a man with great faith. This is because Great faith comes from great hope and Great hope comes from great dreams. The greater the dreams, the greater the faith because the level of dreams is directly proportionate to the level of faith one is operating at. In other words, as our dreams grow, our faith proportionally grows too. That is why we must dream dreams to keep ourselves growing in the things of God. On the contrary, when our dreams stop our faith will stop down the line. But if your dream is big enough , it can contain other people's dreams. That is why when something strikes you as a great dream, let it flow. You may not materialize it but it is the muscles of your spirit and your inner resources exercising so that one day some of those things are achieved.

Dreams Helps Us To Fulfil Our Divine Destiny In God

Dreams are pivotal in terms of us fulfilling our divine destiny in God. In other words, they helps us to become what God has created us for. As we stretch our muscles of dreams some of them may be God's destiny for our life. In most cases when you dream, especially if the dream is in line with God's word and his will, it is actually God directing you to a certain destiny. God can actually use your dreams to establish a divine destiny for you and for others in the world. I remember years back I used to dream becoming a World Renowned Author and writing dozens of Anointed Christin Books but when it actually started happening and I saw myself going to the extent of writing 45 Anointed Christian publications by the anointing of the Hoy Spirit, I realised that it was no longer just my dream but God had translated it into a global destiny and world-wide vision to transform the lives of the masses across the globe through the Throne Room Revelations encapsulated in those books. In a similar vein, when I was young, at the age of 10 years, I used to dream seeing rapture and the visions of the world coming to an end. I would see fire consuming the whole world and people being cast into everlasting torment. Little did I know that God was calling me to a Global Vision. And as I grew up and got involved in the *Ministry Of Revelation And Signs And Wonders*, I realised that that dream was not a personal one, it was a Global Vision God wanted to use me to stir up a global revival that shall shake all the continents of the world with his Mighty power prior to the second coming of our Lord Jesus Christ.

That is why we need to discern our own dreams and have a revelation of whether those dreams are for us as individuals or they are for the whole world. At times when you dream, your dreams might not be self-centred but a global vision God has destined for others since he always has the whole world in mind. You could dream owning a Global Kingdom Bank (GKB) yet God wants to use it to save the whole world in the next global recession. You could dream owning the largest conference centre in the world yet God wants to use it for the next world-wide revival. Likewise you could dream inventing a new technology yet God wants to use it for the betterment of the whole world. If you recall the story of Joseph, you will notice that the dreams which he had were not for himself but God used them as a means to save the whole nation of Israel during drought. That is why you need to be awakened to the realisation that some of the dreams you have seen may be for other people's lives and destinies to fulfil and not just yours. For example, I may not own a Christian hospital with all the Christian doctors, but if I dream it and share my dreams somebody else who is in the medical profession may catch hold of that dream and soon that dream becomes a global vision and world-wide sensation. Which is why the Bible calls it *old men dream dreams and young men see vision,* because the spiritually matured would have finished their work and their call. But they continue to produce seeds that the young men could take hold of and become their visions. The vision of their life becomes their destiny. That is why it is good to be a dreamer of dreams because dreams fulfil destinies.

Dreams Help Stimulate Our Level Of Creativity As Humans

Dreams are a means to activate the inner workings of the spirit man. It is interesting to learn that dreaming plays a fundamental role in terms of sharpening our ability to be creative. Dreaming enables the human brain to function too its level of effectiveness, paving way for new and creative ideas to flourish. On the contrary, Dream Researchers noticed that if a person is prevented from dreaming, their creativity during the day is diminished.. It has been scientifically proven that when you fall asleep your body is actually resting. But when you are dreaming all the biological activity in your body functions as if you are awake. It consumes much energy in your dream state. The eyes move and the body is activated but its like you are in a different realm since you are not conscious. In a biological experiment, when whenever the subjects under study fall asleep and just as they are about to dream when their eyes movement becomes rapid, they are woken up. The researchers tried to stop the subjects from dreaming. Every time they dream, they wake them up. Then they fall asleep again and then they wake them up. They found that these people became less and less creative after they woke up. Those people become reduced to almost mere robots or zombies in their waking state. This shows that their level of creativity was at its highest level when they were asleep than when they were awake.

It suffices to adjudicate that there is something about the ability to dream, which must be cultivated in our lives if ever we want to attain high levels of greatness and creativity. Very soon you might find yourself rubbing shoulders with Presidents of Nations because your dream has produced an invention that has become a worldwide sensation. Did you know that a dream can be a gift in the sense that it can bring you before Kings in a similar fashion in which Joseph was brought to be the Prime Minister of Egypt. I'm talking about a dream that comes when you are asleep just in case you thought that sleeping is a waste of time, you still have a lot to learn. Since creativity is an important part of our lives, we need to cultivate an atmosphere of dreaming and foster a culture of seeing visions so that creative or innovative ideas can flow. You never know, you might be the first to invent a product or machine that will revolutionise the ways things are done in the world. Just keep dreaming and your name might be in line for inscription in the World's Guinness Book of Records, for having introduced a new-to-the-world state of art product that is highly demanded in the whole world.

Dreams Helps Us To Move In The Prophetic Realm Of God

If a prophet arises among you, or a dreamer of dreams. (Deuteronomy 13:1).

Did you know that there is a level in the realm of dreaming that equates the prophetic. It's called the *third dimension of dreams*. Do you notice in our opening scripture that God calls prophets *dreamer of dreams*. This tells me that the way the Writer of the Book of Deuteronomy classifies it, a dreamer of dreams is equivalent to a prophet. However, not all dreamers of dreams may be prophets, but all prophets are dreamers of dreams. A dreamer of dreams reaches a higher dimension and level in the spirit realm that is equivalent to the realm that a prophet operates in. It is on a higher level of consciousness in the supernatural realm. Most of us in the modern world are trained and educated to function only on the intellectual realm. We rationalize and think but there is a higher level that we could move into. It is a level of consciousness beyond our intellectual mind. It's a level of dreaming dreams and seeing visions in the supernatural realm and not just rationalizing something in the natural realm.

Its profound to note that it's the dreamer of dreams that contact the prophetic realm. In Acts 2 we see that due to the outpouring of the Spirit, dreaming dreams and seeing visions are all in line with the prophetic realm. Notice that it says all categories of young men, young women. menservants, maidservants shall prophesy. In other words, they shall contact the prophetic realm of God, which is equivalent to the realm of dreams and visions. Notice also that it didn't say that only prophets will move in prophecy. Neither did it say that young men shall prophesy then after that they shall separately or on a different occasion see visions and dream dreams but rather it puts prophesying, dreaming dreams and seeing visions at the same level. This means that the same grace needed to dream dreams and see visions is the same grace that is required to prophecy. This is how powerful dreams and visions are in provoking the supernatural to flow in our lives. If you can dream dreams, you can be easily catapulted into the realm of the prophetic. In other words, you reach a level where your dreams solidifies and crystallises into solid material that will materialise in the natural realm as a tangible reality. Dreaming is an prophetic act that accentuates an avenue and paves a leeway for you to be elevated into the prophetic realm and translate supernatural material into tangible realities in the natural realm. If you can cultivate in you a habit of dreaming dreams constantly, it won't be long before those dreams burst forth into a river and stream flow of the prophetic. What you see in your dreams will be translated into visions that shall break out into rivers of prophesy. Dreams uses a coded language of symbols and pictures but when we crack that dream code, and secure a revelation of what it entails, it is translated into a prophecy.

Today they have discovered that people can develop ability to control things that are beyond what they thought possible. Did you know that there is a level that you can reach in the dream world whereby you can literally control your dreams and determine the full direction of your dreams by deciding what to dream and what not to dream? I reached that level recently; it's phenomenal. It's like you literally have the remote control of the supernatural realm in your hands and you can control anything. This is to tell you that there is a consciousness that is very deep that God wants us to enter into. To dream dreams. In my sleep, I dream dreams and I could see a building that sits a One hundred thousand people and that cost One Billion Rand. The engineers might be scratching their heads and asking how are they going to build that kind of building? I know that in our dream we defy a lot of natural laws. It is not so much that we want to do so but because we could see in our dream we would discover natural laws and principles and engineering abilities to do what we dream about.

Dreams Can Catapult Us To A Higher Level In The Prophetic Whereby We Have Face To Face Encounters With God

The truth is that dreams give us prophetic direction and if we grow in the knowledge of our dreams, we can graduate to higher levels in the prophetic where God begins to entrust us with deep mysteries of His Kingdom.. To cement this divine truth with reference to scriptural evidence, let's consider what God said about Moses:

> *If there is a prophet among you, I the Lord make myself known to him in a vision, I speak to him in a dream, but not so with my servant Moses, for he is faithful in all my house. I speak to him face to face, even plainly, and do not speak in dark sayings, and he sees the form of the Lord. Why then are you not afraid to speak against my servant Moses?* (Numbers 12:8).

Do you notice that God says he speaks to a prophetic through *dreams*. This speaks of the entry level in the prophetic that has now been made available to dozens of believers in Christ in the New Testament. It is the ordinary level in the prophetic, in which believers touch the prophetic realm of God through dreams and visions. However, God unveils a higher level in the prophetic. I would call it *face to face*. He says *but not so with my servant Moses, for he is faithful in all my house.* **I speak to him face to face**, *even plainly, and do not speak in dark sayings*. This bring us to a realisation that although Moses was a prophetic., God had catapulted him to another higher level in the prophetic called *face to face* where he needed no dream anymore in order to encounter God but experienced him in a tangible manner just like a man speak to his friend. This level in the prophetic is deed and profound and only a few men of God have reached it. It is a level beyond gifts and supernatural manifestations but a solid encounter with God himself. It is a level where you move out of the realm of a dream or vision, into a direct encounter with God. It is the third degree or third dimension in the supernatural. This is a level of divine mysteries and unveiling of ancient secrets to mankind. If God speaks to us in dreams, and visions, and dark sayings, we need to begin to understand metaphorical interpretations of the dark sayings and begin to mature and move from the realm of receiving dreams and visions, to having a face-to-face encounter with him.

There is a level you can reach in the prophetic whereby your dreams solidifies and crystallises into solid material that will materialise in the natural realm as a tangible reality and all of heaven is open up right in front of you. I call it *Condensation of Dreams*, because your dreams condenses and produces solid encounters with God and angels whereby you no longer see angels in an apparition form but as tangible beings just like people. It's a higher realm whereby you don't just hear God's voice through prophecy or sensations, promptings or any other form of usual spiritual communication but you hear a solid voice and see the whole package of God behind the voice that is speaking to you. And if Moses, who operated under an old testament covenant, was able to experience God that way, how much more us who have Christ the hope of glory being tabernacled inside us and literally have the God-being walking inside us, in the extreme quarters of our spirit? The level of intimacy has changed from outside face-to-face with God to inside face-to-face where God literally walks and perambulates in the inner faculties of our being. What a wonder and mystery, Christ in me the Hope of Glory!

God is calling you to the greater depths of God, a level beyond the encounter of Adam with God in the Garden of Eden. Owing to a lack of revelation, some believers presume that we are still yet to reach the level of God's glory in the Garden of Eden yet our experience with God is now beyond the level of Garden of Eden because following the resurrection of the Lord Jesus Christ from the dead, we now have the fullness of God himself dwelling in us, a level which is beyond Moses's face to face encounter. We have reached a level in the prophetic whereby God has decided, "No, I'm not effective when I'm speaking to them face-to-face from the outside, Now let me enter them and begin to speak to myself from within them and carry myself everywhere!" So when you look at people and you start prophesying to them, it is actually God speaking to Himself from within you; When you kneel down to pray, it is actually God praying to himself from with you. What a mystery, Glory to Jesus! I pray that as you graduate in the realm of your dreams, and secure divine elevation in the prophetic, God will catapult you to this level today!

PROPHETIC PRAYER:

Lord, I ask you to give me greater encounters with you. Give me both face to face encounters as well as metaphorical ones. Help me to value each and every encounter you give me, and open my heart to hear your voice through them in Jesus' name.

Dreams Can Provoke The Streams Of God's Miraculous Power To Flow

As aforementioned, God speaks in many forms, and in many ways. While most of us progress from hearing God speak to us through others, to understanding how God is speaking to us in our dreams, others have moved beyond the basics and into face-to-face encounters with God that release a torrential flow of miracles, signs and wonders. There are times when we encounter God in dreams, and when we have regained our consciousness, there is a corresponding evidence of that encounter in the natural realm manifesting in the form of miracles, signs and wonders. There is a substance of God, or evidence of His power that either shows up, or a clear increase of the raw demonstrations of God's power in our meetings, culminating in a change in ministry dynamics. At times you may have dreams of you praying for the sick, and they are getting healed, and when you wake up from that dream, then get your hands on sick people, and watch what God does! If you have a dream about prophesying to multitudes of people, then when you wake up, step out and give people prophetic words. God is activating many people all around the world in dreams, and visions and the manifestation of the activation is showing up in the natural realm. I remember there was a time when my wife suddenly developed skin rush that was itching all over the body. While she slept that night, she says she dreamt that someone was smearing anointing oil over her body and when she woke up, she was healed from that rush.

It is evidently profound that encounters with God in the dream can usher one into the realm of the miraculous. Consider how Moses saw a *vision* of the burning bush and not only did that first encounter revolutionise his life but the destiny of the masses in the world, even today. Yet it all started as a vision in the bush. Moses, our case in point, was a supernatural man who experienced many encounters with God and is probably one of the most amazing examples in the Bible of someone who walked in maturity in the miraculous power with God. He was one who was known for amazing miracles, signs, and wonders, and I believe that the source of his power was his face-to-face encounters with God, that *vision* in the bush! He went from being a coward, and murderer, to a powerful, miracle-working deliverer, as God visited him in a vision of a burning bush, and transformed his life. He entered into an intimacy with God that was, at times literally face-to-face! (See Exodus 3:2.). That realm of seeing God face-to-face can be open to us as well. There are times when you have encounters with God in the spirit realm such that when you come down to the meetings to minister people, God takes over the meetings and you watch him in action from the spectator zone. God would just sovereignty come and heal people in the atmosphere of our meetings as a result of the face-to-face encounter with him. This is when you begin to see a notable increase of miracles that comes by God's presence such as the blind seeing, the deaf hearing, the lame walking, missing body parts grow back, and most importantly the dead raised without anyone laying hands on anybody.

Dreams Can Be A Means By Which You Receive An Impartation Of The Supernatural Anointing

Did you know that one can receive the anointing of the Holy Spirit through a dream? Sadly, many believers have caught a religious mind-set that its only through the laying on of hands that the anointing is imparted. This is attributable to lack of revelation whereby many believers take the scripture where the apostle Paul testified that, *"I need to come to you so that I can impart some spiritual gift"*, and quote it out of context to mean that the things of the spirit can only be imparted through the laying on of hands when the minister is physically present. What they don't realise is that the supernatural realm is so vast and dynamic that God can use anything as a vehicle to transfer his supernatural power, one of which is through *dreams*. We have received numerous testimonies of people testifying of seeing men of God coming to pray for them in a dream. Many people talk about seeing the Lord in a dream. But sometimes, He comes in a form, or as a person who is unfamiliar to us. He hides Himself in the person you dream about. The impartation released through that person in the dream, is no less powerful than if the Lord came Himself. In fact, the person in the dream may actually be Jesus, or the Father, hidden to you in the same way that Jesus hid who He was to the disciples on that road to Damascus, until He broke bread and revealed the truth.

Did you know that there are dozens of Christian who receive the anointing of the Holy Spirit in a dream and many of them are not even aware. Many have received the anointing as an impartation in the dream either from a man of God they know and desire or directly from God and they are not even aware. Sometimes, we may have face-to-face encounters with God and not even know it. This is typical of the encounter of the two disciples whom the Lord appeared to on the road to Damascus. They didn't even recognize Jesus as he preached the gospel to them from the very beginning of the Bible to the very end. We may not recognize an encounter with Jesus. It wasn't until they begged Him to stay the night with them, instead of traveling to another city, that they recognized Him. When Jesus broke the bread for their supper, only then did they recognize Him. Suddenly, Jesus vanished from their sight. (See Luke 24:30.) They had been with the Lord, and did not recognize Him because they thought Jesus was dead. However, Jesus appeared in another form that was unfamiliar that seemed like He came through a dream. Sometimes the Lord will appear as Himself or in another form that is unfamiliar or uncommon to us, and release an impartation through a dream or a vision. While God spoke with Moses face-to-face, God chose to speak to Solomon in a dream.

One of the key anointing that you might receive in a dream is an *anointing for finances* that will catapult you to the realm of Kingdom Millionaires. Let's make reference to Solomon, a man of God in the Bible who received the anointing to create wealth through a dream. In 1 Kings 3:5, the Bible tells us that the Lord appeared to Solomon in a dream by night, and told him to ask whatever his heart desired, and it would be given to him. So Solomon goes on to ask God for Wisdom in order to lead His people. He also asked God for wisdom concerning good from evil. God was pleased with his request, and ended up giving him wisdom, as well as riches and notoriety in the world of his day. Then, God declares to Solomon that there shall be no other King before, or after him, that shall carry wisdom on their life like him. (See 1 Kings 3: 10-13.) Solomon's response to that dream was amazing. He had to do something corresponding prophetic actions of faith in the natural realm involving worship and sacrifice and immediately, he became the World's Richest Man Alive and the word of the Lord that was delivered to Solomon in his dream was fulfilled.

How I Received An Greater Anointing From Pastor Chris Through The Dream

One day when I was at University, I had a dream whereby Dr. Chris Oyakhilome, one of the world's most anointed man, was standing looking at me from a distance. As I looked admirably at him, I noticed that he had a bunch of keys in his hands. He then threw the bunch of keys at me and as I clutched them with both my hands, my countenance instantly changed such that I looked exactly like him. I stood in excitement exclaiming that I look like Pastor Chris. When I woke up, I immediately knew that I had received an anointing from the man of God. In my next meeting when I preached to other students at campus ministry, while I prayed for them, I waved my hands towards the congregation, shouting in a Pastor-Chris-Ministering-Style: *"Take the Anointing"*, and instantaneously, they all fell under the power with some shaking hysterically as the anointing permeated their bodies, into the very core of their beings. Many received instantaneous miracles of healing, deliverance and untold breakthroughs in every sphere of life.

Ever since that time, that anointing has never left me. As someone who passionately loves demonstrating God's power, I used it to demonstrate that anointing unreservedly whenever I went and miracles, signs and wonders would break out like a volcanic eruption. And guess how I received that Greater Anointing? Through a dream!. In the realm of the spirit, keys signify *power* and *authority* and the fact that the man of God threw a bunch of keys at me implies that not only did I receive a Greater anointing but also *power* and *authority* to function in higher realms of the supernatural. In subsequent years, I had dreams of me talking to Pastor Chris on a one on one basis, at times walking as friends with him, at times siting in a lecture room and listening to him teaching me. Through those experiences, I received such a strong impartation of a Revelation Anointing that opened my mind to divine mysteries and heavenly secrets and enabled me to write dozens of Anointed Christian Books, 45 in total, books that are filled with Throne Room Revelations that will thrill you to the last degree.

Frequency Revelator

This is to encourage you not to take your dreams for granted because they have an influence in terms of shaping your destiny and those of others.

A Testimony Of Dream Impartation

A certain minister of God's Word testified about how he desperately wanted a Great man of God to lay hands on him so that he would receive an impartation of the anointing but just like Zacchaeus of the Bible, because of protocol, he couldn't get through to him. The man in question was kind of frustrated that he could not get the man of God to pray for him. However, he said to God, "Lord I want that same anointing that this man of God is operating under". Two nights later God answered him in a dream. In this dream, the man of God walked up to him, and laid his hands on him, and prayed that he would receive an impartation of the anointing and governmental authority of God.. He got blasted and fell on the ground, shaking under the power of God. When he woke up, he could still feel the power of God all over his body. After he woke up, he said to himself, *"I have got to get to another meeting with this Great man of God quickly, and get him to lay hands on me."* But then he heard the Holy Spirit say in reply, *"You don't need to go to another meeting at all. God the Father has just imparted to you the same anointing for miracles in the dream you just had. Now, go lay hands on people and see what happens."* This experience really thrilled him, because he caught the impartation he had desired not from getting a man to lay hands on him, but from the Father in heaven, who loved him enough to activate the desire of his heart, in a dream.

The truth is that God is the greatest imparter or activator there is! Sadly, so many Christians are running from meeting to meeting to get what God has already activated in their lives. It they would just step out in faith, they would see that imparted anointing bear fruit. Just like this this minister of God's word who first thought was that he needed to go get a man of God to lay hands on him, in the natural, at a meeting. But in the dream, God the Father came as the man of God, and imparted the anointing he desired, and the Holy Spirit told him to step out and pray! Its amazing how dreams will revolutionise your spirit and make you a World Bank of God's Power!

Dreams And Visions Are A Point Of Contact With The Spirit World

Did you know that it is in dreams and visions that we contact the spirit world. It is in the lucid state of sleep that we leave this present earthly dimension and enter into the realm of the Spirit -a great realm for creativity. At times you hear dozens of believers asking questions like, *"How do I enter the spirit realm?".* It's simple. Just activate your dream life and you will enter into that long-awaited spirit realm. This is because dreams and visions are a means by which humanity can get to contact the spirit world. In fact, dreaming is the entry level point into the realm of the spirit. In one of my books titled, **"The Seven Dimensions Of The Supernatural"**, I explicitly and elaborately presented the *Seven Dimensions Of The Supernatural Realm*, citing that *Faith* is the first dimension of the supernatural as it introduces one to the realm of the *anointing* and connects us to other higher dimensions of the supernatural such as the *glory realm*. However, before we can get to the level of our faith, there is the *dream realm* which serves as a stepping stone for humanity to be catapulted into the realm of faith. Hence, tactically speaking dreaming is the first dimension of the supernatural realm since it is the first point of contact with the spirit realm. It's in our dreams that we encounter the spirit world. Every time you are asleep, you encounter the spirit world. But if your life is filled with the hustle and bustle of activities, you probably just encounter the physical world although the spiritual atmosphere around you is influencing you.. According to God's original master plan concerning humanity, man was made to contact the spirit world all the time and not some of the times. The supernatural realm does not have visiting hours but rather it is open to all humanity for exploration throughout the seasons. That is why no matter who you are even if you are not born again, you still dream. This is because there is a latent power of the soul and of the spirit of man that is still there. We still dream and in our dreams, spiritual encounters with either angels or God takes place. The Bible in Matthew 27:19 records an encounter with the spirit realm by the most unlikely person, Pontius Pilate's wife.

While he was sitting on the judgment seat, his wife sent word to him, "Have nothing to do with that righteous man, for I have suffered much over him today in a dream."

Do you notice that Pontius Pilate's wife contacted the spirit realm through dreams even though she was not a woman of God? The supernatural veil was taken off her such that she could actually receive communication from the spirit realm, the same realm that God and angels operate. It is always in a dream that you encounter with the spirit world. That is why you must never take dreams lightly. In fact when you lose your ability to dream, it's either your spirit is malnourished or there is too much pollution of this world in your soul and an excess of worldly activities that you don't have enough spiritual activity. Some of you who are so busy in your life say that you hardly dream. You know why? Because once upon a time when you were young, you have dreams but as you grew up and got stuck into the cares and concerns of this life that sucks the energy of your soul, such that your spirit is now malnourished and your soul underdeveloped. That most important area of your life I call the creative part of your soul is now left in a very weak state and the ability to dream ceases. And in actual fact if you lose the ability to dream, you become like a cripple in your soul and spirit since there is a part of you that has not been developed that God wants to develop. However, when you began to spend time in the Word and in prayer, you suddenly begin to dream again. It's like the fountains of creativity are opened once again.

Dreams Are A Channel By Which We Transfer Things Or Blessings From The Spirt Realm Into The Natural Realm

As aforementioned, we have already established that it is through dreams and visions that we contact the spirit world. However, it is not enough just to contact the spirit realm, be excited by its glamour and end there. We need to go beyond that level to maneuverer our way through the spirit realm such that we are able to transfer, our spiritual blessings from the spirit realm into tangible manifestation in the natural realm. Upon being born again, most believers get excited at the idea that they have *spiritual blessings in the heavenly places* as enumerated in Ephesians and as a consequence they tend to adopt a lackadaisical stance towards the things of the spirit in hope that everything will be delivered to them from the spirit realm on a silver platter. Metaphorically speaking, they are like a armature fishermen standing by the river bank, yelling in excitement that the river is loaded with a variety of fish yet they do not know the art of how to use the hook to get the fish out of the water. What they don't realise is that those spiritual blessings supposedly embedded in the spirit realm will not automatically fall on their laps like banana fruits dropping off from its tree. Rather, they need to learn the spiritual art of transmuting spiritual blessings such as wealth, money, healing, wisdom and power from the spirit realm where they are tabernacled into the physical realm where they should manifest. Its only when they are now manifesting in the physical realm that they will be useful to you.

The question you are probably asking yourself is: So, how do I transfer these blessings from the spirit realm into the natural. It's simple. While there are other multiple methods which a believer can employ such as through harnessing the power of imagination, prophetic declaration and meditation on God's word, visualisation and placing a demand on the supernatural through faith, activating your dream life is one of the easiest and most significant method. Did you know that dreams are a means by which we can receive spiritual things or blessings. Because our dreams are our point of contact with the spirit world, they can be so powerful that you actually receive things in your dream. Dreams are a catalyst that provokes, stirs up and destabilises the supernatural realm such that all its contents in the form of breakthroughs and blessings are left with no other option except to drop down to earth. Dreams have a spiritual power that works like a magnet that attracts or draws things from the supernatural realm and forces them to manifest in the physical realm. This is because what you see in your dream is actually a reality being played in the natural realm. It's like watching a movie on television that plays the exact events and activities taking place in real life situations. Only if you can harness the spiritual power of dreaming, you reach a level where your dreams solidifies and crystallises into solid material that will materialise in the natural realm as a tangible reality. Dreaming accentuates an avenue and paves a leeway for you to translate supernatural material into tangible realities in the natural realm. If you can cultivate in you a habit of dreaming dreams, it won't be long before your breakthrough burst forth into manifestation in the physical realm.

The daunting challenge facing many believers is that most people have not learnt the spiritual art of how to *receive* things from the spirit realm. It is for this reason that many have relegated their dream life to something insignificant, yet all it takes to receive great things from the supernatural realm is to delve into the realm of dreaming to conceive and incubate spiritual things in the spirit realm and then coming back to the natural realm to give birth to those things in a tangible way. In the book of I Kings 3:5, *at Gibeon the Lord appeared to Solomon in a dream by night; and He said, "Ask what you want and I shall give you."* Please bear in mind that this was happening in a dream. It was not even a vision of some kind just in case someone might think less of it. God Himself came in a dream and said, *"Solomon, ask what you want."* In the dream Solomon replied to God, *"I want wisdom to rule your people."* God said, *"It is done and I will give you riches and honour too."* The most remarkable thing is that, that very morning when he woke up, there was something deposited in his life because of that dream. The reality is that we contact the spirit world in our dreams that sometimes it's so hard to contact in our conscious state. That's why we need to pay attention to our dreams. And if you lose that ability to dream, you may find yourself missing out a lot on divine opportunities and blessings that you could have received from God. That is why it's highly important that you be a dreamer of dreams so that you can amass humongous wealth, blessings and other financial resources from Heaven especially in this critical end time season whereby the Wealth Transfer Programme is in full force of operation.

Dreams Enables Us To Touch And Enter The Timeless Zone Of God Which Is Outside Our Time Dimension In The Natural Realm

It must be ingrained in your thinking that not only do dreams enables you to enter the spirit world but also to perambulate in what I call the *timeless zone of God*. Dreams can actually catapult us into the realm of God, that is outside our time dimension; an eternal realm where anything and everything is possible. In order to secure a deeper understanding of the time dimension of God, lets first understand few of his attributes. You see, God is, was and is to come. To him, the past, present and future are all in past tense and to him, everything has already transpired. Since God operates outside our time dimension, he is not influenced by either events, or time in our natural domain. The time dimension of God can be likened to a bicycle wheel, in which God is in the centre of the wheel. In a bicycle wheel, although the wheel and the spokes may turn around, the centre of the wheel is not affected by their turning or movement. By the same token, because God exists and operates outside our time dimension, he is not affected or moved by anything that is happening on the earthly realm because where God is, there is no time. As far as God is concerned, time doesn't exist. Yesterday, today and forever is the same. The spokes of the bicycle signifies every fabric of creation in the universe whose life and existence is solely dependent on God. In a similar fashion in which the strength of the wheel and the spokes is dependent on the balance and power remitted from the centre of the wheel, every creation draws life and creative force from God, who is at the centre of the wheel. Although He created the universe and all creation around Him, all creation in the universe around Him functions in time yet he functions in the realm of eternity. So, at the centre of the wheel, time doesn't exist where heaven and the spirit world is. But as God created the material world, we live in the outer spokes of the wheel. That's where time exists and confines us to a limited earthly dimension. When time begins to function, there is a beginning and there is an end.

With this understanding, let's now go back to the subject of dreaming and try and apply it to God's concept of a Wheel and see how dreaming can catapult us into the realm that is outside our time dimension. You see, when we dream, we come out from the outer spokes of the wheel and we enter into the centre of the wheel which is the area where time doesn't exist. In the same way the spinning of the wheel releases a force that can cause material on the spokes to slide into the centre of the wheel, dreaming releases a spiritual force and divine energy that instantly catapults us to the realm that is outside the time dimension. In that timeless zone, we sometimes see the future things in our dreams, sometimes the present and sometimes our past because time doesn't exist in our dream in a sense. Through dreaming, we are prophetically enabled to move or travel in the spirit realm by the quantum of events right into the past to behold certain things which transpired in the past and then come back to the present to establish their present truth and then move into the future to create new realities. It is for this reason that modern day prophets are able to move by the quantum of events to behold certain experiences and events that took place in the life of a person in the past and then come back to the present to explain how such events will affect the person in the present and how they can be prevented from happening in the future.

The most remarkable thing about dreaming is that when our dreams move or progresses, they move with us; they don't leave us behind. In other words, any progress we make in our dream life will produce a corresponding progress in real life. The reason why dreams are important is that they enable us to progress from the time dimension that keeps us confined to the natural realm into the timeless zone of God where there are no limitations of any nature. In our dream, if we are not progressing out of the time dimension of our physical life that means our dreams are bound by the physical forces of this life hence we will not be able to make corresponding progress in real life. For example, if you have lived in three houses from the time when you were born until the time when you were fifty, and if in your dream you still find yourself going back to the first house you lived when you were a child, then God is telling you that there is something in your life that is being dominated by forces from the past that you haven't let go yet. And interestingly, as you progress in real life, you will notice that there is also a corresponding progress in your dreams. Suddenly, in your dreams, you could find yourself moving from one house to the other house and you could in the end be dreaming that you are staying in the house where you are presently staying. Your dreams could even show you the house you will be occupying in the future and the minute you start dreaming living in that future house, that's when divine arrangements of circumstances in the natural realm will start to align with the supernatural (*Zone outside our time dimension*) such that miraculously, you will find yourself getting the money to buy the house. That is how miracles are produced. There is power in dreams, they can create things and produce miracles for you.. That is why the realm of dreaming is the realm of creative miracles because we create things through the power of dreaming. What you call a *miracle* in the natural realm is actually an end-products of what is given birth to in the dream world.

Dreams can take you into the past, present and future, which is the realm outside our time dimension where God operates. This is because dreams are supposed to be timeless. They are not supposed to be affected by time or by some things which happened to us in the past. If you keep dreaming of the old wooden houses that you lived in when you were young, you will not be able to make any progress in real life. That's is why whenever the devil wants to control your life and keep you confined to a certain level, he makes sure that he meddles with your dream life because he knows that dreams are a replay of reality and if he can mess you up in the dream, your life will also be messed up in the physical realm; and if he can prevent your dreams or dream life from progressing, he would have prevented you from making progress in real life. Therefore, if you want to see yourself making progress, start by making progress in your dream life and you will experience corresponding progress in real life because dreams touches the realm that is outside our time dimension, thereby causing us to easily move into the future. With this revelation knowledge at the tip of your fingers, you can never take your dreams for granted!

Dreams are transcendent, meaning they transcend the dimensions of height, depth, breath and time. Dreams and visions allow us to be in two or more dimensions simultaneously. Dreams allow us to be in the future or in the past. Even within the dream, we may leave where we are, momentarily relocating to where we're going. Dreams allow us to transcend age. We can be our current age, living in our childhood home. We may even find ourselves looking through someone else's eyes, as if we were viewing things from inside him or her. Dreams do not seem to be inside us; rather we find ourselves inside a dream. Dreams move us about intra-dimensionally and seem to change matter into energy and turn chaos into order.

Dreams Activate Angelic Activity In Our Lives

Dreams is one of the mechanisms by which we contact the angelic realm. Sadly, many believers have missed angelic visitations because they ignored their dream life. It is through the dreams that we can get to communicate with angels, receive messages and divine instructions from angels concerning our destinies and those around us. We see the role of dreams in the life of Joseph. In Matthew 1:19;

And her husband Joseph, being a just man and unwilling to put her to shame, resolved to send her away quietly. But as he considered this, behold, an angel of the Lord appeared to him in a dream saying, "Joseph, son of David, do not fear to take Mary your wife, for that which is conceived in her is of the Holy Spirit." 24 When Joseph woke from sleep, he did as the angel of the Lord commanded him.

Do you notice that Joseph received a very important message from an angel through a dream? It says *Joseph, being a just man and unwilling to put her to shame, resolved to send her away quietly. But as he considered this…"* Notice the first principle operating, *he slept* with this thought. This tells me that this was a night dream. Joseph was moved by the dream and in the dream he had an angelic encounter. It was almost like a vision except that he was asleep. This is not his first encounter. In Matthew 2:13 *Now when they had departed, behold, an angel of the Lord appeared to Joseph in a dream.* This is his second recorded dream. So God continues to speak to Joseph. The third dream is in Mathew 3:19 which says *But when Herod died, behold, an angel of the Lord appeared in a dream to Joseph in Egypt.* See the right place, the right time, the right position, he dreamt. All his dreams were directional and God met with him in a dream.

My Dream Encounter With The Angel Of Miracle Money Standing On the Grand Stand

One night I had a dream in which I saw an Angel of Miracle Money standing on the Grand Stand in Heaven and calling out the names of people on earth and the amount of money that they were supposed to receive in that season. I waited expectantly for my turn to come as the Angel Called out the names from a book in Heaven. I heard several names being called and, as I listened, I heard the angel call my name saying, **"Frequency Revelator, 5 Million"**. I was so excited that my name was singled out to be a recipient of the Heaven's Wealth Transfer Programme. And when I woke up from the dream and had regained my consciousness, I found that I had literally received those millions from the spirit realm. It was as if there was a supernatural transaction that was effected in the spirit realm such that immediately, millions started manifesting in the natural realm.

My Dream Encounter With Multitudes Of Angels Welcoming Me On The Red Carpet

I had another dream, in which I was walking on the red carpet as in a celebrity style and on my left and right hand, were multitudes of ministering angels which were cheering up and welcoming me on standing ovation. As I walked through the narrow isle, they kept touching me from every side. I noticed that each angel had a pair of wings which they kept flapping as I passed by. I was so overwhelmed by this spectacular divine experience because it was as if each angel was competing just to touch me. If you have seen how Presidents, soccer stars or prominent politicians are received by the fans at a stadium, you will have a picture of what I'm talking about. The good news is that when I regained my consciousness from the dream, I had actually received millions in wealth as a spiritual impartation from the hands of angels. At that very time when I was dreaming Angels pressing on every side just to touch me, in the spirit realm, a group of angels were actually imparting wealth on me as in the case of Solomon. This is to tell you that wealth can be imparted on you from the spirit realm in a dream hence you need to develop a high level of sensitivity and consciousness of the spirit realm so as to detect the movements of angels.

Dreams Connect Us To Our Destiny, Breaks Us Free From Our Past And Reveals To Us What God Has Called Us To Do In Our Future

Did you know that your dreams can reveal what you are destined to do by your Maker. Dreams are designed to reveal your future and not your past. Job 33 tells us that God speaks once and twice in a dream in the vision of the night, to warn us and to keep us from evil and to keep us from wrong decisions. That means dreams are designed to help us handle the future and the things that is to come. But for many people's life their dreams are bounded by their physical circumstances or their past.. And if you were to allow God to dream dreams in your life and remember those dreams God gave to you, this year may be the fulfilment of the dream that you have always dreamt. Ecclesiastes 5:3,

For a dream comes with much business, and a fool's voice with many words. When you vow a vow to God, do not delay paying it; for He has no pleasure in fools. It is better that you should not vow than that you should vow and not pay. For when dreams increase, empty words grow many; but do you fear God?

In the context of this scripture, the multitude of dreams the Writer is talking about is in verse three where in the multitude of dreams that has to do with your daily life. And if all your dreams are just concerned with your past and your daily life and your activity and they have nothing to do with the spirit realm, somehow you are in a dangerous realm. Your dreams that are supposed to contact the spirit realm are no more contacting the spirit realm. It becomes just a hibernation ground of activities from your daily life. That's not what God wants and designed your dream realm to be. It was designed as a contact with God. Angels could appear in your dreams. God could speak to you or God could reveal things to come. It is dangerous ground to fill your dream realm with so many sensory stimuli from your so many worldly activities that you cloud out God's voice and message from contacting you there. The bible calls it vanity. Waste of energy, waste of spiritual energy, waste of soul energy that God could use to His glory. Let's refer to the book of Genesis chapter 37:5;

> *Now Joseph had a dream, and when he told it to his brothers they only hated him the more. He said to them, "Hear this dream which I have dreamed, behold, we were binding sheaves in the field,*

Notice the dream came from his daily activity. But it was not limited by that *and lo, my sheaf arose and stood upright; and behold, your sheaves gathered round it, and bowed down before my sheaf.* Now the binding of sheaves is something they do every day. His dream was not bounded by the past. It used the illustration of the present to point to things in the future that God wants to do. So in a dream it is all right to see yourself as you are but you will find an added thing that you never experienced before. There may be dreams of great and hidden things that you have not comprehended before or seen before. Have your dreams moved up to the house where you are living in. Or are your dreams still stuck somewhere behind. You need God to break it and to shake off that past.

That past is like the dirt and dust that gather onto us when we go out. If you go out in a country road and as you walk and explore, you will find the dirty dust and mud sticking to your shoes and your pants. You are not going to leave the dirt there. If it was a raining day there will be mud all over your shoes. Are you going to leave it there? Most of us will clean it up. But for many people in their soul they never clean up their dreams. When their dreams had the past sticking to them they never clean it up. They go around accumulating more and more dirt until it is so thick that they completely lose the blessings of dreams. Remember when your dreams die your hope dies. Interestingly it's the same type of people who get depressed easily. It's the same type of people who lose their hope easily. It's the same type of people who lose their courage easily. Let's look at another dream in the book of Genesis 40:5:

> *And one night they both dreamed, the butler and the baker of the king of Egypt, who were confined in the prison, each his own dream, and each dream with its own meaning. So, the chief butler told his dream to Joseph, and said to him, "In my dream*

there was a vine before me, and on the vine, there were three branches; as soon as it budded, its blossoms shot forth, and the clusters ripened into grapes. Pharaoh's cup was in my hand; and I took the grapes and pressed them into Pharaoh's cup, and placed the cup in Pharaoh's hand.

Now the butler has always been serving Pharaoh. So his dreams had caught up with him. It was right where he was. You must be dreaming right where you are and then from there you can see the future. We need a platform to see the future that God is revealing in our dreams. As long as your platform is somewhere in the past you can only look from your past into the present. But if you stand on the platform on your present then you can look into the past and you can look into the future. The butler was right where he was. He was still a butler in his dreams. The baker had a different kind of dream, but he was still a baker in the dream. The baker dreamt he was a baker. The baker didn't dream that he was an apprentice in a baker's shop. He dreamt he was a baker. The butler dreamt he was a butler. It is important to see that your dreams must catch up with the present to see the future. Because both butler and baker dreamt of their present, their dreams could show their future. So we need to examine our lives where we are. We could say where are you in your life. Where are you in your spiritual life? Adam, Adam where art thou? "Where art thou?" could be asked in many ways. Where are thou physically. Where are thou spiritually. "Where are you in your dream life?" If you are constantly dreaming of your past, there is something in your past that you must resolve and clear before you get into the will of God for your present. If you are constantly dreaming of your present, then you should look for indications for the future in your dreams.

Dreams Helps To Revitalise, Rejuvenates And Sustain Longevity Of Human Life

In each one of us is a driving desire to live life to the fullest. Sadly for some they are just getting by and by. Some others really want to do something about their lives. Some others just live by. Some others have given up on their life and waiting for it to close. When you have reached the peak of your maturity you thought you have done it all. They tell you today that it is not retirement that kills people. It is inactivity and the lack of zeal in life that kills people. But people who are active in life and who have something always to do tend to live longer and reach ninety, hundred and twenty and they are still full of energy. But when they just sit and watch everything go by with nothing to do, something inside them die. The solution to this quandary can be resolved through dreams. Dreams helps to revitalise, rejuvenates and sustain longevity of human life.

Many older people are looking out for alternatives for them to look younger and rejuvenate their lives. The solution is not in them cosmetics but in dreaming dreams. While cosmetics and surgical procedures might renew the flesh, dreaming completely renews both the soul and the body because once the soul is rejuvenated, results will manifest in the body. It is for this reason that God spoke in Joel 2:28 that *old men shall dream dreams*. Why? Because God knows how powerful dreaming is as a spiritual mechanism for the rejuvenation of the human soul especially at an older age. However, note that the word *old men* here does not literally alludes to physically old men. It's a figure of speech that alludes to spiritual age. That old man could represent people who have reached the zenith of their lives. The good news is that dreams caters for all categories of humanity whether old or young. For example, if you are older in terms of age, you might think that you have tasted everything you could have. Maybe you have reach your highest point and you could see no way out. The solution to your situation is to dream dreams again because when you dream dreams again, your youth is renewed like the eagle. You are charged up once again, and you will have great things to do. The future looks as if you are a teenager again. No matter how old you are you have to remain young by dreaming dreams. They will keep the fire in you alive. Renew your youth like an eagle because you are always seeing more things to do in the Lord. That is why the solution to aging is dreaming. On the other hand, teenagers look forward to growing up in life. Many wonder at many things they haven't seen and tasted in life. The solution to this situation is to dream dreams and you will put fire back into your soul. Once you start dreaming dreams as a teenager, the fire in you will come again alive and you will easily realise your goals.

Dreams And Visions Were Vital In The Ministry Of Our Saviour Jesus Christ

Throughout the Bible, God has always been known to communicate pertinent information to people through dreams and visions. Every time there was something critical to be communicated to the inhabitants of the earthly realm, God would choose to speak in a dream. For anything significant to move from the supernatural into the physical realm, man would catch it through dreams. Dreams have always been the means to by which God reveals ancient secrets and mysteries to mankind. We see this reality being evident in the life and ministry of our Lord Jesus Christ. Just in case you thought that dreams are not important, I want you to know that the life of our Lord Jesus Christ was perfected by dreams. Did you know that the prophetic destiny of our Lord Jesus Christ was actually shaped by dreams? Consider Joseph as an example, the man whom God gave clear-cut direction through dreams concerning the destiny of the Messiah. I don't know why God has to contact Joseph through a dream. But possibly when he is awake he could be quite a rational intellectual man. You could tell that by the way he keeps thinking how to put Mary away. He couldn't understand this virgin birth concept. See he was a rational man. As he thinks rationally how could he believe Mary? It's very hard to believe. Here was his beloved coming and saying that she is pregnant with the Holy Ghost child. He can't compute intellectually. And in fact he has already rejected her.

You look at Matthew chapter one he has already rejected her. He was already making a decision that he was not going to take her neither does he believe her. What would Mary have told Joseph? Mary would have reported everything. If you know the great abilities of ladies they will report everything to you. Usually when ladies tell a story they will go to the details. Mary gave an extraordinary story about how she met an angel and the child that she is carrying is the Messiah. And here is Joseph engaged to her wondering whether this is true or not. And being a righteous man he was seeking to put her away, thinking that she was lying. I believe Mary would have told him how she saw this angel but Joseph was a rational man. He was definitely not given to this thing of the spirit. Matthew 1: 19 *being a just man not wanting to make her a public example was minded.* Let's look at the past tense *he was minded.* This tells us that he has already made up his mind, past tense, *to put her away.* He has already rejected the facts, the evidences, and the testimony of Mary. And because of his state of mind, God cannot speak to him directly. His mind was turned to a different direction. While he was thinking about this thing the bible tells us that while Joseph was asleep an angel of God came and said take Mary as your wife and call her child Jesus. When he was asleep, when his conscious mind was knocked out an angel came and spoke to him in a dream.

Frequency Revelator

The life of our lord Jesus Christ was perfected by dreams. Matthew tells us that the wise men were warned in a dream to go back by a different way. So, if people didn't listen to their dreams they would have missed God. You can listen to God in your conscious state and hear the voice of God and miss the other one third. If we miss what God is saying to us in our dreams we may miss God entirely. And in Matthew chapter two Joseph was warned by a dream to go to Egypt. And when he came back he was warned in a dream not to go back to the place where he was but go to Nazareth. Dreams perfected Joseph, perfected Mary, perfected baby Jesus. For this reason, dreams are important, hence should not be taken lightly.

CHAPTER THREE

THE SEVEN DIFFERENT TYPES AND CATEGORIES OF DREAMS

It is of paramount significance that you understand how to classify dreams so you can determine what to do with them. Over the years, I have established biblical support for seven distinct categories of prophetic dreams. Lucid dreams are the more memorable dreams we have. They may actually be closer to a vision than to a dream, because of their vividness and clarity. A. Lucid means to have clarity of thought and full use of one's faculties. Lucid dreaming is to have a measure of conscious activity and control in our dreams. These **SEVEN** types of dreams does not necessarily mean that are an exhaustive explanation of all dreams in the Bible. Hence I do not intend to create a doctrine in this area but rather provide revelational guidelines which the masses across the world can use to fully understand dreams and visions. Let's take a look at these **SEVEN** categories of prophetic dreams.

Waking Dreams

These are dreams whose occurrence is so profound that such that when you wake up, they leave an imprint on your imagination for the whole day. It is difficult to ignore and forget them because they occur just as you awaken for your day. They are called *waking dreams* because they wake you up from your sleep in the morning, leaving you with nothing but a dream to brighten your day and set the course for all proceeding of your day. These are not your usual or typical dreams that wake you up in the middle of the night, after which you return to sleep. No! These dreams happen right at the end of your night sleep. In other words, they conclude your sleep. They are your first impression of the new day, which is why I usually say they require action. The purpose of waking dreams is to show you something that stays with you and is not forgotten when you wake up. We all know it is possible to dream in the night and not remember it, but it is next to impossible to forget a waking dream. I often find that when God awakens me with a dream in the morning, I am to take action soberly. Sometimes to pray patiently, and sometimes to apply it to my life immediately.

The bottom line is that you cannot shake the feeling that a waking dream is an immediate assignment. The Bible in Genesis 41:1–7 describes Pharaoh's two compelling and abstract dreams that saved a nation and preserved God's chosen people through Joseph, the dreamer and dream interpreter. In Genesis 41:7–8, it describes a waking dream perfectly:

> *"Then Pharaoh woke up; it had been a dream. In the morning his mind was troubled. . . ."*

The first dream was not a waking dream, and no emotion was recorded. The second dream, however, left Pharaoh troubled. Dreams you have just before you wake up leave you feeling definite emotion. They will either trouble you into action or encourage you into peace. Pharaoh was troubled, but not for long, because Joseph's interpretation brought peace. Seven bad economic years were on their way, but seven plentiful ones would precede them so the nation could store up and prepare. Pharaoh's first dream, followed by the second, a waking dream, drove home the point, and fourteen years later the nation was back on track.

Decision Dreams

A decision dream is a dream in which you have to make a decision concerning a matter that is critical either to your own destiny or that of others. It is a dream situation in which you are asked a question or given options, and you watch yourself provide an answer or make a choice. This is the greatest proof we have that we are made up of three parts. Your mind is turned off at night as your body rests, and neither can help you make a decision in your dream, but your spirit can. Your spirit does makes all the decisions. Watch carefully the choices you see yourself make in your dreams, for they are very telling when it comes to what is going on in your spirit, good and bad. Biblically, this is evidenced by the narrative in 1 Kings 3 whereby Solomon was asked in a dream whatever he wanted God to do for him and he made a decision to choose wisdom. We credit Solomon with being the wisest man in the world, all because when given one wish in a dream, he asked for wisdom and made the right decision. But did you know he was asleep when he made it? It was a dream:

"At Gibeon the LORD appeared to Solomon in a dream by night; and God said, 'Ask! What shall I give you?'" (1 Kings 3:5).

Solomon's spirit chose correctly, and he asked for wisdom to lead God's people. I have no doubt that since that same spirit remained in him while he was awake, he would have given the same answer any time of day.

Warning Dreams

Warning dreams are exactly what they sound like, they are dreams that warns you of coming danger caused by a person, the evil one or a wrong decision they are about to make. They are divinely orchestrated by God to prevent the imminent danger the enemy had planned for us. Sometimes God will give us warning dreams, to keep us out of trouble, or to protect us from the plans of the devil. Matthew 2:12 tells us that Joseph, the father of Jesus, was divinely warned in a dream that his family was not to return to the land of Herod, but that they were to move to another country. The result was that Jesus' life was spared! Imagine what would have happened if Joseph did not listen to that warning? Jesus would have been killed with all of the other children who were two years old, and younger, as Herod's evil army slaughtered the children of Bethlehem. It pays to listen to the Lord when He speaks. You never know what blessing is behind the door of obedience! As we read at the start, Job 33:16–18 says about dreams:

"Then He opens the ears of men, and seals their instruction. In order to turn man from his deed, and conceal pride from man, He keeps back his soul from the Pit, and his life from perishing by the sword."

We see here that God can save us from bad deeds, pride or the pit of hell itself. Sometimes we need saving from an enemy, and sometimes we need saving from ourselves. But warning dreams are not necessarily "fate," meaning they are not definitely going to come to pass. The world would have us believe that life is one big happenstance full of unavoidable fortunes, and that a stirring dream heralds either coming good or bad luck. Nothing could be further from the truth. God will often show you things in dreams so you will partner with Him and change them. They are given so you can pray and change the plot of the story. As believers, we not survive without God's warning dreams. Matthew 2 records two of the most important warning dreams of all time. Without them, the salvation of the world would not have occurred when it did. The first warning dream was to the wise men. Commissioned by Herod to find the Christ child, they did not realize that Herod wanted them to report back to him so he could find Jesus and kill Him. Verse 12 says,

> *"And having been warned in a dream not to go back to Herod, they returned to their country by another route."*

Then immediately in verse 13, God's protection continued: "When they had gone, an angel of the Lord appeared to Joseph in a dream. 'Get up,' he said, 'take the child and his mother and escape to Egypt. Stay there until I tell you, for Herod is going to search for the child to kill him.'" Later, in verses 19–20, God tells Joseph in another dream that it is safe to return home again, and they do. All of these dreams involved international travel and faith. God warns us of impending danger and keeps us from so much harm and heartache through warning dreams. I am also thankful for how He gives me warning dreams for my friends and family, even though nobody likes to get that warning phone call that is a call to war in the middle of peacetime. But regardless of how you feel at the time of a warning dream and regardless of when it is given to you, do not dismiss it, even if it means filing it away in a journal somewhere. Warning dreams are valuable in navigating through life. People often discount them, get pummeled and then shake their fists at God for not protecting them. Through warning dreams, it is as if God rolls out hell's blueprints in front of you to divulge what the enemy is plotting. After you pray, such a dream winds up altering your steps. Warning dreams are an invitation to pray, not to fear or relax. They are announcing a day to win, if we will partner with God.

Directional Dreams

Directional dreams gives direction on a particular matter and shows you what to do in a particular situation. They "seal your instruction," as Job 33:16 promises dreams and visions can do. The Bible is full of directional dreams, for example, in Genesis 46:2–3, God tells Jacob in a dream to go to Egypt. In Genesis 31:24, God instructs Laban in a dream to speak kindly to Jacob. In Matthew 1:20, God tells Joseph in a dream to take Mary as his wife. Directional dreams leave you thunderstruck when you awake at the detailed counsel you realize you have just received. These dreams do not always involve warnings; some of them can be quite exciting. A type of a directional dream is what I call a calling dream. Dreams can spark the faith to go in a different direction, and walk into the calling that God has for you.

This is a type of dream that God shows you when he wants to show you your calling. He wants to show you your destiny. Have you ever had a dream of speaking publically? That's a calling dream. God's giving you a vision of what you are to do, in the metaphorical language of the dream. Often, these dreams recur over and over again. Why? Out of the mouth of two or three witnesses, the word of the Lord is established. When it keeps coming it's because there's something the Lord is trying to get through to you. I meet people all the time who say things like, "I just had a dream that I'm called to produce music!" Or "I'm called to preach!"

Recurring Dreams

This is a dream that keeps repeating itself several times. I believe the repetition means God is indeed trying to confirm their calling or emphasize on a critical matter. A repeated or recurring dream may mean the issue is established by God and He will "shortly bring it to pass." Genesis 41:32 "And the dream was repeated to Pharaoh twice because the thing is established by God, and God will shortly bring it to pass. I have talked to people who say they have had the same dream so many times they have lost count. Perhaps it is a dream that started way back in childhood, or a dream with the same plot but slightly different symbols each time. Typically, the people who say this describe their dream with troubled faces. It comes accompanied either with fear, dread or embarrassment. Being in a public place naked, falling off a tall building or dying. Definitely with a recurring dream, there is the chance that something is weighing heavily on the mind. But be comforted by the fact that recurring dreams also happened in Scripture.

The Bible talks of how Joseph was called to interpret Pharaoh's two dreams. They were similar numerically, with their seven cows and seven ears of corn representing the next fourteen years of Egypt's agricultural and economic future, and although they were not the same exact dream, they had the same exact interpretation. Joseph said, "The dreams of Pharaoh are one; God has shown Pharaoh what He is about to do." Yes, it is possible for a recurring dream with slightly different symbols to have one interpretation. Joseph's next statement introduces the idea that through multiple dreams, God is stressing the point that something is ordained to transpire:

> *"And the dream was repeated to Pharaoh twice because the thing is established by God, and God will shortly bring it to pass"* (Genesis 41:32).

I do not want to say that the events in a repetitive dream are 100 percent set in stone to occur, but from looking at Joseph's statement, such dreams must be taken seriously and committed to prayer. Not with fear because God has not given you a spirit of fear and not with confusion because God is not a God of confusion, but with priority.

Incubation Dreams

An incubation dream is a dream that has no immediate application in your life as it relates to an event that will take place in a distant future. It is a kind of dream that you have to file away with a "to be continued . . ." status. Not because a part two will be coming in another dream, as with recurring dreams, but because what you have seen simply has no immediate application for your life. The word *incubate* means to wait, brood over, keep or conceal something. This dream is therefore called *incubation dream* in the sense that its application is kept concealed for a while until it is unveiled in the distance future. The dream which Joseph had whereby he saw is family bowing down to him is a quintessential example of an incubation dream. Joseph's first mistake was telling jealous brothers his dream about them bowing down to him. I can wholeheartedly understand Joseph's enthusiasm in wanting to solve the mystery of his dream, but he was young and should have let this dream incubate a little more instead of committing reputational suicide.

As the dream replayed itself, we see Joseph go from being a boy who cannot interpret his own two dreams and save his own neck, to a man who interprets two highly symbolic dreams for a king and saves a whole nation. Look at what God did through the process: Joseph was thrown in a pit by his brothers, sold into slavery in Potiphar's house, falsely accused by Potiphar's wife, thrown into prison where he met Pharaoh's baker and cupbearer there and interpreted their dreams. Finally, he stood before the king to interpret his dreams and as a result, Jacob, his sons and all of Israel were saved during the horrible famine, and through that family line came the Messiah. But from the time Joseph left that pit as a slave until he stood before Pharaoh, thirteen years passed. Psalm 105:17–19 says,

"He sent a man before them— Joseph—who was sold as a slave. They hurt his feet with fetters, he was laid in irons. Until the time that his word came to pass, the word of the LORD tested him."

The word of the Lord tested him as he was waiting and as his dreams were incubating. I have a lot of dreams I can apply to my life immediately, but I have just as many incubation dreams. Some of your dreams could develop in different areas. When you are here in the outer spokes of the circle, and as you dream you enter into the area into the spirit realm which is a very interesting unique realm – timeless. And in timelessness sometimes some portion of your dreams could be speaking of your future five years down the road. If you notice some of your dreams do not continue in the same night. Some dreams continue over the years like Daniel's. In chapter 8 verse one he had another dream.

In the third year of the reign of King Belshazzar a vision appeared to me, Daniel, after that which appeared to me at the first.

What does he mean by *after that which appeared to me the first time?* The word *after* could mean many things. It could be in a similar form or similar manner. Or it could be something that he knows it is related. But in Daniel 7: 1 the dream happened in the first year of King Belshazzar's reign and in Daniel 8: 1 it was in the third year of King Belshazzar's reign. So what does he mean by *after that which appeared to me the first time?* It was nearly between two to three years in chronology. I mean he had a second dream and the second dream was like a continuation of the first dream and the first dream happened two or three years ago. I am sure he had many dreams between those times. But this was so significant that he knows that the second dream was related to the first.

But how would you know the continuations of your dreams if you didn't write them down? How did Daniel remember? Because in Daniel 7: 1, it says, *Then he wrote down the dream, telling the main facts.* He knew this was different and special. Do your dreams have parts? Yes. Unless we are aware of the messages that are coming in parts and we keep a record of them, you will not be able to interpret that dream properly. That is the third area that we bring forth in the importance of dreams. And because it is so important we need to write down our dreams. If you find it difficult to write everything and every day, at least write down the most impressive dream you have had. The most remarkable one that stayed with you and that sort of stirred your spirit, grieved your spirit or troubled your spirit. Write them down for there may be a next one that will bring meaning to this one. Most of us forget our dreams after two to three years. Let me tell you the most significant dream in my life I have never forgotten even up all these years. We need to always learn that there is significance in dreams and they could be different in time. Therefore it's important to note them down.

How To Finish An Incomplete Dream.

Dreams can leave us with a sense of unfinished business, especially when we awake before the dream has ended. The following techniques can be used to deal with such dreams: **Resolve:** You must have an inner craving to know the interpretation. **Respond:** Pray and ask the Lord to bring back to your spirit what He wanted to communicate to you. **Remember:** Try to recall your dreams, because focus issues, themes, or plots of dreams will often be repeated over several nights. **Replay:** Repeat the dream in your mind. All these are techniques that will help you get interpretation for your dreams.

Apocalyptic or prophetic Dreams

An apocalyptic dream is the one whose meaning or interpretation can only only explained at the end of the story. It is called a prophetic dream in the sense that although it is played now, it relates to a future event. From the time a future prophetic dream comes until the time it comes to pass can sometimes involve years, and as the dreamer, you may experience many stages and emotions along the way—particularly when the dream includes a promise concerning your future. When dreaming becomes more than a song to you and more like a way of life, be encouraged that millions of dreamers before you have waited upon the Lord and seen their dreams come true as they did. Moses, Isaiah, Jeremiah, Daniel, Ezekiel, Zechariah, Zephaniah and Habakkuk all have proven track records of prophetic accuracy when it comes to world events, but they also all have predictions yet to be fulfilled because they deal with the final days of judgment or the end of the world. Moses' 3,500-year-old "regathering of Israel" prophecy from Deuteronomy 30:3–5 is materializing before our very eyes, defining what it means to be alive in a prophetic time. Isaiah's prophecy about Jesus setting up a millennial Kingdom in Jerusalem is about 2,800 years old, and I am sure Isaiah is on the edge of his seat, just counting down the days for its fulfillment (Isaiah 2:4). I wonder if Jeremiah is lamenting and crying over his currently developing prophecies. The truth is, it is possible for a prophetic dream to be several categories rolled into one. It can be audible, encouraging, warning, waking dream.

CHAPTER FOUR

UNDERSTANDING THE ANATOMY AND PHYSIOLOGY OF DREAMS AND VISIONS

Tracing The Origin And Evolution Of How Dreams Came Into Being

In order for you to fully comprehend the evolution of dreams as an integral aspect of humanity, we need to consider the plight of man before the fall. Before Adam and Eve fell into sin, man had an ability to see into the spirit realm. The spirit realm was something very visible to them such that if an angel came to the Garden of Eden, Adam would see it. He didn't need dreams to connect him with the spirit world for the whole spirit realm as open to him for exploration. He didn't need the gift of the Spirit to operate because he had supernatural knowledge of all things. Since Adam was made perfect in God, he didn't need the word of wisdom because he lived in that wisdom. He didn't need the word of knowledge because he lived in the knowledge of God. He didn't need the discerning of spirit because he could see what is in the spirit world. He didn't need the gift of healing because he was in health. He didn't need the working of miracle because miracles were part and parcel of divine life. See, all the gifts of the Spirit are necessary only in the fallen state of man. Man in the perfect state has more than just the gifts, they are supernatural beings and gifts are part and parcel of their nature. The gifts of the Spirit in the book of Hebrews chapter 6 are called *the powers of the age to come.* The age of perfection the heavenly age which we only partake of while in this life. Before the fall, gifts were always a part of our nature and not just something that operates as the Spirit wills. But when sin came, the part in man's life that was affected was the area of the eye of the spirit. It is for this reason that the Bible says in Ephesians 4:18 *having the eyes of your hearts enlightened.* In the context of this scripture, the apostle Paul is not talking about physical eyes. He is talking about the eyes of our inner soul. There are inner eyes that we need to train and have them enlightened. Now these same eyes were darkened when man fell into sin.

There was a paradigm shift that occurred when Adam fell into sin in the Garden of Eden, which culminated in the divine orchestration of dreams. So, something took place in Adam's life when he fell into sin that changed the psychological make-up of humanity. There was a darkness that came on his inside that prevented him from contacting a part of his soul and a part of his spirit. It was cut off from the life of God. And from that day onwards, man began to have dreams as a means to enable him to connect back and contact the supernatural realm again. The conscious and sub-conscious mind of man and the human spirit are now all separated. Scientifically speaking, we use only between five to ten percent of the ability of our mind and our brain and the only contact that we have with the inner recesses of our mind is in the area of *visions* and *dreams*. All these belong to the inner part of our soul that we have lost contact with. For most of us, we only contact the part in our sleeping time. When we are in deep sleep, the other part of our mind begins to work. In fact, when you are in deep sleep and you are dreaming, your biological physical activity is equivalent to being wide-awake. Scientists have hooked up instruments onto sleeping subjects under study and found these electrical instruments responding in a way as if they are awake although they are asleep. It's like a thick line that is drawn. When you are awake, all these biological functions are going on. Then as you fall into sleep, there is a period where there is just stillness. Then you seem to enter into a different realm. It's as if a different part of your mind is working. And it's called REM (rapid eye movement) sleep. Your eyes move as if you are awake. This is what happens when you are dreaming.

A Diagnosis Of The Process Of How Dreams are Divinely Orchestrated From The Spirit Realm

It is interesting to learn that dreaming forms an integral component of human psychological make up. Dream activity is linked to the functions of the human brain which serves as a harbour or power house that drives the nervous system. It has been scientifically proven that when you fall asleep, your body is actually resting. But when you are dreaming, all the biological activity in your body functions as if you are awake. It consumes much energy in your dream state. The eyes move and the body is activated but it's like you are in a different realm since you are not conscious. In a biological experiment, whenever the subjects under study fall asleep and just as they are about to dream when their eyes movement becomes rapid, they are woken up. The researchers tried to stop the subjects from dreaming. Every time they dream, they wake them up. Then they fall asleep again and then they wake them up. They found that these people became less and less creative after they woke up. Those people become reduced to almost mere robots or zombies in their waking state. This shows that their level of creativity was at its highest level when they were asleep than when they were awake.

According to the biological analysis of a person's sleep you go through different stages. There is a stage of sleep where your eyes do not move. According to their study today they recognized that the first stage of sleep is for your body to have a rest. At this stage, to there is no dreaming involved. But there is another stage of dream you enter whereby your eyes start to move. They call it the R.E.M. sleep, which stands for *rapid eye movement*. Why do the eyes move? For in a dream it is as if you are watching a movie and the eyes move and respond as if you are watching a big screen movie accordingly. But it's an internal movie. It's something that only you see. Today scientists who study sleep think an R.E.M sleep has something to do with the mind. There is a necessity for the mind to analyze whatever that thing it was. The activities of the day rearrange information, process the information that has been received thus far throughout the day. Biologists have tested people and whenever a person goes to sleep and whenever the R.E.M sleep starts, they would purposely wake that person up. In other words, they only allow the person to sleep without R.E.M., which is a dream stage. They found that even though a person may have had some sleep but no R.E.M. sleep that his or her mental faculty is affected. A person's ability to concentrate and focus becomes affected when he or she is deprived of dreaming.

As we analyze this thing from the Bible concept R.E.M. sleep is a dream stage and it's at that stage that the Bible says in Job. 33 God places His instructions. God places things that would lead us and guide us. We have actually a large portion of the leading of the Spirit in our dream life. But just as in a conscious stage, so it is in the sub-conscious stage. That is when we are in our conscious stage about 90 or 95 percent of the leading we receive in our life is through the human spirit. It's the human spirit that instructs us and tells us things that are right or wrong; this is the inward witness and the inward voice. The other 5 percent or 10 percent is what we call the spectacular leading like visions, prophecies and even angelic visitations but the main primary leading is our inward spirit or the human spirit.

THREE SOURCES OF DREAMS

It is important that we study the origin or sources of our dreams so that we can be best spiritually positioned to know how to handle them. If you know where a dream came from, it would be easy to interpret it. In terms of origin, dreams can come from **THREE** sources. They can either come from *God*; they can come from the *devil* or they can come from *your own self*. Dreams that come from your self are those that are caused by preoccupation from daily activities, which then gets registered in our subconscious and is replayed in our sleep. Dreams that are brought forth from God are those that show you show destiny and give direction on what God wants you to do, and where He wants you to be in a particular time. This might include your own destiny and that of your family, city or nation. Dreams that come from Satan are those that are demonic in nature and are infiltrated from the enemy. These are *nightmares,* perpetrated by demonic spirit that suppress people, sleep with them in the dream, forces food into their mouths and attack them in dreams. We need to discern between all these sources and have some keys to understand what God is doing in our dream life. Knowing the source of dream will help you in terms of making a decision on what action to take after the dream.

Then there are some dreams that are from God. Dreams can come from three sources just as thoughts can come from three sources. It can come from God; it can come from demonic activity or it can come from our self. And our thoughts can also come from three realms. They can come from God; it can come from our self or it can come from the enemy. As we work with we realize that most of our thoughts are either from God or within us. Our spirit searches within us. In a dream state if we walk with God and the blood of Jesus covers us, there is no open door for the enemy to come in our dream life. That leaves two categories; from God or from our human spirit. About 5 percent or 10 percent of our dreams may be from God. Once in a while you have a dream that is a message direct from God.

1.	**Dreams That Come From God**
2.	**Dreams That Come From The Devil**
3.	**Dreams That Come From Yourself**

Dreams That Come From God.

As aforementioned, it says already been established that God does speaks through dreams. And dreams are one of the most primary easy modes for God to operate, lead and guide our lives. Dreams play the first category and open way where God communicate to us, even to some unbelievers who have not come to know God yet. This is a general statement in Job 33 that says that God in His mercy, God in His compassion does guide and lead believers and unbelievers through dreams. We can classify dreams as one of the leadings of the Holy Spirit. It's the working of the Holy Spirit. Like Pharaoh king of Egypt was led and guided by a dream. He had a dream that was important but he did not understand what it means. Casual readers of the world who hear about Pharaoh having a dream might arrive at a premature conclusion that since he has a cruel and ruthless man who had no regard for the Most High God, obviously his dreams did not come from God. Any religious person in church today, at face value would have thought that Pharaoh was a candidate for the devil to speak to him in a dream and not God. What they don't realise is that God communicate with both believers and unbelievers in a dream, who have not come to know Him yet because these are the very people created in the image of His likeness for which Christ died and shed blood on the cross.

From an arm chair view, you might be probably asking: How does God speak to us in dreams? Its through the dynamic workings of the Holy Spirit who transmits messages from God and imparts them into our spirits during sleep. In the conscious realm, the Holy Spirit might speak to us through multiple avenues such as thoughts, impressions, promptings and so forth. While there are some of our thoughts come from our soul; and some from our spirit man, there are some thoughts that are strong and clear with a ring of authority and presence of God which are the thoughts of the Holy Spirit. On the other side of the coin, in the subconscious realm, there are dreams that are the result of the activity of the soul and there are dreams that are the result of the activity of the spirit and both are linked together. But there are some dreams that are very authoritative with a measure of God's presence involved. Usually you will remember those dreams. You may even get right immediately after those dreams for no apparent reason. Only those dreams are classified as leadings of the Holy Spirit. These are dreams which are directly instigated by the Holy Spirit with a message. Why does God speak in dreams? There are many things that God could not convey to our conscious mind while we are awake. As a result God has to wait until we are asleep then He speaks to us in a dream.

There are certain ways that are clear-cut "Thus says the Lord." There is nothing else you can do about it except pray to God that He will reveal to you fully what He is instructing you. There are certain dreams you notice that are authoritative. They carry a direct message from God like Pharaoh's dream in the Old Testament. Here is a clear-cut dream for his whole nation. If he did not understand that dream and interpret it his whole nation may perish. Those are important dreams. Those are direct messages from God. The two dreams of Joseph that were recorded were direct messages from God. He may have other dreams too but only two were recorded because those instituted messages from God. But these types of dreams only occur in about 5 to 10 percent of our dreams. The vast majority of our dreams come from the realm of our human spirit or our human soul. They interlinked together. And they constitute direction in our life.

The dream is what we call the actual where exactly as you see it, it comes to pass, every details of it. We know that Paul's Macedonian vision cannot be that category. Because if Paul considered it as the third category when he reached Macedonia he should have looked for that man. But he did not. He understood that it is just a message. It is not important whether it's a Macedonian or woman wearing a Macedonian garment calling him. Now the third category of dream is the actual. Like for example Joseph in the gospel of Matthew had a dream of an angel coming to him and telling him to go to Egypt. Then he had a dream to come back. Then he had a dream to tell him where to go and stay. And in the dream he saw an angel. It was an actual vision that came when a person is subconscious. So it was an actual dream; everything came exactly to pass. There is no necessity of an interpretation.

Frequency Revelator

How Do We Know If A Dream Is Of God?

Spiritual encounters in dreams are to be judged not according to how strange or clear an encounter might be. Otherwise this might cost us great revelation when we begin to discard some dreams from God and relegate them to the devil's jurisdiction yet they are actually carrying a message from God. The way we are to judge or test encounters with God, is two-fold. The first thing we must ask is, does the vision or dream line up with the word of God? An earmark of a spiritual encounter from God is that it will line up with His word. The Spirit and the Word go hand-in-hand. The second thing to look for is fruit. Does the dream encounter bear fruit in the partakers' life? Is there a change or transformation of a life, or mind-set, as a result of the encounter? Is there freedom that comes as a result? Does it result in an evidence of God's love and power increasing? Moreover, whenever you encounter dreams from God, you are most likely to have inner peace, sense the presence of God, and receive godly direction. This is because dreams from God do not bring about any condemnation but rebuke in love, they manifest the character of the Holy Spirit, and although some might be parabolic and difficult to understand, they do not bring confusion, divisions, fights or hatred of any nature.

Dreams That Come From The Devil Or Demonic Realm

Are you not surprised that some dreams are actually from the devil? Every dream has a unique atmosphere. Often the atmosphere is the only lingering memory upon awakening. Dreams that come from the devil breeds an atmosphere of fear, oppression, hatred, or an evil presence. The enemy can give you dreams; we do not call them dreams per se, but *nightmares*. It is very common for people who are half asleep to sense a spiritual force that comes and presses on the top of them. At times you dream that something is chasing you or holding your chest down or chocking your neck or you dream falling down from a building. All those dreams are from the devil and not from the Lord. To the extremes, those who were initiated into witchcraft knowingly or unknowingly would dream having their human spirits projected out of their bodies and flying in the air. Some would dream walking by the graveyards or cemeteries, communicating with dead people, others dream swimming in water naked while others dream being in the underworld, in dark places, ghost houses or graves eating human flesh and drinking human blood. All these things are from the diabolical tyrant himself, the devil who has no regard for humanity. What you call a *nightmare* is actually an indirect spiritual attack on humanity by means of dreams.

In fear of direct confrontation and exposition of his evil and dark operations, at times Satan comes masquerading as an angel of light and might not come in the way we expect. At times he comes in disguise and causes his demons to wear the faces of people that we know so that we will loosen up and so that he can get an opportunity to attack us while we have lowered our guard. That is how he managed to fool people especially in the African continent to believe in *ancestors* yet these are familiar demons that would have possessed a person throughout his entire life such that when he dies, these demons come back to the living claiming to be the spirit of the deceased. Demons at times show up in dreams purporting to be ancestors who died long back yet these are tricks from the devil to keep people bound and oppressed. However, when you are in the Lord, the blood of Jesus covers you such that you won't fall prey to the whims and vagaries of the devil. If you don't have open doors, you won't be a candidate to have those kinds of nightmares. In dark dreams or spiritual warfare dreams, others can often be demonic beings, even if they look quite attractive or, conversely, resemble insects or animals. As we become more skilled at discerning the people in our dreams, we will actually be able to fight against demonic forces.

Why Do People Have Nightmares:

See, the devil can access and interfere with your *subconscious* if sin is present in your life or any other thing that grants him a legal foothold to meddle in one's life. Some people fall victims to the devil's nightmares or dream attacks simply because they opened the door for the enemy and granted him access to enter their dream life. Other typical spiritual crimes that can grant demons legal rights to enter their victims' dreams includes initiation into the demonic world, engaging in satanic practices, possession of satanic tools and products, rebelling against God, unforgiveness as well as breaking spiritual laws. It is on the bases of these legal footholds that the devil accuses believers in the Heavenly Courts for their wrong doings and attempt to gain victory and grip over them in their dreams. Remember that the devil's agenda and strategy is to *kill, still and destroy* (1 Peter 5:8). That is why he destroys people's destinies in dreams and steal their joy and peace they are supposed to derive in their sleep.

How Do We Spiritually Deal With Nightmares?

If you choose not to sin and choose to be under the blood, there is no door for the devil or his cohorts to enter your dream life. The only door he has is when there is sin or violation of spiritual laws, which then permits him to attack people's *souls, human spirits* and *bodies* in dreams. Do you know why demons sleep with people in dreams or feed them demonic food in dreams? So that humans will defile their bodies and sin against God such that they won't be qualified or found worthy to be used by God. Do you know why demons oppress people in their sleep such that they even feel a heavy load or oppression over their chest where they can even move an inch, or shout or do anything? Its because demons will be attacking their human spirit, to keep it confined to a lower level where it can't make a significant impact in the spirit realm. That is why it is always important just before we sleep to pray and cover yourselves with the blood of Jesus. As you kneel down besides your bed say,

> **"Lord Jesus if I failed you in any way today, if I missed you in my works in my attitudes in my actions Jesus forgive me. Cleanse me with your precious blood. Continue to speak to me even in my sleep."**

Sadly, many Christians think that their lives for the day end when they sleep. What they don't realise is that sleeping is only the beginning of the next part of God working in their lives through dreams. As much as you pray for the day when you wake up, you must also pray and preparing yourself for your sleep because then you will be preparing to enter another realm which is the dream world, where you might contact either God or the devil. Sadly, many people encounter nightmares in their sleep because they are not cleansed under the blood and did not spiritually prepare themselves

Understanding Prophetic Dreams & Visions

for their sleep. It is important that you put yourself under the blood of Jesus and close any open door that might grant the devil access to block God's workings in your life when you sleep. One of the reasons Satan tries to block your life at night is also because God is trying to bring something to you there. Incidentally if it is a frightening nightmare then that's not from God.

However, if you are a born again believer, you ought not to have any dreams from the enemy. Are you even aware that God promised us in the book of Proverbs that our sleep will be sweet and free from any nightmares?. Look at what it says in Proverbs 3:24 *When you lie down, your sleep will be sweet*. So, we rule out the demonic realm if the blood of Jesus covers us. The demonic realm has no interference or says whatsoever as to how we shape our dreams. Dreams that come from the demonic realm are not supposed to be a part of the Christian life. If ever you encounter them in your life, then it is easily dealt with by confessing to God and a short prayer and meditation on the Word before you sleep will do. Understand your authority as a believer and the power of the blood of Jesus.

How Do We Know If A Dream Is Of The Devil?

In contrast to the dreams that comes from either God or the human soul, dreams that come from the devil are usually it is infested with fear, breeds an evil presence and lack of peace. Therefore, if you dream seeing weird creatures or animals such as snakes, bats or cats or you sense a heavy oppression on you or you dream people chasing you, or having sex with strangers in dream, or eating food in a dream or even communicating with weird personalities in your dream, immediately know that those dreams are from the devil. The Bible says where the spirit of the Lord is, there is liberty. And by the same token, where the spirit of the devil is, there is oppression. So, if you feel any form of oppression in your dream, immediately cast out these demons in the name of Jesus Christ and cove r yourself under the blood of Jesus.

Dreams That Come From Yourself

Frequency Revelator

Dreams can come from yourself tend to be a working of your human spirit and soul. Some dreams come from your inner subconscious thinking and they need to be dealt with. They are not a message from God but yourself. Your own dreams that come forth. To the degree that we are ruled and influenced by the soul (mind, will, and emotions), we run the risk that what we are receiving is a dream, revelation, or interpretation of the soul. It's funny that you cannot lie to yourself in your dream. Your conscience affects it. Your feelings, your personal attitudes colour your dreams. So, to interpret dreams check the people attitudes that received the dream because most of the dreams come from people. So, the second rule is remember in whatever the three types of dreams to check your personal attitude and feeling whether they are colouring the dreams. In helping another person to understand their dreams check their attitude too. Discern it by the Holy Spirit in order to get the accurate picture of what God is saying. So, the Bible says in Jude 33 that God speaks to us. Whether the receiving station is in functioning order, the transmitter is in order heaven never breaks down. But it is our receiving station that breaks down. Sometimes the battery water needs to be changed. The Holy Spirit is not there, the prayer life is not there and the Word is not enough. The voltage has gone so low and the attitudes are wrong it coloured our dreams.

Some dreams come from your daily activities. Every day when you have activity your subconscious mind and your spirit rearranges it. The microprocessor keeps rearranging and putting it into the right slot. That is what I call a natural activity. The Writer of the book of Ecclesiastes 5:3 says *for a dream comes with much business, and a fool's voice with many words.* Notice that it says a dream comes through much activity. In continuation in Verse 7, it says *for when dreams increases, empty words grow many; but do you fear God?* These are the writings of Solomon one of the wisest man in the East in his days. He understood the significance of dreams that they come through much activities. According to his understanding a dream comes through much activity. We realize that king Solomon is the wisest men during his time. And he had some understanding here about dreams. He says a dream comes through much activity. He is indirectly saying that the activities of our life would be related to the dream that we have. This explains that even if you have had dreams, that won't increase your fear of God. Such dreams come from soulish and physical activity and will have little bearing on your spiritual life.

Understanding Prophetic Dreams & Visions

They could not be from God since they do not increase the fear of God in you. Have you noticed that after driving a car during the night for a long distance, by the time you arrive at home and sleep , you can still see those car lights. It's because the dream would have come through so much activities during the day involving driving for long distance and concentrating such that it gets registered in your subconscious and when you dream, all that activity is then replayed in your mind. That is why dreaming is tantamount to watching a movie being replayed in your mind during your sleep. It can come from your own life. It is important that we have to discern dreams that come from God, dreams that come from the enemy or through our own self. If the blood of Jesus covers you, then it is only between God and your own dreams.

As I analyze this area here, I realize that the direction we receive from our dream life is 90 or 95 percent from our human spirit. Deep in the corridor of our spirit are the instructions that are given to us. These are dreams that come from our subconscious and spirit man aligning together. The language of the spirit man is in visions and dreams, and both are in picture forms. You arrange that in your life every time you go through activities. That form of dream is more for your private edification. It exposes you. For example, you could put up a front in your conscious life, where outwardly you are very outgoing and very sociable and cheerful and you put on a front; in front of people you wear a mask. We all know how to do that. Our conscious mind is very clever to put our image before people. But you have what I call a dual life. Behind inside your conscience and inside your heart you feel lonely, you feel inferior, and you feel dejected and rejected inside your heart and inside your life your true self is hidden from people. The interesting thing about your dreams is that you cannot hide your true self from yourself. In your dreams who you really are stands out. If outwardly you look like a brave man, in your dreams you are actually afraid. Every single dream you have is one of your inner fears. If outwardly you look like a very upright person with good social life and no apparent weakness in your life but inwardly you know you have. In your dreams you are exposed - it comes out. You cannot hide from yourself in your dream. Who you really are what you really are comes forth and stands out. They are useful to a certain extend. They are not used for leading. They are useful to understand your inner self. We must understand our inner self. We must understand what our main weaknesses and strong points are. Your dreams will expose them to you so that you are aware of them and you could deal with them. Each time as you grow and your character develops your dreams also improve. So, the dreams come through much activity in your life. Every time when you sleep it has to process the whole thing. What you experienced consciously has to be processed every day.

Are these dreams bad? No! However, what makes these dreams unpleasant is the they might interfere with the message which God wants to communicate to us in the dream. They might disrupts the flow of the message such that by the time you wake up, instead of remembering the message from God, you remember your own experiences in the dream which are a result of the activities you were engaged in during the course of the day. The good thing about these dreams is that they reveal your true self. Only the spirit of man will know what is in the man. Even our conscious mind does not know what your true self is. Our conscious mind can be so trained to ignore certain things. But the bible says in I Corinthians 2 that the spirit of a man within him knows what is inside the person. So your spirit has the most accurate perception of yourself. Each one of you right now has a perception of yourself in your conscious mind. But the most true and accurate perception is in your spirit man. As we renew our mind what our spirit man perceive is translated into our conscious mind. Then you have a true estimation and judgment of yourself, where you are heading, where you are right now, where you have been. We must live our lives in such a way that what is inside and outside is one and not be a double character.

What do we mean by dreams that are from God and from our human spirit? Why do we make a differentiation between the two of them? If you understand how to be led by the Spirit, you must learn to differentiate the voice of the human spirit from the voice of the Holy Spirit. When operating in the prophetic realm, when it is God that says something we say, "Thus says the Lord." By if have our human spirit is instructing us you have what Paul says, "I perceived in my spirit." It's a world of a difference. When we say, "I perceived," we are saying we have only one small part and it is changeable. And the instructions may need more verification and clarification. Whereas when we a have a "Thus says the Lord" there is nothing more you can change; there is nothing more you can add; there is nothing except to obey. In a similar way in dreams, there are certain dreams that are clear-cut authoritative "Thus says the Lord." Which carry a direct message from God such that there is nothing else you can do about it except pray to God that He will reveal to you fully what He is instructing you. On the other hand, there are also dreams that come from within your human spirit such that you can express them as "I perceived in my spirit." Our human spirit can lead us as much as the Holy Spirit. And we are to train our human spirit with the Word of God so that we could be sensitive to our human spirit and do things according to what God wants. Why does God do it that way? God doesn't want us to be robots where we always say, "Thus says the Lord, turn right;" "Thus says the Lord, take your coffee now." We are not robots. So God leads us by the human spirit. And when He does it through the human spirit He demands that we grow. And when we are led by human spirit and human spirit is trained in Him not only are we obedient to God we have become like God because our human spirit has taken the nature and maturity of God. In about 90 percent of our dreams our human spirit is indirectly picking up God's instructions to you. The other 5 to 10 percent of our dreams are God's direct messages to us. Either way, that is a vast amount of dreams and we need to understand them. That is the reason for this book so that we could understand the source of our dreams so that it would be easy for us to interpret them. .

How Do I Know If A Dream Is From Myself?

To discern if a dream came from you or from other sources, consider your own feelings, your personal attitudes as they colour your dreams. The dream is also affected by your conscience. In other words, concerning dreams that come from yourself, there is too much emotions attached. That is why it is important when interpreting dreams to check the people attitudes that received the dream because most of the dreams come from people, check your personal attitude and feeling whether they are colouring the dreams or not. In helping another person to understand their dreams check their attitude too. Discern it by the Holy Spirit in order to get the accurate picture of what God is saying.

CHAPTER FIVE

THE FOUR DIMENSIONS OF PROPHETIC DREAMS AND VISIONS

Do you know that there are **FOUR dimensions** of dreams from God? Prophetic dreams can be categorised into **FOUR dimensions**. A dream from God can come in four ways. A dream can come as No. 1 symbolic dreams. No. 2 as actual dreams. No. 3 as a message dream. No. 4 prophetic dreams. The easiest is the second type. There is a parabolic type of visions and dreams, which means that they are symbols. Then the second type where we call the message dream or vision where it only carries a message. And the third type where we call an actual dream and vision which means actually as you see it, it comes to pass. Then there is a prophetic dream, which refers to a dream that is on par with the prophet's ministry. A parabolic one is symbols. Like Daniel saw a symbol of animals that were coming and going, the rams and the goats in the book of Daniel. Those animals represent kingdoms. Pharaoh had a dream. And in his dream he saw seven fat cows and seven thin calves. Those cows represent seven years of prosperity and seven years of famine. Those are symbolic or parabolic dreams. They are like parables. Symbolic dreams must be interpreted. The second type of dreams needs no interpretation. The third type needs no interpretation. It's the first one that is quite difficult. However, the symbols in your dreams must be the same meaning and symbols as in the bible.

The second two categories don't need much teaching. Like the clear-cut actual dreams, they are just like it is. The clear-cut actual dream or vision does not need interpretation. The message one usually is clear-cut also. There is a very strong message that comes with it. The details of the dream are not important but the major message of the dream is. There is a direct or clear dream or vision that does not need any interpretation. It means what it is. For example we find that Joseph the husband of Mary who was carrying Jesus in the womb being directed by an angel in a dream. Angels do appear directly in people's dream. An angel led him to go into Egypt and then to come back to Israel and settle down in Nazareth where the boy Jesus grew up. So there is a clear cut direct dream or vision. We mentioned that dreams are also referred to as a *vision of the night*. We can see here that dreams and vision of the night are dual phrases referring to the same thing. A dream to the Hebrew mind is a vision of the night. It is a vision that you see in your sub-conscious state.

PARABOLIC OR SYMBOLIC DREAM

These are dreams called symbolic dreams. So the first type of dream is symbolic - it needs interpretation. The interesting thing is that a major portion of most of dreams is in the symbolic realm. In the first category it is called the parabolic dream. And those are the most difficult to deal with and almost 95 percent of the dreams are in that category. They are the most difficult dreams to handle. They are easily misinterpreted. If you have a dream that is symbolical you go to 20 people you will get 20 interpretations. The reason I mentioned this is because there are some people teaching out there, they teach only the second part of the dream is from God. That is unscriptural. They say if God gives you a dream it will be real and there is no need to interpret any more. It will be just as it is. What about the bible? What about the symbolic dreams? Are they not from God? See what you believe must be in line with the Word. So No. 1 there are symbolic dreams. Symbols are involved. In Gen. 39 how Joseph interpreted the dream of the baker and the butler. Who would have interpreted that the baker has those loaves of bread on his head it means that his head is coming off. There is no natural way that we could have gone into that kind of interpretation.

This category is like parable, where each picture in a vision or dream has a symbolic meaning. Daniel had dreams and visions in the night. He saw animals in his dreams. Each animal represents a nation. So these are symbolic visions or dreams. We have also mentioned how Joseph and Daniel got into interpretation of dreams and some of the requirements that were given. And we have given some rules and guidelines on how to interpret dreams in a general form. We have mentioned how that in the parable kind of vision or dream every symbol has to be scriptural. In other words if a snake in the bible represents something evil whatever sort of snake you saw in a dream it still symbolizes evil. Even if the snake is white in color it still is evil. The symbols have to be scriptural. That is what we call the underlining guidelines.

The other *symbolic dream* was dreamt by Pharaoh in Genesis 40. Pharaoh had a dream in fact he had two dreams. Remember when a dream occurs twice it shows the urgency of something. Joseph through the wisdom of God says to Pharaoh the dream occurs twice because it is sure to come and there is urgency involved. So if you have a particular dream that come forth several times, God is trying to tell you that it surely is and there is an urgency involved. Pharaoh had a dream. This was his dream. He says he saw the seven ears of corn and fat ones and seven lean ones ate them up. He woke up and he went back to sleep. Then he saw seven fat cows and suddenly come seven skinny cows. And the amazing thing was the seven skinny cows ate up the seven fat cows. And he said this after the seven skinny cows ate up the seven fat cows, the seven skinny cows were still skinny. That is a symbolic dream. Later Nebuchadnezzar had a dream and Daniel interpreted.

Let's look at the book of Genesis 41:17. Remember that all the wise men and magicians could not interpret this dream;

Then Pharaoh said to Joseph, "Behold, in my dream I was standing on the banks of the Nile; and seven cows, fat and sleek, came up out of the Nile and fed in the reed grass; and seven other cows came up after them, poor and very gaunt and thin, such as I had never seen in all the land of Egypt. And the thin and gaunt cows ate up the first seven fat cows, but when they had eaten them no one could have known that they had eaten them, for they were still as gaunt as at the beginning. Then I awoke. I also saw in my dream seven ears growing on one stalk, full and good; and seven ears, withered, thin, and blighted by the east wind, sprouted after them, and the thin ears swallowed up the seven good ears. And I told it to the magicians, but there was no one who could explain it to me.

A lot of people are in Pharaoh's dilemma where they have some message from God but they have no interpretations. Notice that Pharaoh was standing on the riverbank. A river always symbolizes life of people in a dream. And suddenly there were these fat cows that come from the river. Not along the river but from the river which is interesting because cows don't swim.

But as I said that dreams doesn't quite work in the same realm as our natural realm. I mean, you see very odd things. Then these seven lean cows came up and ate the seven fat cows, and still they remained thin as ever. We know that cows don't eat cows. Immediately we realize that Joseph has a tremendous interpretation and he said that the seven cows and the seven stalks of grain are one. This is reasonable easy because the stalks talk about harvest.

We Need To Interpret Symbols Sin Their Content And Be Mindful That Symbols Can Change Over Time

You must look at the context of the people in those days. See, in those days wealth is measured in cows and grain. If you are rich the way you show that you are rich is your possession of grain and cows. Understand the context of those people. Today in the natural realm if someone is rich they show their prosperity by the cars they drive, by their dressing and by their usage of things or by the house they live in. We need to understand our daily context so that we could interpret the dreams. In those days cows and grains symbolized wealth. Today if God is speaking to you about a famine coming, He may not use cows and grains because they don't mean anything to you now. In our days the symbols have changed. And so don't think that when God speaks to you and suppose that you are a person of authority that when God speaks to you about a famine coming, He is going to use cows again. He will use other symbols that we understand today. The first major principle about parabolic dreams and messages from God is the representation of the symbols that are important. What do the symbols in the dream represent today? See each symbol that is used in a dream represents one major principle or point.

We Need To Interpret Symbols In Line With The Word Of God

A vitally important way to understand how to interpret dreams is to study all the dreams, visions, and parables in the Bible especially the ones that are interpreted. You will learn by the Spirit the interpretive principle that God uses when parabolically communicating. The Bible says in Matthew 13:34 that *"All these things Jesus spoke to the multitude in parables, and without a parable, He did not speak to them, that it might be fulfilled which was spoken by the prophet, saying: 'I will open my mouth in parables; I will utter things kept secret from the foundation of the world.'"* In using parables as a teaching method, Jesus was fulfilling Old Testament prophecy (v. 35 is a quotation of Psalm 78:2). The Messiah would speak to the crowds with *"dark sayings."* But since they seriously doubted (as opposed to honest uncertainty) or rejected Him, even with the evidence of signs and wonders, His teachings would seem *"difficult and obscure."* The truths that Jesus spoke were understandable to those who had faith in him and sincerely desired to comprehend and value His message. Insight into the meaning of the parables is a result of faith in, and passion for, Jesus. That is why to those who are attuned to the spirit realm and led by the Holy Spirit, interpreting enigmatic dreams is a walk through a park.

Interpretation Of The Chief Butler's Dream:

Let's look at the other two dreams Joseph interpreted. In the book of Genesis chapter 40, there was the baker and the butler.

So the chief butler told his dream to Joseph, and said to him, "In my dream there was a vine before me, and on the vine there were three branches; as soon as it budded, its blossoms shot forth, and the clusters ripened into grapes. Pharaoh's cup was in my hand; and I took the grapes and pressed them into Pharaoh's hand.

That was a positive dream. Vine, blossoms, a cup and grapes are all positive representation. Let me explain a little bit. In the scriptures, the winepress can symbolize judgment. One of the laws to interpretation of dreams is consistency with God's Word. Whatever is represented in the Word must be consistent with your dream and interpretation. In other words, if in the Bible a snake represent evil then however you interpret your dream if you see a snake it is evil; whether it's a black or white snake. It must be consistent. With God's Word. Dogs in the Bible are bad symbols and all the unclean animals in the Bible symbolize things that are not good. So, your interpretation of symbols must be consistent. But there are a lot of grounds for variations. A winepress sometimes symbolizes a judgment. Then you must take into context the symbol in his days.

Understanding Prophetic Dreams & Visions

The Meaning Of The Cup:

To the butler that cup represents his employment. All the time he was employed as a cupbearer in the King's palace That was his basic employment. If you were employed in an accountancy firm all the time you are looking at are facts and figures. And that is your expertise. Then you went for some unrelated courses and you resigned from your accountancy profession. Three four years later you came and then you sort of in a dream see those facts and figures and yourself sitting at the table. You know what those represent? Your employment. This is because to you that is the way God speaks to you in facts and figures; that is your field of work. As for the case of the butler that cup represented his work or employment.

The Meaning Of The Vine:

Then we have the vine symbolizing a time span or something that is growing. And blossoms symbolize something new because any flowers or things that blossom represent something new. Either it's a resurrection or restoration. And in his case, since he is still alive, it represented restoration. The three branches of the Vine represents *three days*. Why not three years? It is because flowers have a shorter span of time of life. Flowers don't last many years; they rather come and go in short season. For him, he interpreted it straight away as three days. He understands that flowers can last only a few days hence, the measurement is three days.

Interpretation Of The Chief Baker's Dream:

Let's look at the interpretations of the second dream that the baker had.

When the chief baker saw that the interpretation was favorable, he said to Joseph, "I also had a dream; there were three white baskets on my head, and in the uppermost basket there were all sorts of baked food for Pharaoh, but the birds were eating it out of the basket on my head."

The Meaning Of The Three White Basket On The Head:

Under ordinary circumstances, white normally symbolizes good but it depends on what it is combined with. If it's a white snake it doesn't symbolize something good. It symbolizes deception. But in his context and in his day when somebody dies they were embalmed in white linen. So white is a possible symbol of death in their time. The whiteness of the baskets points to the white linen cloth that was used in funerals. Today funeral services people usually wear black or sack clothes but some times they still wear white. But it's a clear-cut thing in those days in the Judaism custom when somebody dies white was used.

The Meaning Of Loaves Of Bread In The White Baskets:

Then those three white baskets with loaves of bread on them since he was a baker. Isn't it interesting the butler dreamt about wine? The baker was baking bread and seeing bread for many years hence, God used something familiar in his dream, which is bread. Jesus said, I am the bread of life, hence bread represents life. Therefore, the act of birds taking away the loaves of bread from the white baskets indicate the taking away of his own life. Those three loaves of bread, how long can loaves of bread last? Bread lasts for a few days and not months or years. So, he took them to represent *days*.

The Meaning Of Birds Of Air Eating From The White Baskets:

There is a part of the dream where the birds of the air came. Those are bad symbols. In the context of those days, when a criminal was judged and the death sentence is pronounced, they would let the birds of the air get on that person. Joseph was familiar with that because he was a prisoner and there were some prisoners who had the death sentence over their life who have died. He knew what happened to them - the birds of the air came and reaped the flesh off their bodies. So, it was related to the symbols of those days and Joseph understood that it speaks of death. It is emphasized about three times. The baskets being taken meant something being removed. The whiteness of the baskets points to the white linen cloth that was used in funerals. And the birds that came and picked on those things. When God emphasizes a message in a symbolic dream, there is always the same recurring theme.

The Meaning Of The Repetition Or Recurring Of Events In The Dream:

When studying the Bible, contextually we look for recurring phrases or words? Now if you have a parabolic dream, look for recurring words and recurring symbols. That means the symbols will recur three four times to give you the main message and how to interpret it. In this dream there is always one recurring symbol or message. That means that one message is repeated three or four times in various symbols so that it stands out as a stronger key to the interpretation. In the baker's dream, the strongest symbol that stood up was *death*. Those three loaves of bread, how long can loaves of bread last? Bread lasts for a few days and not weeks or months or years. So, he took them to represent days. That's how he interpreted those symbols. Remember that ninety five percent of our dreams is in this category. And that is one of the major ways the Holy Spirit leads us through our dreams. So, your interpretation of symbols must be scriptural.

The Interpretation Of The Symbols Will Be Something That Is Understandable In The Culture And The Context That We Live In.

Wealth today is represented differently from in the Bible. The interpretation of the symbols are affected by your individual understanding and profession. God will use whatever that is in your background in the dream. See, the Holy Spirit is a master of languages. What He cannot say to you in a certain symbol He will put symbols that are related to you because certain symbols may not be present in your life. You might not be acquainted with those symbols. He won't take symbols that are strange to you. You never have a dream where there are symbols that you are not aware of. He chooses the limitation of our symbols to illustrate and to give a coded message. Dreams are the coded message of the Holy Spirit, hence our conscious mind got to decode them.

HOW DO WE INTERPRET SYMBOLIC DREAMS?

The question you are probably asking yourself is: What is the basis of such interpretation of symbolic dreams? So, you see there is no such thing as a universal context. There are some biblical principles **but the symbols God uses to speak to your life will be in the context of your profession, your knowledge, your background.** And God will use a totally different symbol for you that He uses for me. Because of your background, your education, your natural knowledge, your profession, He will use a totally different background to speak about the same. In other words, symbols in a dream like a snake represents evil; sheep represents something good; goat represents something religious. There are fixed symbols in the bible that are unchangeable. But besides that there are other symbols that are changeable. That can represents something in a person's life and another thing in another person's life. That is why the interpretation of dreams is not as easy as you look at it from the outside. We have the Bible that tells us symbols, hence there are certain rules that we want to look at with regard to symbolic dream interpretation.

First Rule:

Symbolic Dreams Are Contextual Hence Should Be Taken In The Context Of The Bible And In The Dreamer's Personal Life.

It is easier to interpret your dreams in some ways but sometimes harder. Let me explain it before you can actually interpret somebody's dream. You must first understand what those symbols mean to him. A snake represents evil but there are others that are not directly covered in the bible. So, to interpret a person's dream, you will need to understand what the symbols mean to him. If to that person a squirrel for example has some significance, then besides the Bible interpretation, you will also need some details to interpret his dream and find out what squirrels mean to him. Perhaps when he was small he had a squirrel as a pet. Maybe, it was something so precious to him that when that squirrel was taken away he cried very much. Then it has some different meaning besides the general meaning that represents unclean animal. It takes on an extra meaning for him in his dream.

Let's take something more common like cats. Let says someone loves cats. He has a cat that he kept all his life when he was a young little boy. This cat means everything to him. So, the cat represents to him something of love. It represents companionship and affection. So, now when he dreams of cat, I can have the general interpretation that a cat is an unclean animal but that doesn't help me in explaining some of the details of his dream. I

Understanding Prophetic Dreams & Visions

would need details of what cat represents to him. I need to know a person's life to help to interpret that. Then for example a cat to another person could represents witchcraft. Perhaps his only experience of cats has to do with witchcraft. Then when he dreams of a cat, there are two different interpretations for the same cat from the one who loves cats. Cat to one person means something nice, to the other, it means something evil. So, If I interpret their dreams, I have to pick up what that person's understanding is. So, you can see why it is sometimes easier to interpret somebody else's dream that you know than the one you do not know. If you take that statement by itself, then the other side logically means it is easier to interpret your own dreams because you know yourself. In a sense it is true but in another sense it's not true. **Our dreams sometimes reveal our blind spots that we cannot see.** And because we cannot see that and the dreams try to tell us of our blind spots, we find it difficult to interpret them. With all these in mind, we look at the book of Genesis chapter 40 the baker and the butler.

So the chief butler told his dream to Joseph, and said to him, "In my dream there was a vine before me, and on the vine there were three branches; as soon as it budded, its blossoms shot forth, and the clusters ripened into grapes. Pharaoh's cup was in my hand; and I took the grapes and pressed them into Pharaoh's cup, and placed the cup in Pharaoh's hand.

In order to interpret the butler's dream we need to know what those symbols mean to the butler. So, Joseph has wisdom that is why in the Bible the great interpreters of dreams are those who are wise. Joseph has God's wisdom. Daniel too has God's wisdom. When you are wise, you understand another person's life besides your own. So Joseph must understand what those symbols mean. What does the vine means to the butler? A vine can means different things to different people. If you take that word generally it means something good. The word vine in the Bible also represents the church. Of course in the butler's dream it has nothing to do with the church. To the butler the vine tree produces grapes. In the dreams, he was taking that cup and taking the grapes and squeezing the grapes juice and giving it to Pharaoh. Remember, this was something he used to do when he worked. All the time when he was serving Pharaoh that was what he was doing. In a modern day context, if you are an accountant and in your dream you dream about yourself doing accounts. Do you know what that means? That dream is talking about your job. You don't need to dream about vine to know about your job because that vine has nothing to do with you. So, the symbols are contextual. Joseph understood that handling cups was what the butler normally does in his job, so the dream has to do with his job. He mentioned that there were three branches. So, that three was significant for it tells three days. And for the baker he had a different dream.

When the chief baker saw that the interpretation was favorable, he said to Joseph, "I also had a dream; there were three cake baskets on my head, and in the uppermost basket there were all sorts of baked food for Pharaoh, but the birds were eating it out of the baskets on my head." And Joseph answered, "This is its interpretation; the three baskets are three days; within three days Pharaoh will lift up your head from you and hang you on a tree; and the birds will eat the flesh from you."

If you study the above portion of scripture carefully, you will pick up that it's a very different interpretation from the normal dream. So, we have to look at the context of the baker. The baker dreamt about bread but the butler dreamt about grapes. To the accountant, he dreams about accounts; To an author, he dreams about books; To the engineer he dreams about engineering projects; And to the minister he dreams about preaching. You know what it means when you dream about preaching your ministry. So, a symbolic dream is contextual; hence we got to understand the context in which it is played.

Second Rule:

To Interpret A Symbolic Dream, We Also Need To Understand Not Only What The Symbols Mean To A Person But The Level That Person Is Functioning In.

In addition to the context of the dream, it is also important that we consider the scale, scope or jurisdiction of dreams. The context of your dream might be determined or limited by your jurisdiction or scope of your work. It's very unlikely if your work is on a national basis for your dream to have an international basis. If your work has to do only with a local district, it is very unlikely that your dream has to do with international things. In other words, its contextual to the size of your job or your ministry. For Pharaoh, he was governing over a whole nation. So, he dreams about things that have national perspective. It was not just a personal soul dream. For Daniel who had an international perspective, his dreams were international. In one dream, he had four nations because he was functioning in an international perspective. He was the key leader and minister over two three nations hence, his dreams took on an international perspective.

For example, if a person is called to be a soul winner but not directly called to the ministry, it is very unlikely that the dream would have significance in an international perspective. That is why we got a lot of misinterpretations. A soul winner who had a certain dream may misinterpret that he will have an international ministry that will impact the body of Christ. I heard people who were not called to the ministry and they interpret their dreams in terms of what their ministry will have internationally. It is very unlikely. For example, a soul winner's dream may looks like he will have an international ministry. He may interpret it as a worldwide ministry that is going to happen. When I heard it and not only judging the dream but also judging from what I am hearing from the Spirit, I know that he is hearing the wrong thing. Or rather he has picked it up with a wrong interpretation with the right dream. You could have the right dream with the wrong interpretation and wrong application.

In retrospect to Joseph's dream interpretation, to the baker bread and carrying bread is something that he does all the time. How did Joseph refer it to death? It looks like he is just losing his job from the description of the three baskets and the birds eating the bread off the baskets. Since Joseph was in charge of the prison, he knew what happens when a death sentence is pronounced. There were many others before the baker who were sentenced to death. He must have seen them hanging on a tree and the birds pecking on their flesh. That was the concept of judgment and death in those days. So, based on that he understood that birds pecking equals death, he interpreted that the baker would die. Today, birds pecking may not equal death. But in those days when a prisoner is sentenced and condemned to death, there would be birds pecking the flesh of the corpse. Pharaoh didn't mete out such a punishment just because it was the baker. It was something common to see criminals sentenced to death by hanging in Egypt. So, with that understanding of what that symbol means in those days, he understood that there was a picture of death.

Frequency Revelator

Third Rule:

We Need To Understand That Symbols In A Symbolic Dream Can Change Even Within One Person's Sphere Of Meaning

The second rule that we need to understand with regard to the interpretation of symbolic dreams is that symbols in a dream can change even within one person's sphere of meaning, let alone a different person. We illustrated earlier that the same symbol to one person can mean two different things to the other. But the other difficulty is that even within one person the same symbol can change. In other words, the same symbol can represent something at a certain point of time in one's life and at another point of time, the same symbol might represent something else. The same symbol changed with time. Let's look at Nebuchadnezzar in Daniel Chapter two specifically the dream that Nebuchadnezzar forgot.

You saw, O king, and behold, a great image. This image, mighty and of exceeding brightness, stood before you and its appearance was frightening. The head of this image was of fine gold, its breast and arms of silver, its belly and thighs of bronze. Now verse 36-38 *"This was the dream; now we will tell the king its interpretation. You, O king, the king of kings, to whom the God of heaven has given the kingdom, the power, and the might, and the glory, and into whose hand he has given, wherever they dwell, the sons of men, the beasts of the field, and the birds of the air, making you rule over them all – you are the head of gold.*

So, in the first dream that Nebuchadnezzar had the head of gold represents himself. This is similar to the second dream that he had in chapter four verse 10:

The vision of my head as I lay in bed were these; I saw and behold, a tree in the midst of the earth; and its height was great. The tree grew and became strong, and its top reached to heaven, and it was visible to the end of the whole earth. Its leaves were fair and its fruit abundant, and in it was food for all. The beasts of the field found shade under it, and the birds of the air dwelt in its branches, and all flesh was fed from it. verse 15 *but leave the stump.* Verse 19 *Then Daniel, whose name was Belteshazzar, was dismayed for a moment and his thoughts alarmed him.*

That means Daniel instantly understood what the dream meant. The moment he heard it, he was filled with shock because he knew what it meant. And it says in verse 22 *It is you, O king, who have grown and become strong.* In other words, the tree represents Nebuchadnezzar. If you analyse it, Nebuchadnezzar had two dreams. In the first dream the head of gold represent himself. In the second dream the tree also represent himself. The two different symbols referred to the same man. It is possible that in different dreams at different times you have different symbols that represent the same thing. If you recall Pharaoh's dream of the seven thin cows and the seven fat cows and the seven sheaves of grain and the seven lean sheaves of grain, you will notice that two different symbols represent the same thing even in one dream. In two different dreams, two symbols represent the same thing. In a single dream, two different symbols represent the same thing. That's why interpretation of dream is not as easy as you see it. But if you understand these points you can make it easy.

If you remember your dreams you know how dreams change and have different parts. You could be in a certain place in your dream and suddenly you are at a different place. Usually it means it is the same thing manifested in different symbols. For example, in Pharaoh's dream about the seven fat cows, seven thin cows, seven fat sheaves of grain and seven thin ones, the two different symbols were two different parts of a dream. It is the same thing referred to. The next time you have a dream that has three parts, scene one, scene two, and scene three, understand that all those scenes can represent one message given in different forms. **Although you are there watching the dream, the dream itself can represent you. It doesn't necessarily mean that it represents somebody else.** Even though Nebuchadnezzar was there and he was looking at the tree, he was right there in the dream himself. He was right there separate from the tree in his dream. The tree was the tree and he was himself. He was a separate person in the dream from the tree yet that tree was him. It was not even referring to the empire. He didn't lose his empire. It was him who was judged. His empire continued to exist possibly because Daniel held it together. During those years when he was cast out as a beast who took control of his empire? If you look at it very carefully the empire didn't collapse; it was Nebuchadnezzar who collapsed.

Even in the other dream where Nebuchadnezzar was the golden head, that represents both him and his empire, even though he was standing there and the statue was separate from him. So, remember when you have a dream it does not mean that you have to be there to represent you. In your dream, you could be there watching something that represents you. It could be a tree, or even be a person. In the dream, it was another person but in the end it was you. Perhaps in a dream you, see a little kid experiencing all kind of things. You cannot recognize the kid. You were wondering whether God is telling you about somebody else's kid. No, most probably God is talking about you. That small little kid represents you. The second point that we are emphasizing here is that symbols change but the meanings might stay the same. Let's look at the book of Genesis chapter 37:3;

Now Israel loved Joseph more than any other of his children, because he was the son of his old age; and he made him a long robe with sleeves. But when his brothers saw that their father loved him more than all his brothers, they hated him more than all his brothers, and could not speak peaceable to him. Now Joseph had a dream, and when he told it to his brothers they only hated him the more. He said to them, "Hear this dream which I have dreamed; behold, we were binding sheaves in the field, and lo, my sheaf arose and stood upright; and behold, your sheaves gathered round it, and bowed down to my sheaf.

That is what made his brothers hated him more. Now, although he was there and his brothers' sheaves were there, his sheaf in his dream represented him. But the other thing here is his sheaf represented his job and his call. In those days they were agricultural based. It was a common thing for them to go out and harvest. So, something from their work was brought into Joseph's dream but an additional thing happened. When they put the sheaves together, all the other sheaves bowed down to Joseph. This implies that Joseph's job, vocation or call will be higher than his brothers. See, it is referring to his call. Not just to his present position but it was a prediction that was to come. Let's cross reference to his second dream which is recorded in verse 9.

Then he dreamed another dream, and told it to his brothers, and said, "Behold, I have dreamed another dream; and behold, the sun, the moon, and eleven stars were bowing down to me." But when he told it to his father and his brothers, his father rebuked him, and said to him, "What is this dream that you have dreamed? Shall I and your mother and your brothers indeed come to bow ourselves to the ground before you?"

Apparently Jacob understood dream. He knew that the sun was him and the moon was the mother, eleven stars were the children. Isn't it strange how symbols are that way? We must realize that the language of the spirit world is symbolic. It's just like I want to convey with my intellect a description to you I have to use phrases that you understand. We cannot use a language which none of us understand to convey something. For example, there is a hotly contested debate over Charismatic terms like infilling of the Spirit, and baptism in the Spirit. People quarrel because of definitions. To them, the different terms could mean the same thing. But churches have fought and split because of definitions. So, when one person stands up and say something, the other person understood it to mean something else. Misunderstanding, and grievances has arisen as a consequence because somebody said something that they don't mean it. They mean it to be something in their context and somebody understood it to be something else because of their background.

Fourth Rule:

The Fourth Rule With Regard To A Symbolic Dream And Its Interpretation Is The Chronological Context Or Time Frame Involved.

Did you now that every dream has a time frame? It may no more be applicable after some time. For example, we want to understand what a person is going through at the time that they have the dream. **To interpret dreams, you must understand not only what the symbols mean to that person, but you must also try to pick up what that person is going through.** This is because what they are going through will have an effect on that dream. If you have been going through a time of difficulty, like perhaps you have just lost your job and you have been applying for job after job, the dreams you have will have to do with the chronology context of what you are going through. If I did not pick up that you have just lost your job, I may interpret the dream differently. But if I have the chronological context of what you are going through, I could interpret the dream better. Those dreams may have a message about your job. It may even tell you when you will get that job. Dreams can project the time. Joseph told the baker that in three days, he will be hanging on a tree and it happened exactly as he had interpreted. **So, a dream has its chronological context in the sense of what the person is going through at that time. Whether a person is fearful, happy, sad, anxious, all these things must be taken into account before you can interpret a dream.**

Solomon says in Ecclesiastes 5:3 that *a dream comes through much activity*. The word *activity* not only does it refer to physical activity but behind it, it also conveys a meaning of your soul state, whether you were fearful or anxious and all these. So, it is important to see when that person has a dream chronologically what context are they going through? We apply that knowledge when we interpret our dreams. That means like David it is important to search our hearts before we sleep. **If you sleep in a state of anxiety and fear that has not been removed or state of unforgiveness or state of anger, let me tell you those will come out in the dream and it will color your dreams.** And that is what prevents an accurate reception from God because our dreams are colored by our emotions. It is important to have emotions of love, joy and peace in the presence of God before we sleep in order to receive accurate messages from our dreams. Otherwise all what the dreams do is just to reveal our soul's condition and what we need to do to deal with it.

I know people who sleep in a state of anger and judgmental attitude and in their dreams their anger and judgmental attitudes come up. The dreams confirm their suspicion. They suspect this and that and it comes out in the dream. It is a projection. What you believe and feel is projected into the dream. It will be the same like negative confession. People say this is going to happen. Later it happened and then they say, "There I told you - prophecy fulfilled." It is not prophecy; they just got what they said in the negative realm. So, it is a kind of projection of their negativities, which materialized because they spoke out their negativities and they dreamed out their negativities. It is quite similar to the conscious state. For example it is very hard to hear from God when you are anxious, fearful, or when something is troubling your mind. It hinders the accuracy of hearing the voice of God and the voice of your human spirit. The best place to hear from God is a place of rest, love, peace and joy in the kingdom of God. If you are filled with anxiety and your thoughts are troubled, it tends to magnetize and pull towards the wrong direction such that your receiving is colored. That is why it is sometimes difficult to tell things about yourself. If you are praying about a job and you really want it desperately. In the natural state when you are awake you keep hearing, "This is God, this is God." Because of your strong desires 95 percent of your dreams are affected by the magnetic pull of your emotions. Your activity colors your dream that's what Solomon is saying in Ecclesiastes 5:3. In order for you to secure an accurate interpretation, you need to know the chronological context, emotion or spiritual context of the person.

A Practical Application Of Symbolic Dreams

Now, that we have explored the basic rules for dream interpretation, lets apply them in real life situations and see if we understand. A lady had two consecutive dreams. In the first dream, she just dreamt she didn't get the wake up call in the hotel and she was late for church by two hours. That dreams doesn't tells me much. It only tells me the state in which she slept in. She was very concerned that she doesn't want to be late. So, that came out in a dream. It tells me several areas about her life. Like to her it is important to get ready for the church. A normal person may not have that kind of anxiety.

She had a dream that she is swimming and walking on water. Now, before we interpret the dream, remember the other context that we mentioned. You have to understand what these symbols mean to her. Walking on water and walking through water are found in the Bible. Walking on water or going through water symbolize spiritual movement. We all remember Moses crossing the Red Sea. That was like darkness and light moving from Egyptian land into the Promised Land. We also remember Joshua and the Israelites how they crossed the Jordan and it was like going from one aspect into something new. So this is the scriptural context. Then we have other areas, which are important to interpret the dream. Because she is in the ministry, the chronological context is important. She doesn't know how to swim in the natural. That plays an important role in interpreting the dream. God specially used something that she cannot do in the natural to show her something that she is doing in a dream. General interpretation would mean that it is talking about some aspect of ministry that she is going to move into. Something that is different for example tantamount to crossing the Jordan to the land of Canaan. Something that is vitally important. Then the interpretation is affected by our own knowledge of what she is going through in her ministry. I understand that at certain points in her dreams it represents a crossover point from one phase of ministry to another phase. So that helps me to interpret her dream too.

Because she does not swim in the natural and yet she has those dreams, it would mean that there is something that she had never done before in the

Spirit. Something that she has never done before that is new in the Spirit. The Holy Spirit brought up things that she could never do. That points to things in the Spirit that she has no experience before that God is preparing her for. Then twice the dream occurs. One when she was within the water and the other when she was above the water. It depends now on when she had that dream. The fact that she had it twice means that she would have two different experiences of what God will do in that phase of ministry. In the first phase, she will be handling those things that she had never done before. As she moves into it, she will get fully involved with it. The second dream means that she is going to dedicate whatever she has done there. She will move into some sort of ministry and going to establish it. See, when she walks on water she is no more in it. She is above it.

OPEN DREAM OR REAL LIFE SITUATION DREAMS.

The second type of dream is the *real life situation dreams*. Dreams are one of the leadings of the Spirit an important leading. Matthew 1:24 When Joseph woke from sleep, he did as the angel of the Lord commanded him. When did the angel spoke look at verse 20 But as he considered this, behold, an angel of the Lord appeared to him in a dream. In a dream he saw an angel coming to him giving him a message. In chapter two we see the same thing in verse 13. The angel appeared again in a dream gave a different message. Then in verse 19 the same angel came and told him to leave Egypt. And in verse 22 God warned him in a dream and he turn aside and went to Galilee. It is dreams that have led Joseph and Mary. And that protected Jesus. These second type of dreams are real life situation dreams. They don't need interpretation. It is a direct dream a real life situation dream. And sometimes some of your dreams that God sent to you are real life situation. Where you may actually see yourself in a place where you have never been before.

In the case of actual dream, its where exactly as you see it, it comes to pass, every details of it. We know that Paul's Macedonian vision cannot be that category. Because if Paul considered it as the third category when he reached Macedonia he should have looked for that man. But he did not. He understood that it is just a message. It is not important whether it's a Macedonian or woman wearing a Macedonian garment calling him. Now the third category of dream is the actual. Like for example Joseph in the gospel of Matthew had a dream of an angel coming to him and telling him to go to Egypt. Then he had a dream to come back. Then he had a dream to tell him where to go and stay. And in the dream he saw an angel. It was an actual vision that came when a person is subconscious. So it was an actual dream; everything came exactly to pass. There is no necessity of an interpretation.

MESSAGE DREAM

The third type of dream is the *message dream*. Where there are a lot of things here and there but there is only one message. Example in Matt. 2 verse 12 the wise men were told not to return to Herod. So sometimes your dreams can be that way. There are a lot of things that happened in a dream and when you get up you forgot everything but you only got one message. The reason we teach on this area is Christians are learning to obey God and be led by the Spirit. But they are still not sensitive to God when it comes to dreams. They take them lightly. They don't record them down. When some one prophesies, thus says the Lord, our ears prick up like a dog. But when we have a dream from God we say, "That's only a dream. I wonder what it means," and afterwards you forgot it. We took it too lightly and we missed the fact the Holy Spirit is working in our lives even when we are asleep. One of the majors leading of the Spirit is through dreams. It is even prophesized in the last days God will lead His people in dreams. Old men shall dream dreams. These are supernatural impartation of wisdom that comes to them when they are asleep.

The second type of dreams or visions is what we call a message type. We don't have any examples of dreams in the bible of that category. But we have a vision like in the book of Acts 16 Paul saw a Macedonian man and it was a message vision. In other words the details of the dreams are not so important as the message it carries. It carries only one message "Come over here to Macedonia". How do we know that dream of Paul was a message dream and not an actual dream? It is because when Paul went over to Macedonia he didn't look for the man. In fact the first people that he met in Acts 16 were women. Then we have the second category that we called the message type where you could have the whole series of dreams but there is only one main message. We have illustrated with Acts 16 Paul before his Macedonian journey he was in Troas waiting. After he was told by the Spirit not to go to Bithynia or Mysia he waited at Troas. Then he had a night vision. If you take the Hebrew meaning he possibly had a dream. To them it was the same; dreams and visions are similar and can be regarded as one. Although he saw the Macedonian man he took it as a message and not as a parable. When he went to Philippi, which was the capital of Macedonia, Paul did not look for a man although he saw a man in a vision. The first people he encountered were women. So we know that it was a kind of message dream or vision.

PROPHETIC DREAMS OR THIRD DIMENSION DREAMS

"In a dream, a vision of the night, when sound sleep falls on men, while they slumber in their beds, then He opens the ears of men, And seals their instruction. It says in Deuteronomy. 13:1-5 *"If a prophet arises among you, or dreamer of dreams, and he gives you a sign or a wonder, and the sign or wonder which he tells you comes to pass, and if he says, "Let us go after other gods, which you have not known, and let us serve them, you shall not listen to the words of that prophet or to that dreamer of dreams; for the Lord your God is testing you, to know whether you love the Lord your God with all your heart and with all your soul. You shall walk after the Lord your God and fear Him, and keep His commandments and obey His voice, and you shall serve Him and cleave to Him. But that prophet or that dreamer of dreams shall be put to death, because he has taught rebellion against the Lord your God, who brought you out of the land of Egypt and redeemed you out of the house of bondage, to make you leave the way in which the Lord your God commanded you to walk. So you shall purge the evil from the midst of you.* (Job 33:15-16).

There is a close association between dreams and the function of a prophet. Hence, prophetic dreams are those dreams that carry a prophetic message either for the person experiencing the dream or for others in his sphere of contact and are at par with the prophetic ministry. They are also called the third dimension dreams. In the context of the above scripture, the word *dreamer* or the phrase *dreamer of dreams* is used together with the word prophet. When this passage speaks about a prophet or dreamer of dreams who gives you a sign or wonder, it is speaking of a different level of dream altogether. That is why there is such a thing as *prophetic dreams*, which are on par with the prophet's ministry and function at the same level as the message spoken through prophecy. For this reason, a dreamer of dreams is equal to a prophet's ministry. In other words, these are dreams that carry a prophecy as if a prophet himself were prophesying. These dreams are a vehicle of prophecy; hence they are called prophetic dreams. In regard to prophetic dream we need to consider that a dream is a vision of the night and it goes beyond the second dimension of spiritual encounter. Sometimes there is a word of wisdom or a word of knowledge that comes from the dream. Not all dreams are in that category. Most of it is in the first dimension of giving you a warning. From time to time it is in the second dimension of giving you a direction in life. But if you have a call to a prophet's office or you have the gift of prophecy operating in your life that same anointing that helps you to prophesy while you are awake, while you are in your conscious state, that same anointing while you are asleep makes you a dreamer of prophetic dreams. In other words, now you prophesy in your dreams. That same anointing works whether you are asleep or you are awake. So prophetic dreams come because of the anointing upon. The anointing within covers the first two dimensions of dreams. But prophetic dreams come because of the anointing upon. Sometimes when you sleep under an anointing you have prophetic dreams. I remember the three day fast that I went through in the second year of my seminary. I had many prophetic dreams.

Let's refer to Acts chapter 2. We must consider in Acts 2 the prophecy in regard to the Holy Spirit coming down has to do with prophetic dream. It is not ordinary dream of either the first dimension or the second dimension. We can call it *third dimension*. We can say there are the first dimension, second dimension and third dimension of dreams. How do we analyze that? Compare it with the conscious state. Most of the time the Holy Spirit leads us by the inward witness and by the inward voice. That is the first dimension of the leading of the Holy Spirit. Then you would have the voice of the Holy Spirit and supernatural leading. That would be the second dimension in the conscious state. Then there is the third dimension where you are in a ministry or you are operating a gift. It's a different thing when you are hearing God under an anointing and without an anointing. When the anointing is upon you the voice of God sounds clearer than when it is not upon you. When an anointing comes upon your life in ministry in your conscious state, whether through a gift or an office that you are functioning in, the voice of God and even the voice of your spirit man is amplified. It takes on a different dimension. I will call it the *third dimension*. It's a deeper level. It's as if you are hearing God from the outside but it's not; it is still from the inside. But because of the anointing upon you what you hear inside your spirit comes from the anointing that is upon you and you are hearing it on the outside. It's loud and it's clear. It's easier to hear God when the anointing is upon you than when it is not upon you.

For that reason sometimes people under the anointing say something and predict something accurately. But outside of the anointing, outside of the ministry, outside of the gift, in the normal state they will predict something that will really go off the mark. Although Eli was not a very dedicated priest, but his position as a priest was still there. The anointing of a priest was still on him. When Hannah was praying for a child Eli said, "Go your way the Lord has heard your prayer." That was a statement made under an anointing. See, the anointing works in spite of and despite his life. But in the end a careless person will lose the anointing completely. So, that is an example that what was said under the anointing has power. But outside of his office there is no power. It's a different thing when the anointing is upon and a different thing when the anointing is not upon. In a similar way in dreams there is a third dimension, where there is an anointing upon that comes upon you when you are asleep.

And in the last days it shall be, God declares, that I will pour out my Spirit upon all flesh, and your sons and your daughters shall prophesy, and your young men shall see visions, and your old men shall dream dreams; yes, and on my menservants and my maidservants in those days I will pour out my Spirit; and they shall prophesy
(Acts 2:17).

The whole context talks about the outpouring of the Holy Spirit. The word translated as dream here is not the ordinary Greek word for dream. The ordinary Greek word for dream as used in Matthew chapter one and chapter two in the life of Joseph and in the wise men life is the word onar, which is the official Greek word for the word dream. Notice that onar has been used for the first dimension and second dimension. The word onar in Matthew one and two refers to Joseph having a dream about this angel coming to him and talking to him. Onar is used even in the second dimension of dreams. But in Acts 2 the word *dream* is not the word *onar* but is the word *enupnion*. What he is saying here is that root word means in a state of rest. It's not just dreaming. So when they combine the word together they have the word enupnion and the word enupnion talks about receiving a leading, an impression, a direction, a vision, a spiritual encounter, while in the state of rest. That definition will be just nice for the second dimension of dream. But we put it under third dimension because here it includes the anointing upon. In the second dimension you don't need the anointing upon. Joseph did not have anointing upon when he saw the angel. But this third dimension is where we have anointing upon come upon you while you are in a state of rest. When you are in a state of sleeping, and when the anointing comes upon you the dreams that you see are not *onar*. They are prophetic dreams. You move into what Deuteronomy 13:1 says a dreamer of dreams.

If you study the word old men in Acts 2, you cannot take it literally. Because if you take it literally a lot of you would be old since all of you have dreams. It says here in Acts 2, Young men see visions old men dream dreams. Everybody dream dreams so everybody must be old. Understand that the Greek word used is different. It is talking about a third dimension of dream, where the prophetic gift operates in a dream. And here the word young and old signifies your walk with God. It's in the similar usage as in First John it says little children, young men and old men, three spiritual stages. So here old men is talking about the final spiritual stage of your life. There are always three spiritual stages, children, young men and old men. That's in the book of First John. When we are children we need the milk. Then you progress from spiritual milk to spiritual maturity. Then when you reached fatherhood in the spirit realm you have a different dimension. Let me illustrate what is like at the fatherhood stage. When you have grown into the Lord from childhood to manhood to fatherhood, there is a stage where you become quite prophetic. You may not be a prophet but you are prophetic. You have the advantage of your spiritual past and the advantage point of seeing into the spirit.

Towards the end of his life, Jacob was going to bless his children and two of his grandchildren. Although Jacob was not a prophet when he was going to die, he suddenly taps onto that old man's ability, the kind of ability that Acts 2 speaks about old men shall dream dreams. And in the book of Genesis chapter 49:1 he began to prophesy and those prophecies came to pass. He prophesied over all his children. He spoke about what they were and what they shall be. It is actually classified under the spiritual truth of blessings. But those blessings were not ordinary blessings. It is more than that his blessings moved into the word of wisdom. That's where prophetic elements came into his blessings. Jacob's prophesying over his children was a case of old men dreaming dreams but in his conscious state. It says in Genesis 49:2-3 *Assemble and hear, O sons of Jacob, and hearken to Israel your father.* Now he is about to die and he is going to tell them about their future. You notice this happened several times in the bible. Then he talks about Reuben, talks about Judah, talks about Simeon, talks about Levi, he talks about Zebulun, talks about Issachar, talks about Dan, talks about Joseph, he speaks the past and he speaks the future. When he has blessed them and given out all the prophetic blessings he died. Notice his blessings of Joseph's son in chapter 48. You must understand his condition now. Now he is an old man. When he saw Joseph's children he asks, "Who are these?" Joseph said, "My children." Then he says, *"Bring them to me."* And he places the elder one Manasseh on one side and Ephraim on the other. And Israel stretched out his hands and he placed his right hand, (which is a symbol of higher blessing) on. Ephraim and his left hand on Manasseh. And Joseph thought he made a mistake. So Joseph said, "I think you are making a mistake that is not the elder," and he shifted Jacob's hand over. Jacob said, "I know." So he knew what he was doing. He had a word of wisdom. True enough Ephraim became the bigger crowd in a sense. Notice verse 17 When Joseph saw that his father laid his right hand upon the head of Ephraim, it displeased him. He predicted correctly about the future of Ephraim and Manasseh; he had a word of wisdom that was a prophetic blessing. Notice this type of thing is never done when a person is not going to die.

Unless they function in the office of a prophet you don't see this kind of thing manifesting. There seems to be some special thing manifesting when a person is about to go home to the Lord. Notice that Moses pronounced blessing on the Israelites when he was about to go home. And he was a prophet. Even though he was a prophet before he died there was an extra power in his last words. Jesus Himself did that as He was being lifted up to heaven. He raised his hands and blessed His disciples. That spiritual truth of prophetic blessing has a connection to what we look in Acts chapter two and called it old men dream dreams. In other words there is a difference when you are in the beginning of your ministry. You are just moving in. You are like a child. Then there is a difference when you are at the middle of your ministry and you are like a young man. But when you reached your final stage, when you reached your final years then there is a special impartation that comes upon your life. When that element works while you are asleep you are a dreamer of prophetic dreams.

Understanding Prophetic Dreams & Visions

Most of Smith Wigglesworth's prophecies about our times today and the last days came towards the end of his ministry. Most of Daniel's prophecies about these last days came at the end of his ministry. Notice in the book of Daniel it was only in his later years that he received a lot of those prophecies regarding the end times. So most of the prophetic dreams come when a person had reached that fatherhood stage in their ministry. They are going to leave the place and leave something behind. That is why it is not so common because God has to put an anointing upon while you are asleep. Or He has to quicken a gift of prophecy in your life. And it is powerful when the anointing is upon your life. Perhaps you have been to a very anointed meeting. When you left the meeting and you went home, the anointing was still all over you. You could hardly sleep, you worship God and you fell asleep worshipping and that night you had a prophetic dream. Again remember our teaching you have to understand the background. What was your last thought before you slept? It makes a difference when your final experience before you slept was under the anointing. You were soaked in the anointing and you dreamed a dream. Most probably it would have a prophetic significance. It would have been a third dimension dream, a prophetic dream. That is the area we must understand in order to be opened to it.

How does a person move fully into it? There is no short cut. No. 1 the anointing upon has to be there. It does not mean that it always has to be towards the end of your life. When Deut. 13:1 talks about a dreamer of dreams it didn't say that the dreamer of dreams was going to die then that person becomes a dreamer of dreams. A person could have a special gifting. If you have a gift of prophecy under normal circumstances most probably the same anointing will operate in your dream life. As long as the gift of prophecy is in your life you can have prophetic dreams. So that's No. 1 the anointing upon must be there not just the anointing within. No. 2 the principle behind it is not that you have to kick the bucket before you do it. The person must have reached a fatherhood level of spiritual maturity. It may not mean that you have to be going home before you move into that. The principle behind it is that you are in the fatherhood stage in your spiritual life. Perhaps you have moved in the perfect will of God and you have grown from spiritual childhood to spiritual manhood into spiritual fatherhood. And now you are at that stage and your maturity is such you could easily move into prophetic dream. Spiritual children do not have that. These are not step one, step two, step three. These are keys. In other words if one of the keys are operating you could move into prophetic dreams. You could be a young child but if the anointing upon is so strong you could have prophetic dreams while you are asleep. So No. 2 is where your maturity is such. You have developed your spiritual maturity and you have developed your spiritual ministry. You are a spiritual father. It is easy for you to move into that stage in the prophetic dream.

Let's look at an example in the life of Daniel. Daniel 7:1 In the first year of Belshazzar king of Babylon, Daniel had a dream (Now that dream is not first dimension nor is it in the second dimension; it is in the third dimension. It was a prophetic dream) and visions of his head as he lay in his bed. Then he wrote down the dream, and told the sum of the matter. The dream basically showed the different Empires that will arise, the different kings that will arise in Daniel's time. And in verse 13 I saw in the night vision, and behold, with the clouds of heaven there came one like a son of man and he came to the Ancient of Days and was presented before Him. Verse 15 As for me, Daniel, my spirit within me was anxious and the vision of my head alarmed me.

As I studied that very carefully it looks like this that within that chapter there were two parts. One was while he was asleep and the other was while he was awake and as he was still meditating on that it seems he has some sort of a vision. One was definitely a dream. The other looks like he was awake and he was seeing a vision of the Ancient of Days and he was grieved because he didn't understand. A prophetic dream must have a prophetic interpretation. Anything received by anointing upon needs an anointing upon to unveil it. So Daniel was grieved and he must have been praying over these things. And finally it was the angel who told him what the dream meant. Although he himself had the gift of interpretation he could not interpret that particular dream for it was beyond him; it was too far in the future for him to compare to anything he knows of the present.

> *In the third year of the reign of King Belshazzar a vision appeared to me, Daniel, after that which appeared to me at the first. (In other words this was his second prophetic dream. And I saw in the vision; in Susa the capital, which is in the province of Elam; and I saw in the vision, and I was at the river Ulai (Daniel 8:1-2).*

Now, that signifies while he was dreaming. And in verse one he says it's the same like the one in chapter seven. And the one in Dan 7: 1 is a dream.

So logically Dan 8: 1-2 must also be part of a dream and possibly part of a vision too. Although he was in Susa he dreamt he was by the river. And he saw all these significant things happening. Then in verse 15 When I, Daniel, had seen the vision, I sought to understand it. See he had a prophetic dream and he didn't understand it. He was seeking its interpretation although he had the gift of interpretation of dreams. If there was anyone that was expected to interpret that dream or vision, he was the one. Here he could not do it and he needed spiritual revelation.

PROPHETIC DREAM CODE MEANINGS

A certain brother had a dream that he was connecting wire on the ceiling What does electrical wiring symbolize in a dream? Electrical wiring in our days is spiritual power. It can be good. It can be bad. Depending on the dream. But most of the time it symbolizes Holy Spirit power. This brother had a dream that he was connecting wire on the ceiling. Remember if you dream of a house that house is usually your soul. If you are dreaming of the upper portion of your house it talks about your spiritual life. If you are dreaming about the lower portion of your house it talks about your physical body. So he is dreaming about the ceiling. A ceiling talks about his spiritual life. He is seeking to channel his spiritual life into his natural life. He was asking God before the dream how to hear the voice of the Spirit. The Lord is showing him that the connection between his spirit man and his soul man has to be done very carefully.

What happens if you dream about furniture in the house? Furniture represents things that you add to your life either in your soul or in your spirit. Your house represents your soul, your spirit or your body. So any furniture within the house represents an addition that is made to your house. If you dream that the furniture was damaged then it means that there is something wrong inside. It could be your physical body that your dream is warning you. It could be your spiritual life that is dying and you need to do something about it. You cannot see it when you are awake and its being shown in the dream. What about dreams about someone who has passed away? If it is not demon powers working then it has to do with your past. Your dream about your mother or your father may not mean that they are appearing to you. Since your mother and father were the ones who brought you up and taught you about life values and principles, dreaming about them may mean the voice of your soul or your conscience that has been training your life.

This lady said that she was dreaming about laundry and cleaning. That talks about spiritual cleansing, spiritual prayers. I believe it talks about prayer ministry. Dream about getting married. It could mean an answer to prayer. It could also mean tying up to spiritual things. If it's applies to your soul then its talking about areas in your soul that you are beginning to grasp certain principles that you didn't have before. You are beginning to take them into your life, marrying them into your life. If it talks about your physical realm, then your dream could be pointing to areas of physical affection in your life that perhaps you are neglecting or not paying attention to. How do you interpret time frame? Time frames come when in your dream you remember numbers. If in your dream you dream about just walking to a place and you are just seeing a lot of trees. When you woke up you don't remember the number of trees. Then time frame is not important. But when you wake up and the number hits you. You saw ten trees. Time frame can come in. So time frame comes in when the number is very significant so that you do not forget it when you woke up. Like Joseph's dream and Pharaoh's dream the number seven comes very clearly. Then the butler's dream and the baker's dream the number three was very significant. So that talks about time frame.

There is a rainbow and underneath there are a lot of colored fishes. When you dream about fish usually they represent Christians. Rainbows symbolize spiritual covenant and spiritual promises. So the person is looking at the spiritual condition or spiritual area. This man here dreamt about telephones that were not working. Telephone talks about relationship and communication. Perhaps you would wish that there was some connection with someone or with some people but there was none. Perhaps you like to be closer and its not there. White clothing. White clothing talks about spiritual life. Army clothing. Depends on the context of the dream. If you dream of war, please don't interpret it as a third dimension dream or a prophetic dream. It could be revealing the state of your spiritual life. So army clothing talks about readiness and the battle that is being fought. One last one; Snake. Snake represents the devil. It could be things that you got to take authority in your life. So we pray that through these sessions you would be more sensitive to your dreams

CHAPTER SIX

INTERPRETATION OF DREAMS AND VISIONS

As for me, Daniel, my spirit within me was anxious and the visions of my head alarmed me. Here we are not sure whether in a vision or in a dream possibly vision. I approached one of those who stood there and asked him the truth concerning all this. So he told, and made known to me the interpretation of the things
(Daniel 7:15).

There are a lot of awesome tools out there for understanding visions and dreams, but you need to keep it simple, and get the basics of dream interpretation to start with. As you go, constantly ask the Holy Spirit for His interpretation. Listening to God interpret symbols that are personal to you, is the only way to fully understand how God is speaking personally, and uniquely to you. As evidenced in our opening scripture, Daniel had a vision and he asked for the interpretation of the dream and he got the complete interpretation that God gave to him. This is to tell you that before we can interpret dreams, we need to understand what those symbols are in our life. The reason I point to it is there is such a difference in the meanings of symbols in different people's lives. It is very difficult to use one's own dream language to interpret someone else's dream without clouding the integrity of the dream. For example, in scripture, *"seed"* has various meanings depending on the context: A seed can mean the Word of God (Matthew 13:1-23); A seed can also represent the Kingdom (Matthew 13:31-32); and a seed can also refer to Faith (Matthew 17). So, you got to understand his context and where God is speaking to him from. In the case of Pharaoh's dreams, cows and stalks represented money and prosperity in those days. Pharaoh was standing at the riverbank pointing to his position of authority. Then the number seven will leave only the other interpretation of years. A river and a mountain in the context of God symbolize in the bible time span. That's how Joseph understood that to be years. If you have dreams about yourself walking through a path or mountain, today modern concept you see yourself standing by the highway. Remember roads and paths and things that flow like a river or perhaps like yourself going up a mountain symbolize time span or a period of time in the Word of God. And that's where the time span is emphasized. Sometimes the river symbolizes the Holy Spirit. So from that time span that Pharaoh was standing by comes these seven cows representing seven years. Seven fat years followed by seven lean years. Joseph has his dream interpreted.

How Do We Receive Interpretation For Our Dreams?

God may choose to give us the interpretation in these ways: Instantaneously revealing the meaning of a dream or vision through an angel, as God did with Daniel (Daniel 10:10-15). Daniel 10:14 *"Now I have come to make you understand what will happen to your people in the latter days, for the vision refers to many days yet to come."* Simultaneously speaking the dream's interpretation to us as we sleep. Through the process of writing it down. 1 Chronicles 28:19 *"All this,"* said David, *"the Lord made me understand in writing, by His hand upon me, all the works of these plans."* Daniel 7:1 "In the first year of Belshazzar king of Babylon, Daniel had a dream and visions in his head while on his bed. Then he wrote down the dream, telling the main facts." Unfolding a dream's meaning as we mature in understanding His ways. Proverbs 25:2 *"It is the glory of God to conceal a matter, but the glory of kings to search out a matter."* Proverbs 1:5-6 "A wise man will hear and increase learning, and a man of understanding will attain wise counsel, to understand a proverb and an enigma, the words of the wise and their riddles.". God places great value on our searching for the things He conceals. Often we learn as much if not more in the discovery process of interpreting a dream as we do in simply obtaining the dream's answer itself.

FOUR LEVELS OF DREAM INTERPRETATION

In order to secure a holistic understanding and interpretation of dreams, it is important that dreams be broken down into various parts and be interpreted at different levels. There are **FOUR** main levels by which dreams can be received, applied and interpreted. This symbolism is revelation from

God. With revelation comes the need for interpretation, application, and proclamation.

Level 1: Revelation:

This includes anything we receive from God that we did not previously know or that cannot be known by natural means. Consider the episode of Gideon in Judges 7. The Midianites and Amalekites were arrayed against Gideon and the 300. The Lord told Gideon to go to the camp of the enemy and he would "hear what I (God) shall say." When Gideon gets there, he overhears a man say, "'I have had a dream: To my surprise, a loaf of barley bread tumbled into the camp of Midian; it came to a tent and struck it so that it fell and overturned, and the tent collapsed.' Then his companion answered and said, 'This is nothing else but the sword of Gideon; Into his hand God has delivered Midian and the whole camp.'

Level 2: Interpretation:

Once you have received a revelation through a dream, the next step is to interpret it. Interpretation connotes to securing the meaning of the dream. Dream interpretation seek to address the following questions: What does the dream mean? For who is the dream intended? The guiding principle is that all symbolism must be understood and interpreted without violating scriptural principles. In response to the dream about a loaf of bread which came to the enemy's camp and struck it so that it fell and overturned, his companion answered and said, 'This is nothing else but the sword of Gideon; Into his hand God has delivered Midian and the whole camp. 'This was the interpretation of the dream, that God has given their enemy, Median into their hands.

Level 3: Application:

After securing the correct interpretation of your dream, it is imperative that you apply it. Application addresses the following fundamental questions: When? Where? Why? How? Interpreting dreams is taking that which is spiritual and giving it natural application. Application requires the wisdom of God and the leading of the Holy Spirit. The above mentioned dream was applied when the Children of Israel took practical steps to invade the enemy's camp and attacked the Medianites based on the confirmation they had received in the dream.

Level 4: Proclamation:

The manner in which we communicate what we have received is very key in dream interpretation. Proclamation connotes to the conveyance of the message or revelation that we have received to its intended recipients or those to whom the dream is intended. Proclamation was made when his companion answered and said, 'This is nothing else but the sword of Gideon; Into his hand God has delivered Midian and the whole camp. Proclamation also connotes to sounding the horn to announce the fulfillment of the dream.

KEYS FOR UNLOCKING THE INTERPRETATION OF DREAMS

As aforementioned, there are different types of dreams and these are rules that you apply when you interpret dreams.. The principle is that the symbolic dreams must be interpreted in such a way that the symbols in your dreams have the same meaning and symbols as in the Bible. They must be biblical symbols in your interpretation. For example if in your sleep you dream about a dog, a dog in the bible symbolizes *Judaizers*. Paul was fighting with those people called the *Judaizers* and he called them dogs. There is only one statement in the Bible where Paul says beware of dogs. Dogs also refer to people outside the covenant of God. When the Canaanite woman came Jesus said the bread is for the children and not for the dogs. She was outside of the covenant of God. So you can see that dogs represent things that are outside the covenant. They don't represent things that are good. And so even if in your dream you had a white dog or even a golden dog, when you get up, you thought that's a good dream. I wonder what the dog represents? Blessings? A dog in whatever colour of the rainbow in your dream still represents something not good.

Base Every Dream Interpretation On God's Word

The principle is that the symbolic dreams must be interpreted in such a way that the symbols in your dreams have the same meaning and symbols as in the Bible. They must be biblical symbols in your interpretation. You can see obviously that the more Word you have in your life and the more understanding you have of the Bible the greater your ability to interpret dreams. If you understand the Bible and the symbols that are in the Bible, it will help you to interpret dreams because you know what the symbols represent. If you see a snake whether it is a white snake, black snake, even they sing some nice songs in your dreams they still represent evil and deception. So, there are many symbols such as land, gold, silver and all kind of things in the Bible. When you get a dream and you don't understand the symbol, simply search for it in the Word of God. Don't try to interpret something outside the Word, lest you fall into error. Your symbols must always be in line with the Bible. That's the first key when it comes to dream and how to understand and interpret them. Soulish interpretive methods are accepted as legitimate in the secular arena and by some in the religious realm (i.e. Jung, Freud), with no recognition that, in fact, the interpretation belongs to God. Someone using one of these humanly devised models will not come to the same conclusion as one applying the principles of interpretation that are found in Scripture. Those that are of God's light and household are unlimited in their interpretive potential due to God's unlimited nature. They are privy to an infinite panorama of knowledge and understanding.

You Must Discern What Kind Of Spirit The Person Who Had A Dream Has

The second key in dream interpretation is for us to discern what kind of spirit the person who had a dream has. The Bible in Ecclesiastes 5:3 tells us that dreams come through much activities. In your dream, your personal attitudes and feelings can affect its accuracy. Remember this key otherwise you will misinterpret your dreams. If someone tells me a dream and ask for an interpretation, one of the first things that I must do is discern what kind of spirit this person has. I must discern the kind of attitude this person has so that I could interpret the type of dream he has. If for example, he is a person filled with hate and he has a dream that some body is angry with him. It may not necessary imply that the person is angry with him. It could simply mean that what he is seeing is his own attitude colored his dreams. In other words, his dream didn't become the color God wants it to be, but it added, polluted, and blurred the vision. Just like in our waking hours when we are awake you hear God's voice. But sometimes God's voice feel like an inner thought and you wonder, "Did I think about that or is it really the Holy Spirit?" And sometimes those dreams reveal your inner most feeling. That means your dreams come from your daily activities.

Some dreams come from your inner subconscious thinking and they need to be dealt with. They are not a message from God but yourself. Your own dreams that come forth. Its funny you cannot lie to yourself in your dream. Your conscience affects it. Your feelings, your personal attitudes color your dreams. So to interpret dreams check the people attitudes that received the dream. Whether the receiving station is in functioning order, the transmitter is in order heaven never breaks down. But it is our receiving station that breaks down. Sometimes the battery water needs to be changed. What is that? The Holy Spirit is not there, the prayer life is not there and the Word is not enough. The voltage has gone so low and the attitudes are wrong it colored our dreams. So the second rule is remember in whatever the three types of dreams to check your personal attitude and feeling whether they are coloring the dreams. In helping another person to understand their dreams check their attitude too. Discern it by the Holy Spirit in order to get the accurate picture of what God is saying. So the bible says in Jude 33 that God speaks to us.

You Must Determine The Urgency Of The Message In The Dream By Its Recurrence

The third key in interpreting of dreams is to determine the urgency of the message in the dream by its recurrence. In the book of Genesis Chapter 41, look at how Joseph interpreted the dreams and have the third key coming forward. Here, we have Joseph interpreting Pharaoh's dream. In verse

28 that's where the interpretation starts. *It is as I told Pharaoh, God has shown to Pharaoh what he is about to do. There will come seven years of great supply throughout all the land of Egypt.* Imagine if they missed the dream. They would have been finished. The whole nation would have been famished if they didn't pay attention to the dream.

> *But after them there will arise seven years of famine, and all the plenty will be forgotten in the land of Egypt; the famine will consume the land, and the plenty will be unknown in the land by reason of that famine which will follow, for it will be very grievous.*

And the dream was repeated to Pharaoh twice. Because whenever God establishes the thing, He will shortly bring it to pass. If a dream is repeated, it's a sign that it is established and that there is a sureness about it. It is urgent and it is coming to pass shortly. Notice a few things here. It is a dream that is not good. If you have a dream about seven lorries coming to your house, bringing all kind of goodies and emptying them in your front yard. Then after the seven lorries came the seven tractors and flatten your house. By the time the seventh one passed by, there is nothing remaining of your house. What would be your feeling? When a dream is like a warning, it's not supposed to come to pass. It is supposed to be prevented. If you have a dream of your daughter drowning, you are not going to say bless God. You are not going to do that. First of all you are going to check whether this is the enemy coming. Whether you live in fear so much it comes out in your dream.

You Have To Check Whether There Are No Emotions Or Feelings Attached By The Person Having The Dream

The fourth key is to check if the dream is not coming from the person herself and if no emotions or feelings are attached. Your best friends may like you too much to be unbiased in their interpretation. Thus, you may receive from them an interpretation that God did not intend. Recently you have been swimming for seven days. Then after you have checked these areas if you finally feel that is a warning from God, all you have to do is to pray against that fear. And it will never come to pass. Most of the time this type of dreams come from the enemy. Sometimes from our own life, our own fear brought the dreams. For this reason those of you who just fall in love and you are praying to God, "God is that man (or woman) Your will for me?" And then you dream about you and her or him in a wedding. You cannot trust that dream. You know why? Your feelings are involved. It is very hard to hear God's dream when your own feelings are involved. Those are the times where you should trust your dreams least, especially dreams in the area of marriage and life partners. Your own feelings, your own desires are coming out. You got to examine them. So you cannot say after you wake up from that dream, "Bless God, I have the confirmation." So when your feelings come into play it is not necessarily that the Lord has sent you that dream.

God never send a warning like this type in order for it to come to pass. And some of you businessmen you are so rational. You have been hearing from God in dreams but you are not paying attention to it. God warns you in your dreams some times in your business. He warns you. He gives you direction. He tells you of situations not to enter. In your dream you could be dreaming about certain partnership that you are praying about. And here in your dream you saw some thing happening that you never saw in your conscious state. You wake up and ask, "Is it going to come to pass? Is this going to happen?" No, it should not happen. It's a warning to prevent you from allowing that event to happen. It must always be positive. The interpretation must always be positive. It must not bring fear, grief into people's life.

So, here is Joseph interpreting the dream and did you know his interpretation stops in verse 32. Verse 33 onwards is not an interpretation. The interpretation has finished there is nothing more to interpret. But verse 33 is the application, the wisdom and that is the third key. In order to apply dreams in our lives you will need No. 3 the wisdom of God for two areas, the wisdom of God to interpret and the wisdom of God to apply. The third key is the wisdom of God for interpretation and application. Now Joseph was not applying the dream. It has nothing to do with Pharaoh's dream. This is from Joseph's spirit. He says, "Pharaoh this is going to happen. Choose a man who is wise. And gather all the abundant of grain in the first seven years, so that the next seven years we will excess and extra." That is wisdom. It is not the gift of the word of wisdom. That is a revelation of the future. But it's a gift a spiritual wisdom an application. It's the same kind of wisdom that Solomon asked. It's the same type of wisdom that James tells us to ask. If any lack wisdom let him ask from God. So the third key to interpret dreams is wisdom.

You Must Understand The Timing For Interpretation Of Dreams.

Rule 5 is to understand the timing for interpretation of dreams. Some dreams may be shut up until its time to be opened. So what we have to do is record them down. And the Holy Spirit will bring it to mind even though you may consciously forget it. The Holy Spirit will remind you when its time to open it up. A similar type of situation can be seen in Daniel's life. Daniel had a lot of vision some of them in the night dreams. And he did not understand them because the time was not ripe to unfold them to him. But through his prayers he was able to understand some. Towards the end of the book of Daniel the angel told him, "Go thy way. These things are shut up for the end of time." So the full understanding did not come to Daniel. But sometimes the fourth key is to remember if the Holy Spirit did not give an interpretation don't try to put your own. Don't try to get into human rationalizing or human intellectualism. If you sense that there is nothing in the Spirit write it down. If you are a growing Christian you should have kept three books. One book to record dreams and visions and prophecies. One book to record your bible studies, notes that you have from your bible study so that you continue to grow. The third book to record your prayer items. Note down all those things you are believing God for. So that when they are answered you can note when they are answered. So we need to record them down for the time that the Holy Spirit determines for the interpretation to come forth.

FOUR METHODS OR DIVINE STRATEGIES OF DREAM INTERPRETATION (ACTS 2:16-21)

"And it shall come to pass in the last days, says God, I will pour out My Spirit on all flesh; your sons and your daughters shall prophesy, your young men shall see visions,

your old men shall dream dreams. And on My menservants and on My maidservants I will pour out My spirit in those days; and they shall prophesy." (Acts 2:17-18).

There are various methods or techniques that can be used to interpret dreams and secure their meanings. Remember that in the context of our opening scripture above, these levels are an illustration of spiritual maturity - neither the age of a person nor the length of time saved or born again. Using the familiar verses of Acts 2, in the art of hearing God, one can apply the following four methods of interpretation.

Literal Interpretation:

This connotes to the act of taking the dream as it is and interpreting it in a literal sense. This is typical in scenarios where there aren't much symbols or codes in the dream. It's not every dream that will have parabolic symbolise; some of the dreams might be so clear-cut and straight forward in terms of the meaning of the message such that they do not require any symbolic interpretation. When Joseph dreamt an angel telling him to take the child to Egypt because Herod wanted to kill him, that dream required a literal application: to simply take the child and run away. However, even though the literal interpretation of scripture is important, it should not be applied exclusively.

Allegorical Interpretation:

This connotes to the act of revealing the meanings behind the codes or hidden symbols that are appearing in the dream. For example in Acts 2:16 when the Bible says your sons and daughters shall prophecy and young men shall see visions and old men shall dream dreams, the use of the words, young men and old men does not connote to physical age but spiritual maturity. The same applies to the symbols in the Baker and Butler's dreams which required allegorical interpretation rather than a literal one.

Philosophical Interpretation:

A philosophy is an idea to execute a particular concept. Hence, philosophical application connotes to the act of interpreting dreams based on set principles known rules as depicted in the Word of God. It is highly advisable that every dream should be interpreted in line with the word of God. The word of God has all the answers you need to interpret even the most complicated of all dreams. However, it is important that you draft your own personal dream vocabulary, since the dream objects or symbols may not mean the same to you as it would to another person.

Enigmatic Interpretation:

This involves interpreting dream symbols that are divinely coded and whose meaning is hidden. This is a typical scenario in parabolic dreams which demands a maturity continuum for the spiritually mature (understanding dreams). In some cases, the meaning of the dream may be so hidden or enigmatic that it takes only the Holy Spirit to reveal the meaning of the dream. That is why a complete dependence on the Holy Spirit for all dream interpretations is mandatory. For example, the Book of Revelation uses hidden codes and imagery to represent different things, making it difficult to someone who is reading while in the flesh, to understand.

PRINCIPLES OF INTERPRETING DREAMS

There are some principles that are involved in dreams that are very vital that we need to see and understand from the Word of God. This is why we need to see some principles of interpretation of dream. To a certain extent all of us dream dreams. Throughout your life you do have dreams. What do they mean? What are they saying? We have to understand what they say so that we could determine the message of God.

You Must Check The Background Of The Dream And Understand The Circumstances That Took Place Before The Dream

Frequency Revelator

For God speaks in one way, and in two, though man does not perceive it. In a dream, in a vision of the night, when deep sleep falls upon men, while they slumber on their beds, then he opens the ears of men, and terrifies them with warnings, that He may turn man aside from his deed, and cut off pride from man; He keeps back his soul from the Pit, his life from perishing by the sword. (John 33:14).

Before you interpret a dream you must understand the circumstances that took place before the dream. In other words, if you are writing a dream for me to interpret for you, if possible write down what is occurring in your life at that time. In other words, write down what was going on in your life about that time. It will give us an accuracy of interpretation to 100 percent. But if you don't highlight the circumstances that took place before the dream, the accuracy may be reduced to 80 percent. So, to interpret a dream the best person is yourself except where it shows a blind spot. In order to accurately interpret a dream, we need to note down what took place in your life prior to the unfolding of the dream. Let's look at the book of Daniel. *To you, O king, as you lay in bed came thoughts of what would be hereafter and He who reveals mysteries made known to you what is to be* (Daniel 2:29). In Nebuchadnezzar's life that night before he had that dream, he was thinking about what is going to come in the next kingdom. What will take place after he died and his kingdom passes away. And he slept with that thought in his mind. That was important for the dream reveals his thought. So, the background for the dream could be things that took place a week or it could be things that dominate your life.

First Dream:

For example, there is a certain lady who had a dream that needed interpretation. This lady had a tremendous pressure in her family life. Her husband was not fully in the Lord although he was supposed to be in the Lord and she had a very unhappy family life. She had been in a sense abused physically. This was the dream that she had. She dreamt that she was in this hospital. And it seemed that there were musicians who were sick. The doctor was running around trying to minister to these musicians. She was one of the nurses. And in the dream there was this one doctor who was gently firm and kind, whom she liked very much in the dream. She remembers in that dream the kindness. And then as she was arranging these beds, this doctor comes and tells her to hurry up. And for the first time she feels a bit hurt. Because she felt that she wanted to make it very clean and make sure there were no germs. Then suddenly the scene changed. Although in the first part of the dream she had sort of she really loved the doctor, then the dream changed and she was now on the phone. And she was talking to this doctor. This doctor was about to fly somewhere on an airplane. But somehow in that dream she knew that the plane was going to crash because there was something wrong with the engine. So, over the phone she was saying to the doctor, "I love you. Do you love Jesus too?" The doctor says, "Yes I do. I know Jesus as you do know Jesus." Just as she was saying that the plane crashed and the doctor died. Then subsequently she woke up.

Dream Interpretation:

If you are not careful and knowledgeable in dream interpretation, after this type of dream, you will be running around panicking, thinking that someone who is a doctor is going to die, yet the dream symbols are not to be interpreted literally but figuratively. But imbued with an understanding of her background, this was what the Lord was saying through that dream. Her relationship with the husband was such that the music in her life had died. And the husband was killing that music in her life and taking the joy and the music out of her life. That doctor represents a part of her life, the firm but gentle part that was dying. And somehow in her circumstances she was allowing that part of her to die. The part of her that was creative, that was firm but gentle. And the dream was warning her that if she allows that part of her to die, in the end, it would destroy her marriage. That was an important dream and throughout the dream, she was afraid that her husband would find out about the doctor. Actually the dream was revealing that the firm gentle nature in that doctor was a part of her. We may not realize it but our emotions and our will, our intellect, our soul and our spirit have many intricate parts.

Can you imagine that in your physical body, you have the heart, liver and all the intricate organs within us? And they all must function in balance. If there is something wrong in your heart, it will affect all the other organs. All our physical organs must function in balance for optimum physical health. Do not think that your spirit and soul have only one part? There are a lot of attributes of our soul and spirit. We have to balance for example between authority and gentleness. We have to balance so many of these forces. We have to balance between being tender hearted and easy to cry and weep and the ability not to be emotional. Can you see the balance there? Everything within us must be held in balance. So, sometimes in a dream they are in subjective areas as they are revealing imbalances in your soul, and personality.

Second Dream:

There is another man who had a dream. In this dream, he saw this policeman. This policeman illegally entered the house with a gun. In the dream, he saw it and phoned the police station. And in that dream, another person came, a policewoman. Then the dream was such that the policeman and the policewoman were facing each other with the gun. Suddenly, the scene changed. He was now in the house and he was facing his mother. His mother was holding a gun; and him too was also holding a gun and he shot his mother, then he woke up. What was the interpretation? A few days before this dream, he had a quarrel with his son. His son was being educated in the university and came back with all kind of doubts and all kind of questions on the Christian faith. He scolded his son and the son in a temper walked out on him. Then he had that dream. You see, the background is important. He did not understand the interpretation for sometime until slowly it dawned on him.

Dream Interpretation:

You notice in that dream that there were two authoritative figures, the policeman and the policewoman. They symbolize the authority that has been built into him. His background was that a very strict father and a very gentle mother had brought him up. In his life, the dream was revealing that gentle part of him. You see, his mother in the dream, it was not that he killed his mother, but it was revealing that motherly part of him that was influencing his soul was dying. And somehow the dream revealed that this harmony between his authoritative part and his gentle part was being threatened. The conflict in his own soul was resulting in the conflict with his own son. If he had been in harmony with his own being where he knows how to be firm but gentle, he may never had that quarrel with his son. The dream was trying to show that the problem he was having externally in his family was the result of his own inner conflict. It is his own soul that was in disharmony.

In view of above, it is evident that dreams are important, as they are warnings, they tell us things that are not right in our life. Just as if your physical body is sick; you may have fever, you may have all kind of symptoms, running nose and so forth. your body gives you symptoms. Your soul gives you symptoms in your dream. Your dreams reveal problems in your soul; disharmony in your soul. And if we pay attention to what God is saying through our dreams, warning us of extremes in our life, we will have wholeness. In our interpretation of dreams, we have to look at the background. What was the background of your dreams? What did you go through during that time? What were the things facing you? These are important for an accurate interpretation of dreams.

Third Dream:

Let's analyse another dream which a certain man had. It says: I dreamt of a place where there was a party. In this party a vampire was on the loose. After a few victims, I knew who he was. The dream was strange because there was a swimming pool at the party. I was swimming with a girl who could be a future victim. After the swim, I told some people that I knew who the vampire was and that we needed a plan to trap him. Then the scene changed. The vampire was now at the side of the pool sitting down. And I told a pastor who was there by eye contact that he was the one. Then the scene changed again and a new dream related to my work. I was now making phone calls mostly from public booths to my clients while my friends waited for me in my car parked at the side of the road.

Frequency Revelator

Dream Interpretation:

Notice that there are three scenes in that dream. The key to the interpretation is the last scene. They are all one dream. The Lord through that dream was trying to tell this brother about his job. It is important to have certain details in your dream because those details are the key to the interpretation. You notice in Daniel's interpretation of Nebuchadnezzar's second dream that the tree and some of the descriptions of the tree apply directly to Nebuchadnezzar. Of course, the tree is Nebuchadnezzar. Those details help you to link them together. So, the third scene tells us that these three dreams are the same. Just like Pharaoh's dream interpreted by Joseph. They were two separate dreams; two different scenes yet they have the same message. The second dream is a clearer direct application. Because he sees the sheaves of corn which applies to famine.

So, in the contest of the above-narrated dream, the third scene is the key to the interpretation. All three scenes refer to the work. In the first part of the dream, the swimming pool and the party represent a public place. The vampire symbolizes evil that is there but hidden. But somehow in this dream that person recognized it. So, it has reference to that person's work, job, project or business. That somehow as he is right now in whatever job, this person recognizes that there is a person who will in the end destroy the whole business. It's the image coming out. The girl in this dream represents the new business and the new project that this person has launched into. You see, he was swimming with the girl. That was an important key to show that this picture of a girl is not a prophecy that he was going to find a wife but it is speaking about one of his businesses at the time he is involved with. He is now involved in that very business in which this vampire or something that he knows is going to destroy that whole business.

In the second scene it tells that this person has sought spiritual help either through counsel or in prayer. The pastor represents spiritual help. And through that spiritual help, he is able to detect and pinpoint exactly what is the thing that will destroy that business. Now in the third scene, notice that there is an emphasis on him using the public booth. There are a few details missing. He says there are people waiting in the car. I am not sure from this dream whether they were the driver and he was the passenger and they were waiting for him. Or he was the driver and left them in the back seat. Those details are missing here. What is apparent is that he was phoning and they were waiting. He was the driver of the car. Without that we attempt to give some understanding and interpretation. It is speaking about how he is launching into this other project. All these other friends of his we do not know whether they were business friends or people involved in his business. In other words, they will be directly involved with his business. But it seems that he is the one who has to move out. And the public phone represents a public place.

This dream is a warning as it gives a certain direction. Not all dreams have direction. Usually dreams have a warning. The direction would come from our spiritual walk with God. This dream is revealing that he is involved in a business at the moment and is in danger from certain areas. And the dream is warning him that there is danger. He has picked it up from his normal Christian life and his inward voice and his conscience. Notice in the dream that nothing is done. There is nothing done about the danger yet. So, the dream is revealing a danger in a realm of his business.

The third scene reveals what the other two scenes were trying to depict. It gives a clearer picture form but the direction is not so clear except that it shows him that he has to do something about that. What he has to do about that goes back to the Word. It could be a warning about your personal life where perhaps you are neglecting one area. We have to balance between spirit, soul and body. When you begin to neglect one area of your soul, or physical life, your dream will warn you. If you are sensitive to your mind, your conscience and your inward voice will warn. You could hear it in your conscious state. But if you ignore it as we usually do because when you are not sensitive to certain things, then it comes up in your dream. The secondary line of defence is activated through your dreams. So, that dream is a warning about the dangers in that person's business and project. And he has to take note of and deals with it before it happens.

So, that confirms the two points we have covered so far. Firstly, the dream is a warning. And secondly, check the background. The background is vitally important. If another person with a different background dreams that same dream, we may have a totally different interpretation. As we see here, Nebuchadnezzar was lying down thinking about the things of the future. Then he had a dream. So, that helps us to streamline the interpretation to one area about those things that were disturbing him and troubling his thoughts. And that dream carries a revelation in those areas. The background could be something that troubled your life for years but its still there. In that case you may have recurring dreams in the same area. So remember recurring dreams can tell you about certain things have been really deep rooted in your life that you have to deal with it. If you don't deal with it, it is going to endanger your life. Before it takes place your dreams are warning you.

The Second Area Is Not To Neglect The Details Of Dreams.

If you have dreams about car and you are inside, it is important to find out whether you are in front or at the back. Details like for example the clothes you wear. Like in the dream that I talked to you about the woman and the doctor who crashed in an airplane. In that dream she remembered she was in her normal clothes not in her work clothes. That was important because the dream was trying to reveal a defect in her life not in her working life but in her normal daily life. Even children's dream are very important; like one child dreamt of how he was on a railway track and he was lying on the railway track and the train was coming. That dream is telling us that kind of strict rigid training that child was having. The train was coming and the child was on the track. It tells that in the upbringing of the child there is no wholeness. Somehow the parents were too strict. And that strictness and rigid military discipline in the home was destroying that child's wholeness. And if nothing is done that child's soul will be damaged and the child will have problems in his later life. See we influence the personality of children. And when children have those dreams its important to understand the interpretation because it may reveal things that we are putting wrongly into their life. When that boy had that dream it is telling us something about the family. Something needs to be done. We need to talk to the parents and say your bringing up of the child is too strict. The child needs to learn gentleness for his soul to be formed properly. So dreams are important. Details are important what they represent.

Understanding Prophetic Dreams & Visions

In the book of Daniel chapter 4 notice that while Nebuchadnezzar had that dream, suddenly the tree becomes him and he cried aloud and said thus,

"Hew down the tree and cut off its branches, strip off its leaves and scatter its fruit; let the beasts flee from under it and the birds from its branches. But leave the stump of its roots in the earth, bound with a band of iron and bronze, amid the tender grass of the field. Let him be wet with the dew of heaven; let his lot be with the beasts in the grass of the earth.

Notice the sudden change: the tree becomes him. Details like these we must not miss. Then there are other details. Like verse 17 *The sentence is by the decree of the watchers, the decision by the word of the holy ones, to the end that the living may know that the Most High rules the kingdom of men, and gives it to whom He will, and sets over it the lowliest of men.* Now, the final part becomes important in the interpretation because it talks about a king. A ruler and Nebuchadnezzar was the one who had the dream logically it points straight to him. The moment Daniel heard it he knew the interpretation. It was quite a simple interpretation for this. Such is the skill that we could train ourselves in interpretation. When we hear a dream we could sense what it is talking about and the warning it carries. Now that dream was not supposed to take place. That dream was just a warning saying Nebuchadnezzar if you don't change your direction that's how you will end up. It was not supposed to take place at all. As a result for one year he changed a little bit. He walked humbly. But he forgot after a year. His old self came back and he fell. He got into this judgment. Nebuchadnezzar was not one who knew what to do. And that is the fourth part where the dream alone doesn't give you enough direction. Daniel with his spiritual experience, his spiritual principles, was able to tell Nebuchadnezzar what to do. In verse 27 now verse 27 is not from the dream. Verse 27 is the advice and verse 27 came directly from Daniel's life.

Therefore, O king, let my counsel be acceptable to you; break off your sins by practicing righteousness, and your iniquities by showing mercy to the oppressed, that there may perhaps be a lengthening of our tranquility.

He was saying unless you break off those things yourself you yourself would be broken. Daniel counselled the king, "O king break off those sins, remove those sins in your life." Then he advised him the wisdom that only the bible can gives, "Be righteous, be merciful, and these things won't happen." Dream is a warning but the direction we still need to get from the Word of the living God and our walk with God. The first time Nebuchadnezzar also didn't pay much heed to his first dream. In Daniel chapter 2 in his first dream after Daniel interpreted the dream which represent all the different Empires that will follow after Nebuchadnezzar. Nebuchadnezzar did not apply that dream for himself. Because that dream was so frightening he must have woken up and forgotten it. He saw this huge big statue. In the dream it zoomed on the head and he saw that it was made of gold; slowly the focus came down to silver and then bronze and then iron and clay. Then just as he was looking at the feet he saw this huge stone coming and knocking the statue's feet and in the dream the stone expand and coming nearer and nearer to Nebuchadnezzar he got up.

Now that stone represents the kingdom of God, the reign and rule of the Lord Jesus Christ to come. And it did not humble Nebuchadnezzar. In fact immediately after that in chapter 3 because of that dream he built that golden statue of himself. That dream didn't help him at all. In fact he made use of that dream in a wrong way. He built that big huge golden statue and asked everybody to bow down before it. These are called blind spots. Had he took that dream correctly that dream would have humbled him. He would have known that his kingdom was nothing compared to the kingdom of God. But he took that dream the wrong way. Just like many people when they go to a place or when they meet people they always seek to hear what they want not what they actually need that will change their life. Sometimes people go to other people for advice. They are not really going to seek advice. They only want to hear what the person says that they can agree with, they can confirm what they want to do themselves. Not really what God wants of them.

The greatest danger that we have is blind spots. Things we do not see. Which is why dreams are sometimes useful. If we come with an open heart to God and say, "God teach me, mould me as you will," God will teach. We have to be pliable to God so that God could mould our lives. Nebuchadnezzar never had that. He had to have the second dream and he had to have a terrible experience before he learned. He took that dream and said, "Good I am the head of gold." He forgot the ending of that dream. He only took the first part. Head of gold that means his Empire is the best. All these others are silver, bronze, iron, clay lesser than him. He must have felt proud. That dream he took it wrongly to built his ego bigger. His ego expanded until he built that huge statue. He never changed. He only came to acknowledge the Lord after the judgment in his second dream.

So dreams alone do not constitute direction. Direction comes from the Word of God. There is no short cut. You cannot say dreams are so powerful I will spend my whole life dreaming and getting all my directions from dreams. Dreams do not direct so much; they only warn what may happen. That is why a dream projects to you what your road leads you. In other word you could be walking in this direction and you cannot see that path there. In your dream it shows you what will happen at the end of the road. Whether it's a dead end street or it's a street that leads anywhere else while you are still here in your daily life. If you turn the wrong way it shows you that way so you could turn back. To turn as the book of Job 33 tells us, to turn us into the path of God. To humble us, to remove pride from us so that we realize we need to walk humbly with God daily. To turn us from the Pit. To turn us from the destruction by the sword. That is what dreams are for.

Check If There Is Any Incidence Of Repetition In The Dream

But when they had eaten them no one would have known that they had eaten them, for they were still as gaunt as at the beginning. Then I woke up, I also saw in my dream seven ears growing on one stalk, full and good; and seven ears, withered, thin, and blighted by the east wind, sprouted after them (Genesis 41:21).

Now Pharaoh had actually two dreams. The fifth area as we look at interpretation why the second point, the background, is important. This is because dreams tend to have a continual story. We can actually have repeated dreams but repeated in a different way. So, as you notice in Pharaoh's dream there was a *repetition*. So, we note here the sequence of dreams. Repetition of dreams means seriousness. Something deeply rooted you better deal with it. If you have series of dreams that repeat themselves please note it down. It's important very important. You must take note of that otherwise it won't repeat so many times. Then dreams can have progression. There is a progression in the author's life from the baby to the girl. So that is why you need to keep a dream book because our dreams progress with us. And some of your dreams are continuation of stories that were in the past. So if you once in a while record your dreams you may not get the full picture of your life from the spirit realm.

As I mentioned this author dreamt about his old school mate. That was just one isolated incident. It was trying to show him this is how you look to others. So, in that dream he saw his old school mate was very dogmatic which he never saw himself to be that. He thought he was gentle, kind, understanding and one who hears others. That is how he sees himself. That dream was telling him, "This is how you look." He was seeing a mirror of himself. If not for that dream he will not take note that he is getting too dogmatic. Now because of that dream, he tells himself, "Better deal with this area in my life because that is how others are looking at me now." So that is a different type of dream an isolated kind of dream that reveals your circumstances as it is. But there are other dreams that are progressive, sequence of dreams. So, in the fifth point we see that repetition and progression of dreams needs to be taken note of. The moment you have become aware and sensitive to these areas of dreams then you will have a richer life. Areas that your conscious mind neglect that your sub-conscious mind brings to you. Your life becomes whole and more balanced. You sense an inner peace all the time.

In the dream there was a lot of chaos. Three men came to burn the place where I was. They managed to burn the place and things around. Then the men took a piece of burning wood and tried to hurt me, which he succeeded. When he succeeded he placed the burning wood on my shoulder. But there was no pain. The wood became soft and gave a feeling of softness.

Some details are missing here. What kind of the clothes was that person wearing? In this dream if the person is in clothes where you normally wear in your daily life, it tells you whether your dream is revealing about your personal life or your work in your office. There are three people; notice the number three and there was chaos. Some of this is in the past. Although I do not have the background what the person was going through before this dream, I could discern from this dream that something has occurred. Because that person didn't mention what kind of dress, then it is either in the home life, work life or personal life. There are some circumstances that have taken place that have been completely destroyed. But here the wood touching the person's shoulder is important. A shoulder is where a person carries responsibility. So it is speaking about a person's responsibility. Whether this is a family obligation or work obligation, it is something that the person has a duty in. So it is in reference to obligations and duties that the person has. The dream here is a slight warning. There are some obligations and duties that the person is avoiding because of the confusion that prevail in that situation. So the dream is trying to say don't run from that chaos. Perhaps in the conscious state the person wants to run from the chaos. She is thinking of running from that duty and obligation. But the dream is trying to say, "Don't run and don't be afraid of facing that chaos. You have a duty to perform." Because the end of the dream says, "If you take it, it will be pleasant to you."

Gathering from this dream that the person wants to run to flee from that chaos. The natural instinct when you look at chaos and fire and people burning your place is to flee and run. If you face those things in your dream they change. Those who are growing up sometimes there is a biological effect and there is a soul effect. Sometimes when you sleep you have a falling sensation. Now if it's a falling sensation without a dream then it is biologically caused. Your blood pressure drops so the sensation of falling is interpreted. But if in your dream you fall in some way, it is revealing that your foundations are collapsing. Those who are growing up into adulthood tends to have a lot of that because it is telling them that the physiological framework of their life Is weak. In other words they don't have a foundation in their life. All of us have life principles. Principles of how we behave. What happens when a person going into adult life is those life principles sometimes are not formed yet. So they are going through life without any life principle; they feel very aimless. And usually you will have dreams of falling. Your dream is telling you, you don't have a foundation.

Frequency Revelator

How To Receive The Gift Of Interpretation

It is important that we learn the art of how to receive the gift of interpretation. This is one of the most critical gifts needed in the Body of Christ right now. In the book of Daniel chapter one. There are two things that are similar between Joseph and Daniel. Daniel was a man of dreams and also visions. Joseph was a man of dreams. You notice Joseph in the book of Genesis and Daniel in the book of Daniel both were similar characters. Both were faithful to the Lord when they were young. Both sought to do the right ways of the Lord. So you will find these three keys to receive the gift of interpretation in both their lives. Sometimes these keys were developed in the silent years in Joseph's life but its clear cut in Daniel's life. I believe it also was in Joseph's life. So here in Daniel chapter one verse 17 *As for these four youths, God gave them learning and skill in all letters and wisdom and dreams.* Look at it there is such a special gift. And notice something about Joseph somewhere between the time he was in Potiphar's house to the time that he was in prison he received the gift of interpretation. He interpreted the butler's and the baker's dream. And he interpreted Pharaoh's dream. Somewhere along the line Joseph received the gift of interpretation of dreams. And it is available for every one of you here.

If you develop the first four keys you have already moved in that direction to understand and interpret dreams. Here we see in Daniel's life, he was given a special gift. Daniel when he was brought to Babylon together with all his other three friends. They were with many other young men. If you were chosen as the cream of the flock to be brought to the king's table, a lot of people will start breaking their principles and compromising their principles. But not these four young men. They kept strictly to the Jewish covenant. While the other young men said look at the food, the promotion, the learning and they gave up whatever Jewish covenant they have and they join the Gentiles. But these four men said no. We don't want to partake all these idols worship. We want to partake of the things of the Lord. The same applies to Joseph. Potiphar's wife came told him to sin. He said, "No, the master has given me everything except you. And I cannot sin against God." Even though he was alone he knew God was with him. If you are conscious of God you find it very hard to sin. If you are not conscious of God it's easy to sin. People sin because they are not conscious of God. Develop the consciousness of God and you find it hard to sin.

Faithfulness

Joseph made a choice to choose the path or righteousness. Daniel also made that same choice. What did you see in common about them? Faithfulness. So the first requirement for one to move in the realm of interpreting dreams and visions is faithfulness to the Lord, to His Word, faithfulness to His covenant, faithfulness to keep yourself for Him. Many people don't realize that the Lord has more to give you than the devil. If any one of you dedicate yourself to the Lord let me express the help of our Father. I have never known our Father not to give you a gift. I have never known our Father not to reward faithfulness. One of the things that Gordon Lindsey mentioned was that he realize that in the ministry he spent so much time with the Lord that sometimes his family pay a heavy price because their father and husband is a man of God. But then as he looked back, he found that God gave special grace to his family for the sacrifice that was made. God gave different types of gifts to them. See God never robs you. He is a Father. When you dedicate yourself to Him first you will have the opportunity to choose. During the time of choosing you may not see God's reward. James chapter one says when you endure temptation you are rewarded. When you choose no I don't want these things of the devil. No I don't want the things of the world. I want the will of God. It looks like you are giving up everything. But later you find that you found everything. God begins to start giving you things. God begins to bless you financially. It is God Himself who say I will add this to you (Matthew 6:33).

Acquire The Gift Of Interpretation

Daniel and Joseph had a remarkable ability to interpret dreams. Do you know that it was that gift that promoted Joseph to Prime Minster? If Joseph did not interpret dreams he could be a good man. He could be a hard worker. He would never made it to be Prime Minister. He made it to be Prime Minister because he interpreted dreams. The gift of God was on his life. When God gives you a gift that gift promotes you. The gift of God promotes you. Promotion comes not from the East or from the West it comes out from God. It was the gift of God that Joseph developed that promoted him. Do you realize in Daniel's life it's the gift of interpretation that promoted him to the level of Governor and the most influential man in the land of Babylon? Doesn't that weigh more than money? Worth more than anything in the world can buy. So one of the first keys to receive the gift of interpretation is faithfulness.

Prayer

The second key after that an incident occurred in which Nebuchadnezzar in Daniel chapter 2 gave a command for all the wise people to be slaughtered because they could not interpret a dream. And when they wanted to interpret his dream he said, "I forgot the dream. You all have to tell me the dream and then tell me the interpretation." And they could not. He said, "Off with their heads." So the word got to Daniel. Daniel asked why this urgency to kill everybody. And when he heard what it was in Daniel chapter verse 16 *And Daniel went in and besought the king to appoint him a time, that he might show the king the interpretation.* Do you notice Daniel in chapter one he already had the interpretation but it was not fully operating yet. He was not in the same position like Joseph. In Joseph's time the king gave the dream and he gave the interpretation. Here Daniel had to give the dream and the interpretation. That is harder still. But Daniel said give us time. In verse 18 ;

And told them to seek mercy of the God of heaven concerning this mystery, so that Daniel and his companions might not perish with the rest of the wise men of Babylon. Then the mystery was revealed to Daniel in a vision of the night. Then Daniel blessed the God of heaven.

This is important: how did Daniel get it? Through Prayer. Daniel told his friends in verse 17 he says pray together. It is in time of prayer that the gift comes. So the second key is to live a life of prayer. Some of you don't realize what has happened to your life when the gift of the Spirit has been dropped into your spirit in seed form when you went to the overnight prayer. But I could pick it up with my spirit. And some of those seeds start growing you can point it out through prayer. In the time of prayer with the Lord the seeds of God's gift drop into your life. So it is important to spend time with God because it is in those times that God drops things into our spirits.

Fasting

The third key to receive wisdom, understanding and interpretation of dreams. Daniel chapter 10 Notice something here in verse 3 it says Daniel was fasting and in verse 11 it tells us the reason why he fasted but the answer came;

> *O Daniel, man greatly beloved, give heed to the words that I speak to you, and stand upright, for now I have been sent to you." While he was speaking this word to me, I stood up trembling. Then he said to me, Fear not, Daniel, for from the first day that you set your mind to understand.*

Do you know why one of the reasons for his 21 days fast, is to seek revelation, is to seek understanding. So fasting brings revelations. It puts you in a position to receive revelations. And you could put one of the objectives of the fast to receive revelations to understand something. It may not come during your fast. But the answer may come sometime after your fast. But the answer is traced to your fasting. During the time that you fast, revelation may not come but at least you have the satisfaction to know that you fasted over it and you committed it to the Lord and God in His timing will bring it back to you.

CHAPTER SEVEN

DREAM INTERPRETATION PRACTICALS

THE INTERPRETIVE PROCESS OF DREAM INTERPRETATION

In the context of dream interpretation, it is important to note that any dream that is not understood remains a mere occurrence. However, when understood, a dream can become a life-changing experience, touching the destinies of the masses across the globe. When interpreting a dream, it is highly advisable that you reduce it to its simplest form. This involves developing an understanding that symbols do not always mean the same thing as they vary from dream to dream. It is important that you ask yourself the following questions: "Where am I in this dream?" Determining this will tell you who the dream is about. It is also important that you determine your role or position in the dream whether you are an observe, participant or main centre of focus:

The Observer:

As an observer, you merely observe the action but do not take part in the events or activities of the dream. The observer is external to the dream as a spectator watching the proceedings of the dream from a distant. As an observer, its like a move is played right in front of you, of which you are not a part. However, if you are an observer, it is important that you analyse the key things you are observing in the dream.

Understanding Prophetic Dreams & Visions

The Participant:

As a participant, you appear to be actively taking part in the proceedings of the dream, but not the centre of attention. The participant in some cases find himself playing the role of a main character in the dream whereby everything revolves around you. If you are a participant, then find out how is your emotions, behaviour, and attitude towards the people and scenes you encounter in the dream. This is because these emotions or behaviors are key in terms of securing the interpretation of the dream.

The Main Focus:

As the main focus in the dream, everything revolves around you. You are the principal actor and centre of attention. Occasionally, you can shift positions in the dream, for example from observer to participant. To determine if you are the main focus of the dream, ask yourself this question, "Who is this dream about? Who, or what, is the center of attention? In addition, it is also important that you establish the Sub-Focus of the dream. Sub-focuses are the elements in a dream that are necessary to find the theme or plot and make it have meaning. They are important to rounding out or completing the story.

Imbued with this understanding, let's now consider some of the dreams below as well as their practical interpretations:

DREAM 1

I was at a well near my house. The well has a rope. The rope looks like an ordinary rope and was not too thin or too thick. There was plenty of water in the well. But the water level was about 13 to15 feet from the mouth of the well. It looks like a very deep well that will never run dry. In this dream I had already drawn out a big bucket of water. The bucket, which was red in color, had water to its brim and it was besides me. Yet I was not satisfied. I let down another big bucket and was filling it up to the brim again. Strange in the natural I know I could have easily taken half a bucket at a time. However in this dream I seem to be greedy and quite unreasonable. I could see myself causing the bucket to fill up and overflow with water. So of course I had real problem getting the bucket up. It seems to be a struggle. Each time I managed to bring the bucket of water up to the mouth of the well. My greatest struggle was getting a hold of the bucket and holding the rope at the same time. I had used all my strength and energy in pulling up the bucket of water but was unable to reach out to the bucket without falling into the well. I have tried so many times with one hand holding the rope and the other hand holding the bucket. Then in the dream there was someone near the bathroom nearby. And I heard the voice of the person inside. It sounded like my mother. So I called out to her to come and help me to pull the bucket of water out. But she was not able to. I cannot remember what she said. Then I tried to call to someone else for help. But it looks like there was no one around. I knew I could easily pull the bucket by causing it to be half filled. But strangely I was not satisfied or reasonable. I wanted to fill it up right to overflowing. I saw myself giving it another try. Looks like I wanted as much water as I could from the well. I found myself in the sea-saw position desperately trying to reach the pail of water. I looked frustrated desperately clinging to the rope and no one to help me to hold to the pail and then suddenly I woke up.

Dream Interpretation:

This dream is speaking about the person's ministry. You notice the depth of the well was about 13 to15 feet. That was roughly the time that person has come to know the Lord. At the age of 13 to 15 years she really knew the Lord and sensed the Lord's call to the ministry. There was a pail of water that has already been drawn up. That represent the person has already moved into the ministry. Secondly the person is drawing another aspect of ministry. See there are different phases of ministry. So the struggle that this person is having is with another phase of ministry that is coming up. But that phase can only be done half of it. The person wants all of it. So there is a spiritual struggle. This happened after the person moved into the measure of the second phase of ministry. So just after the person did that there was this dream. So this dream is in reference to the second phase of the person's ministry that she is struggling with. The mother represents some abilities within her. But all the natural abilities could not cope up with this new thing that is happening. And in this dream the person is being told to slow down. Don't do so many things; don't take so many things, slow down. Go slower and let it grow out of the person. If you are called to the ministry or you are called into the secular realm to function as some sort of a ministry, know that a ministry must grow out rather than forced out. And there is a time and pattern for it to flow out in our lives. You cannot hasten it because it would be like harvesting green apples. You have to let it ripe of its own accord. So here is a dream that is tell the person to slow down. What happen if that person doesn't slow down? The person will begin to feel naturally frustrated and have all kind of problems that would occur.

DREAM 2

We are in the palace ground as a family in a van. There is a road leading to the palace. As we drew nearer to the palace about five huge dogs surrounded the van. Nothing happened to any of us as we were still in the van.

Dream Interpretation:

A van or a car always talks about the direction of your life. If you ever have a dream about car, van and you are inside it is talking about the direction of your life and the road of life that you are heading. If there are people in the car like your family, then it depends on who were in the car. Earlier, we interpreted a dream of a car and the clients were in the back. So that car represents his work life not his home life or his personal life. Now here is the whole family so it represents the family life. If you are alone then it is about your personal life.

Now those dogs represent opposition. The palace ground represents something spiritual. It's the spiritual walk in the family. And the whole family is going on into a higher realm of the kingly ministry, a higher realm of the kingly and priestly ministry. In other words, the palace represents the realm of the kingdom of God and all the promises of Jesus Christ. They are moving into a higher dimension that exercises the kingdom and authority of God. But there are opposition represented by these five dogs. The whole family wants to move into the higher dimension. But there are oppositions represented by the dogs. Dogs in the bible represent religious folks who oppose the things of the spirit. Remember Paul call the Judaizers dogs. He says, "Beware of dogs," he is referring to the Jewish folks who have come to know the Lord but still follows Jewish ways. But most of them don't know the Lord and just wanting to follow Jewish customs. But apparently some of them must have absorbed some Christian values. They are not plain Jews. They call themselves Christians but they want all Christians to follow the Jewish customs. That is why Paul calls them Judaizers. They came to trouble the Christians and said you all must be circumcised too. So these five dogs represent to a certain extend five people or five different situations where they are religious people. They may be Christians who are moving in the flesh and not moving in the Spirit. As they move in the flesh, they are hindering this family from moving on into the spiritual level. The dream is saying forget about them. Don't be affected by the words they say or by the things they do.

DREAM 3

An armored truck with two heavily armed American soldiers. The back of the truck was all covered with canvas. Through a small hole in the canvas came the head of a huge snake. And the snake was yawning. Soon it withdrew itself into the canvas.

Dream Interpretation:

Now it depends what America and American soldiers symbolize to this person. But a dream about war zone or soldiers speaks about struggles. As far as I see and interpret this dream the fact that the truck was covered with canvas and the fact that the soldiers are American symbolizes foreigners coming in. Here I would say that it would refer to a situation in their life which has to do with their family members or the whole family having some event to do with a foreign country; like perhaps sending their children over there for education. Or some sort of relationship they have with a foreign country that has not taken place yet. Here it is covered with canvas. Could be anything but a matter that relates to a foreign country. Not necessary America but that is a symbol of a foreign country.

The snake represented spiritual opposition. Whether it could be anything that they need a breakthrough either in communication or some realm that relates to a foreign country. And there was a barrier. Now the canvas shows that it was not fully timed yet but there was also a barrier. It means that they need to have some authority taken over demon power. This dream is revealing the difficulty they are experiencing in process whatever it is that has to do with a foreign country. It is not natural but there are demonic powers that are involved. And they need to take spiritual authority. It is not just natural circumstances. It is revealing that hiding behind the natural circumstances are spiritual opposition.

DREAM 4

> *I got up in the middle of the night and found my husband sleeping without a pillow. I found the pillow on the floor and a huge black frog sitting on the pillow. I woke up my husband and in the meanwhile the sun was already there. The black frog tried to fly out and come to rest on my pillow. I took a piece of tissue and chased the frog away. The frog turned into a fly and flew out.*

Dream Interpretation:

This is a dream about waking up. This dream actually talks about the financial situation. Because I know the background so I know the interpretation. The husband was going through some financial need. Then the financial difficulty was going to affect also the wife. So in the dream it was showing that as they were taking authority and chasing all these demonic powers out of their life their financial difficulty is growing smaller and smaller. And it will go out of the window. That is the interpretation for that dream.

Frequency Revelator

DREAM 5

I dreamt of an adventure. The adventurer was about to go to a place across the sea. I asked the adventurer if I could follow. But he said no. Then when he went to buy some food, I tied my boat to his boat. When he came back he did not know that my boat was with his boat. So when he went I followed.

Then finally we reached an island. As he was coming to the shore I was on the beach with two friends. The island looks deserted. When I looked behind I saw a woodpecker. It looked normal but when it pecked on the tree the tree fell. At the same time while lying on the beach there was a dead fish ashore. And when my friend wanted to eat the fish I knew that it was poisonous. So I told him not to. At the same time the adventurer reached the shore and knocked the fish out of my friend's hand. The next thing that happened was the woodpecker came near me. I put my hand to touch its bill to see what kind of bill it has whether it was made of iron. The adventurer pulled my hand away and said it was dangerous. Then the dream changed and this time it was in a camp like a detention camp. While we were having our food in the hall the warden chased a few naughty boys away. When he chased them away he found a pair of slippers. This pair of slippers belonged to one of my friends. The warden was angry I told my friend not to worry because the warden was also my friend. When he came into the hall and asked whose slippers it was, I heard the name of my friend called out. When the name of my friend was called up I woke up.

Dream Interpretation:

From the beginning you know that adventurer was somebody in the person's life. Another interpretation is that adventurer is the person himself or possibly a spiritual aspect of a person. Now here the second part of the dream gives the first part the interpretation. The second part apparently refers to the person's fellowship and friendship in the realm of the gospel. Shoes and slippers as you know in the bible represent the gospel. So it is an aspect of spiritual life, soul winning, and testimony. So somehow in this dream the person seems to have some sort of a struggle in the testimony life. It may not be a revelation about the other friend. But this dream could represent the aspect of the other friend's life that may affect his testimony to him. It ties back to the adventurer. The adventurer is the spiritual life of this person. The woodpecker symbolizes something that was effective but dangerous that takes place and relates to something that happens in this person's testimony. It is effective but dangerous. It could be a spiritual truth or spiritual aspect that must be handled carefully. If its not handled carefully it would be harmful. If handled correctly it would be a blessing. It could be a spiritual truth that this person has come across. It could be a revelation, a truth, a principle, could have been prophecy that is dangerous and yet can be a blessing.

Now this dream also has a poison fish. You know fish is a good symbol in the bible. But here is a poisonous fish. So it talks about a spiritual principle that has been misapplied that this other friend of his had. So it talks about the person's relationship with his Christian friends. And some of his Christian friends are having spiritual truth but they don't see it and they are using it in the wrong way. This dream is sort of telling the person to watch out for the person is telling this principle but the principle is not fully correct. See it goes back to the slippers. Slippers represent the witness. The witness was not so strong because of the misapplication of spiritual truth.

DREAM 6

I dreamt that I was visiting my sister. She took me around the place where she stayed. We came to a squatter house. I said no you don't stay here. So she took me behind. We passed by broken doors. Behind was a house that was quite clean. It was a long house with many rooms. In front of every room was a tap. I was surprised and said why was this tap in front? And she did not answer me. I did not remember going into her room. When I came back my slippers were gone. And instead of the slipper I found two slippers that don't match. On the side of one shoe there was a scratch and it very dirty. The other shoe was different and it was dusty and dirty too. I had no choice but to wear those slippers. They were too big for me. I was dragging them as I walked. All of a sudden my nephew was waiting in the car. How he came I do not know. He asked us to get into the car. When I went into the car my brother was in front of the car. And he turned the seat completely around. I got a shock. And I turn to see my sister-in-law she also was about to sit together with us. But she got in before us. I woke up.

Dream Interpretation:

This dream is talking about the person's ministry. There are actually two dreams here. The two different types of slippers represent two ministries that people offered to the sister. And she had accepted that offer. And she has moved into the aspect of ministry that doesn't fit the person. And the person is struggling in those ministries. Its dusty and old represent that it is steeped in traditions. It could be a church work it could be a ministry work but the people involved who had opened the door for her are stiff in tradition. So the person is dragging in the ministry and found it difficult because the person is not flowing fully a hundred percent in the exact ministry God wanted that person to be in. The second part of the dream confirms it. Because the person was in the car and in the car she was not the driver. Here in this car there is the nephew and the brother. Now whatever they represent to her, if you have a dream of one of your relations who symbolize a strong religious tradition and those are the things that are directing her life right now. So this dream is sort of a warning. There are other people directing her life. There are other people telling her what to do. There are other people telling her this is what God wants you to do and they are opening the door and letting her go in. The dream is telling the person to wake up and find your own ministry. Get your own slipper. Get your own ministry. Find your own place in the ministry. Don't do what somebody tells you. Do what you know what the Lord tells you to.

DREAM 7

I was in a car, but I was in the back seat trying to steer. Someone I knew was in the front seat sitting behind the steering wheel. This person was demanding that I drive, but I had to reach around the person to do so. It was very difficult to steer. Then the car had a flat tire, and I was the one who had to change the flat. When I got out of the car to do so, I noticed all the other tires were very low. I wondered why the person siting on the front seat of the car had been so neglectful.

Dream Interpretation:

This dream is talking about a ministry that is not in full force operation. A car could either represent a ministry or a family, but in this case it speaks of a ministry that is dormant. God is showing this person that there is a ministry that he is supposed to be operating yet its under the influence of someone else who is dragging it into the ground. Trying to drive a car from the back seat symbolises the act of trying to spearhead a ministry from a position of a follower. A flat tire represents problems and in this case the ministry is experiencing problems because the person siting behind its steering wheel is not fit to be heading it.

PLOTING THE DREAM MIND MAP:

Write down the vision and make it plain on tables that he may run that readeth (Habakkuk 2:2).

The Bible records that when God showed Prophet Habakkuk a vision, he gave him a prophetic instruction to write the vision down. This means scribbling, recording and documenting every detail of the vision. Therefore, in order to fully understand and interpret your dreams in an exhaustive manner, a Biblical dream application technique based on Habakkuk 2:2, called a Dream Mind Map can be used to map out all the details of the dream. This involves capturing the details of events taking place in the dream, the people appearing in the dreams, the emotions or feelings of people participating in the dream, as well as determining the role of people appearing in a dream, whether they are observes, participants or the main area of focus.

To map out the Dream Mind Map and interpret the dream, you must answer the following questions:

DREAM MESSAGE DETAILS:
What would you title this dream?
Who is the focus of this dream?
What are the sub-focuses of this dream?
What other details in this dream are important?
What emotion did the dream evoke? (Was there a feeling of tension or aggression or harmony?).
How did the people, or creatures, in the dream relate to one another?
THE STATE OF PEOPLE APPEARING IN THE DREAM:
Is the person known to the dreamer?
How are they connected to the dreamer?
What is their name?
What stands out about them?
What does the person portray in the dreamer's life?
What spiritual quality do they portray?
Does the dreamer like, dislike, or is neutral toward them?
Has this person appeared in other dreams?
Is this a person unknown to the dreamer?
How would they be described?
From their actions or manner, what name could they be given?
What role do they play in the dream?
Does the person exude any qualities, positive or negative?
FACELESS PEOPLE APPEARING IN THE DREAM:
Is the person's countenance dark or light?
What feeling or tone does this person exude or add to the dream?
Does this person seem to hinder or help the dream's direction?
Does the person display any special powers or heavenly qualities?
NAMES OF PERSONS APPEARING IN THE DREAM:
What is the name of the person apearing in the dream (The name may be the meaning of the dream).
Is the name in scripture? (Their name may be a prophetic pointer to what is going to happen).

What position do they hold in life (The name of the position they hold, or represent, is significant).

THE PLACES WHICH APPEARS IN THE DREAM
Is it a place of liberty of prison?
Is it a city or remote area? Is it a complete building or still under construction?
Is it a mountain or valley?

Identifying Places, Scenes, Characters, Objects, Creatures and Colors.

It is imperative that you break the dream down and 'dissect' it. Once you become more accustomed to dream interpretation, you will not need to break the dream down as much as you will see the interpretation without having to 'dig through' all the details. But for those who are still 'trying their hand' at dream interpretation this is a good way to go until you learn how to flow better in the Spirit. Make a list on your page from A - F then under each letter list the corresponding Place, Scene, Character, Object, Creature and Color as they appear in the dream. Reading through the helps that I list below, systematically identify the symbol for each of these points one by one.

A: Places

Make a list of the various places encountered in the dream. Often you may dream of places that are familiar to you. It could be that a time of healing is being brought to that period of your life or that the Lord is exposing something that happened during that time. Churches can speak of a place of worship. If it is an old style church, it could be speaking of the religious status quo system. A house could speak of your life, your body as a temple of the Holy Spirit. Places such as monuments or historical buildings may speak of things relating to the past – things gone by.

At times you might find yourself running through alleyways or dark streets. This often speaks of running blind and not having direction. If the feeling that comes with the place is negative and fearful, it could be that the Lord is revealing to you that the enemy is wreaking havoc in your life and sending you running all directions – none of which are of the Lord. Of course if you find yourself in a meadow where the sun is shining and you feel peace, the Lord could be revealing to you that you have entered into a time of rest and peace with Him. This could speak of a time of freedom and escape from the pressure around you. Each of these would have a specific meaning pertaining to you as an individual. Look to the Lord for revelation concerning what the places you dream about mean to you.

B: Scenes

Write down the scenes in the dream. Once again you might find yourself in a scene that is familiar to you. Restaurants can speak of 'feeding'; bathrooms can speak of 'exposure' or a place of 'washing'. Then again bedrooms may speak of intimacy and privacy. You would need to identify what the scene mean to you and if you sensed a positive or negative feeling towards that scene in your dream.

C: Identifying the Characters

Take each character in the dream and identify what part of you they represent if the dream is internal. If they were people you know, then write down your relationship with them or what they mean to you. If they were people you did not know, note what your impressions were of them in your dream. If they are relatives, note how close you are to them. If a spouse, then your relationship with your spouse will determine the symbol. It could be positive or negative. Learn to identify this one because it will recur. Often a spouse can speak of your recreated spirit in Christ. If you had a really good relationship with your earthly father, he could speak of the Lord in your dreams. If you have a bad relationship with a certain person, it is possible that they represent your 'flesh' or 'sinful nature' in your dreams.

If you often find yourself dreaming of a man or woman that you do not know, but yet seem familiar to you, they could represent your masculine and feminine nature. The masculine often represents left-brained, intellectual thinking, while the feminine representing prophetic, right-brained emphasis. If there is a person in your life that is strong and you look up to, they could speak of the Holy Spirit and His protection. Your relationship with the person in your dream, in real life is vital in identifying what the represent. Your sub-conscious mind will use those emotions and thoughts you have to convey the appropriate message to you clearly.

Often your sub-conscious will use people that represent something in your life. Perhaps the music leader in your church could represent your musical gifts. If you as a prophet are at constant logger-heads with your pastor, he could speak of the church, status quo system in your dreams. Often your children speak of your ministry or those things you have 'birthed' in the spirit. So, it is vital to take a look at how you feel about the person in your dream before identifying the symbol. Once you have identified those characters you will find they are used repeatedly in your dreams as the same symbol.

D: Objects

Note if the object means anything special to you? Does the object convey a negative or positive impression to you. Often if you keep dreaming of a wedding ring, it can speak of a covenant and a wedding dress of your union with the Lord or those things you are 'married' or 'tied' to. It is also common to see vehicles in your dreams as your ministry – those things that 'drive' your ministry. Often you may dream that you are driving and you are encountering difficulty. The Lord could be saying that you need to give over the wheel to Him and to stop taking your ministry out of His hands. Perhaps you will dream that a person who symbolizes the Lord is driving in which case it is a good interpretation, indicating that the Lord is in control and that you can sit back and relax for a while. Dreaming that your vehicle has broken down can speak of some kind of damage you have faced in your ministry. There are even those dreams where you dream you get new keys and are given a new car! This speaks of promotion and the Lord could be confirming that He has given you a greater anointing to carry out the ministry he has given you.

Then there are those objects from the Word that are often displayed in our dreams. Gold objects speak of the Lord and His deity, while a clay pot may speak of us as His vessels ready for service. Wine often speaks of the anointing, as does water and oil. Arrows or weapons piercing you can speak of the work of the enemy who is known for his darts of destruction. Then again wielding a sword speaks of carrying the authority of the Lord and using it as a weapon against the enemy. If you are not sure on the interpretation of an object take a look through the Word. It is rich with revelation and symbols. The Lord has been speaking in dark sayings and symbols to His prophets since the beginning of the world and you are certain to find the answer to your revelation right in the scriptures!

E: Creatures

Animals and insects can refer to demonic powers but it depends also on how you view them. Plants and trees - can refer to growth, or barrenness if they are in bad condition. Babies or children - things that have been birthed or are still immature. Snakes, spiders and black creatures very often speak of the work of the enemy and his attacks. Dreaming about giving birth or being pregnant can speak of something you are about to birth in the spirit or have given birth to. If you dream of babies dying it could be a warning dream that the thing the Lord has given you is dying. A lion can speak of the strength of the Lord. A lamb, of innocence and salvation. If you dream of your pet, you would need to identify what that pet means to you. Often pets are substitutes for children in which case they would represent a positive aspect of yourself.

F: Colors and senses

Take note of the things that were said or that you heard in the dream as well as the things you felt, tasted, smelled. Often the color red can speak of the blood of the Lord. Blue is a heavenly color, while black does not have a good connotation, being likened to the nature of the enemy. Gold often speaks of the Lord and His majesty, while silver speaks of humanity and redemption in the scriptures. White can speak of purity and green of fertility. Once again you would need to identify what they mean to you as an individual and what they represent in the Word.

Get Revelation!

Once you have made your list and identified what each symbol represents. Put the dream aside and summarize now what you have received from the

Holy Spirit. Write this final summary as a journal and so let it flow not from your intellectual thinking, but by using the internal anointing the Lord has given us for revelation. Do not use the same formula on every dream you interpret. Allow the Holy Spirit to speak to you and give you additional visions and revelations to back up what you feel the dream means. Here is where you are going to give the subject (or yourself) the direction and answers you are looking for. It is not good enough to just give an interpretation without following it up with the Word of God to encourage, exhort and to promote faith, hope and love.

If a warning is being indicated then give the warning and with it scripture and direction on how to be victorious in that particular situation. If the dream is internal then guide the subject through a better understanding of what is going on inside themselves and how to move on from where they are. If the dream is Internally prophetic, then prepare the subject for what lies ahead and how to prepare for the work the Lord is about to do in their lives. If the dream is external receive revelation from the Spirit and Word on what to do with the revelation. In other words if it needs to be spoken forth as a decree, kept for a later time, to be travailed over in intercession, or to be shared with a group that you might intercede in unity.

DREAM PRACTICAL APPLICATION:

"As the dream began, I found myself standing at the edge of a very high cliff. I knew with certainty that I had a decision to make — either step off the cliff or turn around and walk to safety. I decided to step off; instead of falling straight down, I began to glide gently downward. I landed in the driver's seat of a blue and white convertible that was moving at a high rate of speed."

Begin by giving the dream a title: _____
Dreamer _____
Blue and White _____
3. To find the sub-focus consider the following:

a) Often, when we remove the "detail" or "filler" in the dream the meaning will become clear. "Detail" refers to items in a dream that are not important to the coherence or meaning of the dream.

Study the dream recorded and assign a status to each of the symbols in the space provided:

Cliff edge _____

Convertible Car _____

Gliding _____

Car already moving _____

Driver's seat _____

Speed _____

F. Ascertain the Context of the dream: The context of a dream determines whether a symbol is positive or negative.

1. Keep the main thing.
2. Determine the attitude and agendas of those in the dream.
3. Recognize what God is presently dealing with in your life.
4. Note the goals God has given you.
5. Determine the importance of Color: Color helps determine the context of the dream. The color of a symbol reveals its meaning or purpose.

G. Determine the Tone of the dream: Did the dream produce fear, hopelessness, uneasiness, peace (or a lack thereof), anticipation, etc.?

Was the atmosphere of the dream: harsh, ominous, exciting, light-hearted, or neutral?

Find the theme or plot of the dream: Write down the main facts. Daniel 7:1 "I understood the meaning, and I Daniel had a dream and I wrote down the main facts."

Note the object or thought that occurs most often, or what object or thought remains with you when the dream ends.

Consider natural order. (For example, when a house is built, walls are put into place before the windows.)

What questions linger about the dream?

What are the most arresting images in the dream?

Do you have an immediate sense of the meaning?

What are your strongest associations (feelings, esteem, disdain) toward the individuals in the dream?
Do any people symbolize something to you?
Is your feeling toward the people in the dream biblical?
What do you need to remember most about the dream?
Were certain things in the dream exaggerated such as some physical item (person with a big nose, ears), emotion, or action?
Learn to walk through the dream with the dreamer.
Finally determine the meaning of the dream.

How To Prepare Yourself For Lucid Dreaming:

It is imperative that you embark on the following prophetic instructions if ever you really want to remember your dreams: Ask the Holy Spirit to increase the level, intensity, and clarity of your dreams; Be consistent in going to bed with the intent of recognizing when you are dreaming; In the early stages, we often wake ourselves up when we recognize we are dreaming; Before you go to sleep, ask the Holy Spirit to help you stay in the dream until you learn and respond properly to His purpose for the dream; Try to form a habit of never going to sleep anxious; Meditate on an attribute of God. Consider one of His names and what it means; Imagine the Holy Spirit hovering over you. Taking the chaos out of your life, and bringing order to it as He brought order to the chaos of the Earth for you were made of dust; Feel the Holy Spirit breathing over you, blowing all the dust out of your life. Remember, God wants you to walk in the spirit and to live in the spirit; Remind yourself that God wants His Spirit to blanket you and tell you the things hidden deep within His heart (Genesis 2:7; 1 Corinthians 2:10).

How Will You Know That You Are Developing In Lucid Dreaming?

The following are indications that you are developing and making progress in your dreams: You will start to remember former dreams in the current dream you are having; You may find yourself in the dream saying, "I've

Frequency Revelator

dreamed this part before; You will begin to recognize patterns of people, places, and things and who or what they represent as you are dreaming; You will begin to influence events in the dream rather remaining as a passive responder; and one very high level of lucid dreaming is interpreting the dream while you are having it.

CHAPTER EIGHT

DREAM ACTIVATION: HOW TO ACTIVATE YOUR DREAMS

How Do We Stimulate Dreams? What Are Those Things That Will Help Us To Stimulate *Dreams?*

Have A Dream Book Or Diary By Your Bedside Every Night Where You Document All Your Dreams And Their interpretations

Write down the vision and make it plain on tables that he may run that readeth
(Habakkuk 2:2).

It is worth mentioning that dreams seem to reside in a non-dimension, free from the limitations of time, space, and logic. When the dream enters into our memory, it moves into a world bound by time, space, and logic. Our minds then translate the dream into three dimensions, while our hands must translate the dream into the two dimensions of ink and paper. Dream images are written in our minds with disappearing ink. If we do not re-experience them immediately, dreams become invisible as the fast turning pages of our waking consciousness take over our mind. One of the best ways to remember and understand the significance of our dreams is to write them down immediately, upon awakening, so we don't forget them. While it might be a daunting challenge to write down an entire dream sometimes, if you take time to write down the main facts of your dreams, a clearer interpretation of the dream will come across. Did you ever have a time when you woke up in the middle of the night from a dream that was so clear that you thought; "Oh I will remember that in the morning"? Then, when you wake up you remember very little, and say, "Aww man... I know I had a significant dream last night, and I just lost it." It's because you have no system in which you could document your dreams. If you had a system of documenting your dreams, it would be easy for you to keep track of them and also determine the direction God is giving you through dreams. To substantiate this view with reference to scriptural evidence, let's look at how some great dreamers in the Bible handled their own dreams:

> *In the first year of Belshazzar king of Babylon. Daniel had a dream and visions of his head as he lay in his bed. <u>Then he wrote down the dream</u>, and told the sum of the matter.*

Do you notice that the first thing Daniel did when he woke up was to write the dream down. Daniel was a man known for having strange and amazing encounters with God. He was a man who served four different kings in his lifetime. The gift that made room for his ongoing success was his ability to dream, and his interpretation skills. One of the main things you see in Daniel's life is spiritual discipline. He was a man of prayer, and he took seriously what God showed him. Daniel 7:1 says that God gave Daniel a dream, and he wrote down the dream telling the main facts. Then, he was able to pray about the dream and receive an interpretation. Writing the dream down enables us to remain focused on what God has said even when we encounter trials. It is for this reason that God instructed Prophet Habakkuk saying, *"Write down the vision and make it plain on tables that he may run that readeth" (Habakkuk 2:2)*. Why because he knew that there is a possibility of man forgetting what God would have said. It is the same reason why we have all the various books documented in the Bible so that firstly, it can serve as written evidence to back up what God has said concerning us and secondly, to help us not to forget divine instructions, directions, experiences and encounters from God. The Bible is a documentation of spiritual encounters and experiences that Great men and women had with God? And if God could inspire people to write down these encounters and document them in the form of a book called the BIBLE, why is it difficult for you to write your own Dream Dictionary where you document all your spiritual encounters and experiences with God in your dreams?

PROPHETIC INSTRUCTION:

I want you to take this seriously as a prophetic instruction from God.

Understanding Prophetic Dreams & Visions

From today onwards, go and buy a small book from any stationary shop and label it as a "**DREAM BOOK**". Divide it into two columns; the first column is where you shall write down all your dreams the first thing every morning when you wake up. And the second column is where you shall write down their meaning and interpretation. At the end of every week or month, make sure that you do an audit of your dreams to determine what God is saying to you. As you go through them, you will realise that there is a specific pattern and a specific message that God wants you to pay attention to. Date and title each dream and start each dream on a new page. In certain cases, you may want to group dreams by subject, symbol, image or intrinsic/extrinsic. Sometimes the biggest breakthroughs happen in a believer's life by simple prophetic action of faith of placing a writing pad by your bedside. What you are doing when you put the pad of paper next to your bed is showing God that you expect him to speak to you, and that you will take seriously what He reveals in a dream. That simple prophetic act of faith often opens you up to the realm of dreams and visions. So put a pad of paper and a pen next to your bed, and watch what happens!

Now, you might he asking yourself a question: Should I write the entire dream as far as I can remember? No. Simply write the main points, facts or theme of the dream. Too often people focus on the one, odd thing in a dream, and miss the theme or focal point of the dream. Look for a theme or focal point in your dreams. Determine if you are a participator in the dream or a spectator. Is the dream about you or someone else? Don't get caught up in the random things that happen so often in dreams, and get side-tracked from the focal point of the dream's meaning.

PROPHETIC PRAYER

Heavenly Faither, I ask you to speak to me through dreams and visions in the night. By faith I will put a pad of paper and pen next to my bed. As I do so, I ask for you to open my heart up to receive revelation from you, as well as give me the tenacity to become a good steward of the revelation you give me. In Jesus' name, amen.

Frequency Revelator

Your Dreams Should Be Channelled In The Area Or Field That You Want To Dream.

There is such as thing as *channelling your dreams*, which means directing your dreams in the area you want them to. You need to think in the general area of those dreams for those specific visions of your life to come to pass. For example, if you are in the business world your mind needs to hang loose what will become of your business, what is God's will for you. As your thoughts revolve around in the area of wondering, you are hanging loose you are not limiting yourself to what you know or what you have. You are just wondering. In a state of mind of wondering what is to come to pass, the answer may come to you in your dreams. Let's look in the book of Daniel. In Daniel chapter two Nebuchadnezzar had a dream; Daniel received an interpretation for Nebuchadnezzar's dream and brought to Nebuchadnezzar some of the reasons of those dreams and why they occur. As he brought forth the dream, he gave some background in verse 28-29 *But there is a God in heaven who reveals mysteries, and He has made known to King Nebuchadnezzar what will be in the latter days*. Now, Nebuchadnezzar was only the first part of the dream the golden head and the others had nothing to do with him, the Middle Persian Empire etc. But yet in his dream he could contact areas that go beyond his life span.

Your dream and the visions of your head as you lay in bed are these; To you, O king, as you lay in bed came thoughts of what would be hereafter, and He who reveals mysteries made known to you what is to be.

King Nebuchadnezzar, one day before he slept he wondered what would come to pass after his kingdom. What is the end of all these things? And with all these thoughts coming strong on him, it brought him into a position where God gave him a dream. The question you might be asking yourself is: If Nebuchadnezzar did not wonder about what is to come, would he have had that dream? The answer is no! Because by channelling his thoughts in the direction of his dreams, he drew God's attention and provoked Him to speak to him through dreams. Which explain why many people do not allow their consciousness to rise beyond their natural ability of what they have. God never could reveal to them what is to come in that area because they never let go of their limitations. They began to wonder what goes beyond their limitations what will come to pass. Daniel does it in a different way.

In the first year of Belshazzar king of Babylon. Daniel had a dream and visions of his head as he lay in his bed. Then he wrote down the dream, and told the sum of the matter. (Daniel 7:1).

Apparently, Daniel who served in the kingdom was wondering what is to come to pass too and in seeking after God's best for his life, he had this strange dream. Now, that dream that he had in chapter seven there are several verses that he mentioned. In verse eight he says *I was considering the horns.* Verse nine says *As I looked.* Verse says eleven *I looked.* Verse fifteen also says *As for me, Daniel, my spirit within me was anxious and the visions of my head alarmed me.* He didn't understand but it did disturb him. Daniel was like a watcher and one who seeks God's understanding.

In the third year of Cyrus king of Persia a word was reveled to Daniel, who was named Belteshazzar. And the word was true, and it was a great conflict. And he understood the word and had understanding of the vision. (Daniel 10:1).

Daniel was a seeker after truth and after things to come. And there is something about people who long to know the future, who long to know what is to come. Right now, in God's book everything written about your life is already there. Everything written about what you are to do is already in God's book. And if we desire after it, God will reveal and bring it forth into your life. So, one of the first keys is to be able to dream dreams in the category or have thoughts in your mind in the area that you would like to move into. It can get beyond these areas but it is the same general vicinity and it will stimulate those dreams in our life that is your destiny and vision for your life.

In the book of Genesis chapter 41 in Pharaoh's dream, we see Joseph coming to interpret Pharaoh's dream. There are some statements that he made as an introduction to his dreams. In verse 25 *Then Joseph said to Pharaoh, "The dream of Pharaoh is one; God has revealed to Pharaoh what he is about to do."* Now, there is no record of what is the condition of Pharaoh before he slept and had the dream. But he had two dreams occurring in the same night. When he woke up and he slept he had a second dream. Two dreams that took place one after the other. Joseph said God has shown Pharaoh what He is about to do. Doesn't that sound like Job 33? God seals it upon our lives what He is about to do.

PRACTICAL APPLICATION

In the dream I saw I was eating a green apple. Halfway after having taken several bites of the apple, I suddenly saw two tiny worms in the apple. One was peach in colour; the other was white. When I saw the worms I tried to vomit out what I had eaten. What was I doing when I was awake? I was offered to enter a new business by contributing some capital to that business. That night as I slept I asked the Lord to show me whether I should get involved in the business. That dream is a direct answer. The Lord is saying that there are worms in that venture. Worms in what that person is going to enter into. So the Lord is saying don't enter. The white worm symbolizes things that look all right to the natural eye. The principles looks O.K. everything looks O.K. and there is nothing wrong. It looks so honest about it. And green signifies that is something new. See it directly speaks about that business and God is saying no to that dream. A lady here said she had a dream about angels singing in heaven. That looks like Jacob's ladder. Now Jacob's ladder may be classified under the second dimension of dream. Her dream was a spiritual encounter. What she needs to take note is what is said during the dream and what she saw in the dream. It means her spirit was moving into the spirit realm.

The Dreams That God Gives To You Relate To The Area In Which You Either Have Something To Do With It Or Some Influence In That Area.

Pharaoh had the ability to protect all these millions of people from starving. God was not just concerned about Pharaoh. Instead, he was concerned about all human kind. So, God gave a dream to Pharaoh so that through Pharaoh He will do something to protect His innocent people from dying. The dreams that you have relate to the position you are in. And by position here in Pharaoh it has to do with the area where he was supposed to do something about. See God does not simply gives dreams. Dreams have a purpose in our lives. We saw in our earlier areas how it stimulates faith. Now we are looking at areas that could stir up more dreams in our lives.

If God place you into business world, let go and let God dream dreams through you. And cause dreams to come in that area of your life. Don't stop those dreams. If you are in the ministry let go and let those dreams of your ministry come forth. Don't stop there. Those dreams may save other lives and help other lives. Do you notice something about those dreams? Pharaoh didn't have the interpretation. It was Joseph who having the interpretation helped to fulfil that dream. That doesn't take place necessary all the time. But we cannot understand fully some of our dreams until we come up together with people who are a part of the fulfilment of that dream. Perhaps you dreamt of something in the business world or something in the ministry. And you cannot fully comprehend that dream. But one day when you are with the people, who become a part of that dream, the interpretation becomes clear both to that person and to you. And together as a team you will be able to fulfil and bring that dream to pass. So write down those dreams even if you don't understand them or even if they look ridiculous to you. They are the fertile ground of your faith working in those areas.

Position Yourself You Stir Up Those Dreams.

It is important that you position yourself you stir up those dreams. You see if Joseph were anywhere else, he would not have the interpretation of dream. By position we are saying be in the right place at the right time and doing the right thing. When you are in the correct place dreams will come. Some are in the wrong place and the dreams are not coming forth. You need to be in the right place for those dreams to come forth in your life. Firstly, you need to be filled with thoughts in regards to those areas of your dream. You need to be always wondering about things to come. Secondly, being in the right place at the right time doing the right thing. Joseph was in the right place at the right time doing the right thing. Pharaoh was in the right place at the right time doing the right thing. And the dreams just came to pass. If you are in the wrong place doing the wrong thing, something stops your dream and it just won't come to pass.

One more example of that. Paul and Silas were traveling from place to place seeking to preach the gospel. No matter where they go they seemed to be in the wrong place doing the right thing. So in Acts 16:6;

And they went through the region of Phrygia Galatia, having been forbidden by the Holy Spirit to speak the Word in Asia. And when they had come opposite Mysia they attempted to go into Bithynia, but the Spirit of Jesus did not allow them.

It seems that they were just knocking on blank walls. *So passing by Mysia they went down to Troas.* Troas was a seaside town. Only when they came to a place where they could take a boat did the vision occur. But he knew that he was in the wrong place doing the right thing preaching the gospel. And he had to get into the right position for the dream to come forth. And Troas was the right place because God wanted them to take a boat. Troas was a seaside town and when he went there he had a Macedonian vision that began his second missionary journey. Do you know what the second missionary journey was? He had to go into areas he had never gone before. You see Paul tried to go into areas that he had gone before. God wants him to totally make a break and just go by boat and go forth into areas he had never gone before. He tried to stick around areas where Jews congregate and not in Gentiles areas. And so the vision may not come. Why did they go to Troas? I believe that there was somehow an inner inclination to go there perhaps something more will come from there. It is just like going and lying down at the airport. You know that God called you somewhere some place but you don't know where. So you go to the airport and just look at the planes and dream. And then God speaks in your heart, "Go to Macedonia." It doesn't mean that after this a few of you are going to gather in the airport and dream. But you need to be in a place where you could make a move to fulfil that dream. Are you in the right place doing the right thing at the right time? If you are those dreams will keep bubbling out into your life. If you are not, then get into position.

Sometimes God might you out of your home into a mountain into another place so that there He can give you that dream. Why is that so? Because there is a multitude of others things that prevent that dream from getting in your life. Ecclesiastes 5:3 says a dream comes through much activities. He is talking about the type of dreams that come from your daily life. It is like a noise that continues from your daily life. You need to get out from those activities and get into position. So that God could cause you to dream dreams. The basis of this message is to bring you to this point to face your life to ask, "Have the dreams in your life stopped?" Because the day it does creativity stops. It's the hassles of this New Year. Do you know something about being dreamy? You have to somehow detach yourself from this world and its activities. It is really hard to get dreamy while you are in the peak of activities. It is just impossible. You can only do it when you get out of these activities into the right position. Then those dreams will come. Sometimes it means just getting out to a hillside by our home and just looking over the whole place dreamy. . You must be in the right position to dream those dreams. Get into position. By position it could be physical, it could be social, it could be geographical. Let me give one last point on things that stimulate our dream life.

How Do You Position Yourself To Receive Gods Prophetic Promises?

So many Christians don't see the fulfilment of the dreams and visions that God gives them, because they don't do anything with them. It is not good enough to just think, and talk about the dreams, and visions that God gives you. Visions and dreams require a response of faith – faith that takes action. The first thing you must do with a dream is **seek God for the interpretation**. What kind of dream is it? What is God trying to show you about yourself? About your spiritual calling? Is the Holy Spirit warning you, or imparting some gift to you? Once you have the interpretation, then what? You must get into God's presence, and begin to decree what you see until the manifestation of what He shows you comes to pass. Job 22:28 says, *"You will also declare a thing and it will be established for you; and light will shine on your ways."* We must put action behind our faith. If you are crying out to God to speak to you in dreams and visions, and He does, then you must take what He shows you to prayer, and declare His word over your life and situation. As you begin to declare what God shows you in prayer, your declarations of faith will release favor, and the light of God will shine on all your ways.

The next step of faith requires that you **position yourself to receive that which he shows you in the natural.** For instance, if God gives you a dream, or shows you in a vision that you are called to be a CEO of a large company or a business owner, it might be a good idea to begin to go to school, and obtain a business degree. When you do this, your education provides God with a wineskin to begin to pour out the blessings of God, into and through you. Too many people want the new wine of heaven but don't position themselves to receive it. Callings require a response. That's why the Bible says that many are called, but few are chosen (Matthew 22:14) - because people don't position themselves to be chosen.

You Must Foster Exposure To An Atmosphere Of Music Which Is Necessary To Stimulating The Dream.

After that you shall come to Gibeathelohim, where there is a garrison of the Philistines; and there, as you come to the city, you will meet a band of prophets coming down from the high place with harps, tambourine, flute and lyre before them, prophesying. (I Samuel 10:5).

Music plays a fundamental role in terms of cultivating a conducive atmosphere for dreams to flourish. If you sleep with music playing in the background, there will be a tendency to stir up some of those dreams. Or sometimes in the conscious state while listening to music, it can bring you to dream dreams of the areas that God wants to build in your life.. God has put a song in our heart to sing to Him. Ephesians 5:19 tells us *be filled with the Spirit speaking to one another with psalms and hymns and spiritual songs, singing and making melody in your heart to the Lord.* If the melody and music in your life die the dreams will stop. The music needs to continue. And sometimes we need external help. If you are not a dreamer of dreams possibly you are also someone who seldom hear music. Perhaps you are so engrossed in other things, in study, in research and you are not one who just listens to music. I am not talking about music while you are in our beehive of activities. If you just put on good Christian music and you just sit and allow the music to take your spirit off into a dreamy state, you will once again stir the ability to dream in your life.

Understanding Prophetic Dreams & Visions

All of us before we became adults we were dreamers of dreams. Somehow as we get educated as we get into a profession we get into the beehive of earthly worldly activities we lost the ability to dream. We need to put that music back into your life so that we could dream dreams again. Learn to wait on God. Do you notice that the greatest period of mankind has been the period when great music came forth? In the Renaissance period that's when the great classical music all came forth. And people took time to just listen to music. Their ability in the natural even rises. By all means have music in your life 24 hours while you are in activity. But learn to just be still and let the music take you off. And you will be able to dream dreams again.

Be In Control Of Your Dream Life By Praying A Lot In Tongues.

There is another fourth little thing that you could do. If you really want to dream dreams the last fifteen minutes or half an hour before you sleep is important. Spend some time with God pray in tongues and you will notice that there is a greater frequency of dreams that come from God. I would like to advise that if you really want to remember your dream especially those that are from God, then spend some time with the Lord before you sleep, especially praying in the Spirit. Usually those dreams that you could remember have a significant message in your life. When you wake up from a bad dream, you could tell yourself what to do and sleep again. Start the show by seeing the last part of the old dream. And then continue with something good like for example in your dream there was this hairy monster that came and grabbed you by your neck. You feel yourself shaking and you woke up with cold sweat. You look at the time it was 3 a.m. So you are not sure what to do now. You spend some time in prayer. But do you know what you could do? You could pray and you could cause that same dream to reverse provided you have the Word of God inside you.

It is only possible through the Word of God and through faith and you don't allow fear to come in your life. You could say no that is not going to happen. And you just began to get into *enupnion* in a dream like state see the whole thing but see yourself chasing that demon. See yourself grabbing that hairy fellow and kicking it away and then go back to sleep and dream what you have premeditated. Part two of your dream continues. Is that possible? Yes, because part of our dream is the inner healing of our self. Some of us have uncompleted dreams. And we get frightened and disturbed by them. We need to have completed dream. Sometimes your dreams can be completed over three or four nights and some times over many months. We need to learn that dreams are not beyond the area of control like what we think. You could actually control them to a certain extent. Remember what the key to control that area of the deep recess of spirit is – vision. What you see will enter into the.

Cultivate An Atmosphere Of Prayer And Worship In Your Sphere Of Contact

The environment or surroundings in a key determinant to the type of dreams we are likely to encounter. That is why it is imperative that we cultivate a conducive atmosphere that will be conducive for godly dreams. Have you ever thought about why you seem to dream more on Sunday nights or Monday mornings? Years ago, I began to recognize this pattern with myself and soon realized why. I had spent time in worship on Sunday morning at church, and sadly, had not done so any other day of the week. I was praying, but not truly spending time in thanksgiving and adoration of the Lord. Some people have never been taught to sit still long enough to practice God's presence, but if you will wait on God, you will notice a change in your spirit. It may not be in that moment of worship and you may be tempted to think it is time wasted, but it is not.

In fact, what happens as you sit there in prayer is that you make a deposit into yourself and into your inner man (or woman). Tomorrow or the next day or the next, when you are presented with a situation in which an immediate decision must be made, you instantly will be able to make a withdrawal and choose rightly. There will be a sudden wisdom that you cannot explain, or a "knowing" about how you should proceed. It came from God, and it came while you sat with Him and—by faith—allowed Him to pour His divine nature into you. It is a supernatural exchange that many miss these days because they are too busy and too distracted. These very people fall into bed exhausted, needing counsel, often begging God to speak to them at night with a dream, but no dream comes. Not because God is unkind, but because these people never prepared their spirit to hear from God that day. And because, on the practical side, they were so exhausted and had such a sleep debt that they spent much of the night in a deep N-REM dreamless sleep.

Train Yourself To See Regularly In The Spirit

God wants to open up our hearts, and open up our eyes to the realm of the Kingdom, but here's the thing I've learned from walking with God, as well as from the scriptures. You won't walk in the supernatural unless you see in the Spirit, and hear the Spirit. Why? The defining anointing that was upon Jesus was in John 5:19. He said, "I never do a thing unless I first see what my Father is doing." Then it goes on further in the same chapter, and He talks about how He never does a thing unless He first hears what the Father says to do. It's out of that place that He makes judgments. Because those judgments come out of the bidding of God's voice, they're right – and they are powerful. What God wants to do is open up our eyes, open up our ears and give us maturity. Acts 2 says God's going to pour out dreams, visions, miracles, signs, and wonders. If he's going to do that, and the result is souls coming into the Kingdom, we need to understand dreams, visions, signs, and wonders. We need to understand the supernatural! This stuff of dreams, visions, and encounters, is to be found all throughout the Bible.

For example, I could teach from the Old Testament to Revelation about dreams and visions. But if you want to become activated in your spirit to greater experiences with dreams and visions, you need to search out the stories of other dreams and prophets, in the Word – for yourself. God will speak to you as you read. The Bible is your ultimate guidebook, and dream symbol interpreter. Start reading! Also begin to ask God to give you dreams and encounters. Remember to put that pad of paper next to your bed and seek God out for the interpretation of your dreams and visions.

An Empowerment Prayer To Get You There:

Lord, I ask you to open my eyes in the spirit to see what you're doing, and teach me how to step out in faith with what you show me so that my dreams become a reality. Also I pray that you would help me to develop a dream language with you that I might know you more and hear your voice more clearly. In Jesus' name, amen.

Master The Spiritual Art Of How To Control Activities In Your Dreams

It is important that you master the spiritual art of how to control activities in your dreams. Did you know that you can reach a level in the spirit realm whereby you can literally control your dream life and determine the direction of your dreams. When I sleep, I can determine the direction of my dreams and decide what to see, and what not to see. I can decide where to go, the type of people to meet, and if I realise that my dream is headed in the direction I don't like, I can choose to either change direction or wake up. In dream, I have the power to change the plot of the story, or at least avoid the trap set for your feet. Sort of like those movies with alternate endings where you can use your DVD remote to decide the outcome. This level comes with being more conscious of the spirit realm and sensitive to its movements. As we learn to change dark dreams and spiritual warfare dreams, we will notice that when they are changed to God's purposes the dreams will also transform from dark or black and white dreams into full blown color.

CHAPTER NINE

DEEPER REVELATIONS OF PROPHETIC DREAMS AND VISIONS

He said to them, "Hear this dream which I have dreamed, behold, we were binding sheaves in the field, and lo, my sheaf arose and stood upright; and behold. Your sheaves gathered round it, and bowed down to my sheaf." His brothers said to him, "Are you indeed to reign over us? Or are you indeed to have dominion over us?" So they hated him yet more for his dream and for his words. Then he dreamed another dream, and told it to his brothers, and said, "Behold, I have dreamed another dream; and behold, the sun, the moon, and the eleven stars were bowing down to me." But when he told it to his father and to his brothers, his father rebuked him, and said to him, "What is this dream that you have dreamed? Shall I and your mother and your brothers indeed come to bow ourselves to the ground before you?" (Genesis 37:6-10).

Here are two dreams that Joseph had in his early life about seventeen years old. Apparently it's a very simple dream that they understood. In the last message we saw how that when we have dreams God will take from the background that we had to speak to us. God will also speak to us dreams that concern our life in some ways. Although you may dream of some area that is further from your life yet in some way your life will be connected to that. He won't just suddenly give you a dream about something taking place in the North Pole where you have no involvement at all. If you have never hunted polar bears before, never seen what a polar bear is like it would be very exceptional for you to suddenly have a dream about polar bear. God doesn't do that He usually takes from our resources that is within us. Let me illustrate something like prophecy. God can give a word of prophecy and the instrument or the vessel that delivers that prophecy will be limited by the vessel's vocabulary and language. If for example you find that your vocabulary is very small and limited, then when God speaks something using whatever word you have to describe what God is seeking to say to you or through you to somebody else, God will make use of all that is within you to bring forth a message.

When the Holy Spirit gives a dream it will be so clear cut its different from the dreams that you have by your soul or your spirit. Those are from the different category. We are talking about dreams from the Holy Spirit and how to interpret them. Notice that the dreams that Joseph dreamt he had a part involved in the dreams. We realize that it took many years for the dreams to come to pass. But those dreams concerned himself. Although he dreamt about his brothers and his father it concern himself. One of the things that Joseph dreamt in the first dream was about sheaves. That is something that Joseph and his brothers are working on all the time. It was an incident taken from his daily life. It was something that he was familiar with. Apparently they worked at the farm and they constantly have been doing that. So the Holy Spirit took something from his life to illustrate and to give him a word of wisdom in a dream regarding his future. It is very clear-cut because there were the number of sheaves there and the fact that they bowed to him signifies that he had the lordship or some measure of authority over them.

Now the second dream where he dreamt about the sun, the moon and the eleven stars speaks of a greater realm of authority. Joseph's father seems to understand that the sun and moon represent him and the mother. Obviously they knew the interpretation of the dream. Thus he says, "Will you really reign and rule over us?" Let's show again Genesis chapter 40 and 41 that in the butler's dream it was something from his own life too. In chapter 40 verse 9 the butler dreamt about the vine and the cup and they were things he was familiar with. The baker dreamt about baskets and bread, which again were things that he was familiar with. Pharaoh in chapter 41 dreamt about cows and river and there was a message in regard to his rule and reign. It affected his life.

We saw in the preceding chapters how in the book of Job chapter 33 that God in a dream will reveal and will show forth things to come. In verse 11 and 12 how God hid the hidden mysteries of things to come. And all these in regard to the dreams that come forth. So let's lay down some rules

Understanding Prophetic Dreams & Visions

of this interpretation of dreams. Usually a person who dreams a dream, after isolating all those dreams that came from his soul and spirit would find that some dreams are from the Holy Spirit. The dreams would usually have something to do with your life. God will not reveal something way out. It would be something that you are acquainted with that you may be directly or indirectly involved. And that being the case the best interpreter of that dream would be yourself with the Lord's help of course.

Let me just give one more illustration so that it will seal into your life. Take Daniel for example. Bear in mind that Daniel was at the peak of the political system in his days. Daniel was a man acquainted with the change and coming of kingdoms. God in His time shows forth visions and dreams. The incident is about Nebuchadnezzar who had a dream. But when Nebuchadnezzar woke up he forgot his dream. And what was required was that the wise men were to not only interpret his dream they must tell him what the dream was. Nobody could do it but Daniel said to Nebuchadnezzar in Daniel 2 verse 24-28;

Therefore Daniel went to Arioch, whom the king had appointed to destroy the wise men of Babylon; he went and said thus to him, "Do not destroy the wise men of Babylon bring me in before the king, and I will show the king the interpretation." Then Arioch brought in Daniel before the king in haste, and said thus to him, "I have found among the exiles from Judah a man who can make known the king the interpretation." The king said to Daniel, whose name was Belteshazar, "Are you able to make known to me the dream that I have seen and its interpretation?" Daniel answered the king, "No wise men, enchanters, magicians or astrologers can show to the king the mystery which the king as asked, but there is a God in heaven who reveals mysteries, and he has made known to King Nebuchadnezzar what will be in the later days. Your dream and the visions of your head as you lay in bed are these; To you, O king, as you lay in bed came thoughts of what would be hereafter, and He who reveals mysteries made known to you what is to be.

Daniel proceeded to describe the dream. Basically the dream about the statue of Nebuchadnezzar in gold, silver and bronze and clay and iron that went down was basically talking about the four kingdoms. Daniel himself was involved. He was involved in the first kingdom in the Babylonian kingdom. In the end he was promoted to be the Prime Minister over the whole entire empire. In the kingdom of the Medes and the Persian, Daniel again continued in the high position. So he was involved in some ways with that dream. Later on in his life notice that the visions that he received that were symbolic about all the animals related to him being in that position. So in other words when God gives you a dream if it is from the Lord it would directly or indirectly but in a closely knitted was have to do with your involvement in it. A dream is not only just given for your entertainment.

We talked about three types of dreams and we are only concerned with the **parabolic dream.** The other two types of dreams don't need any interpretation. But parabolic dreams are dreams that are in symbols. So symbolic dreams are the hardest to interpret that is why we are teaching on those symbolic dreams. So the first thing we mentioned that God will use something. In the last message we talked about how God will use symbols in society to speak onto us. Like in Pharaoh's time in Genesis 41 cows and cattle are the symbol of prosperity in their days. So God use those symbols to speak to Pharaoh. Today cows are not necessarily symbols of prosperity any more. There are other symbols of prosperity and God will use the symbols that we understand today. Remember that symbols change with time. Something that is symbol of prosperity long ago may no longer be a symbol of prosperity today. God will speak to us something current that we can understand. So the interpretation of dreams is not so way out that we have to go back into long historical time. But it is always in terms of something we understand today.

The first factor is that the dreams that we receive from the Holy Spirit has to do with our life and our position and what we are involved with.

Sometimes it could be like Joseph a seventeen boy and you never understand how that will one day his dreams will come to pass. There is no natural way he could think of. He was only seventeen years old having such a dream. That is why the father scolded him. There is no natural way that Joseph could know how that could come to pass. But yet when God gives a dream it was because he was directly going to be involved in that. Those dreams were going to come to pass in his life. So when God gives a dream it would involve you directly. So the next time you have a dream don't come and say to somebody else and say I dreamed about you and it involved you. If you dream about somebody else then perhaps you may have something to do with that. God is not going to just give you a dream so that you know about a person that's all. God doesn't waste time like that. When He gives a dream you are directly or indirectly involved maybe through prayer, maybe through an active role like Daniel was involved in those kingdoms that he dreamt about. He had a very active role in the rule and reign of those kingdoms. So when you have dreams from the Holy Spirit there will always be a direct involvement with you.

I was thinking of not sharing these other areas but I felt in my spirit that I must touch a little bit on that too just to make it clear. The dreams from the Holy Spirit are clear-cut and they follows the same rules that we talked about in hearing the voice of the Holy Spirit. The voice of the Holy Spirit, the voice of the human spirit and the inward witness are different. There are five inward witnesses, and the voice of the human spirit is in a category by itself and it is just like the normal flow of things. Remember one of the rules of the voice of the Holy Spirit is that before the Holy Spirit speaks, it is always accompanied by His presence. See God speaks all the time through our human spirit. Our human spirit can pick up all kind of things. But when the Holy Spirit speaks there is a presence that comes with it. You know that His presence is there. In the same way dreams of the Holy Spirit carries that same kind of presence. You may wake up immediately after the dream although its 3 a.m. or it will be distinct in you that you will remember. Sometimes like Nebuchadnezzar's case he forgot about it but he knew that it was important.

Dreams can be caused as you see in the book of Ecclesiastes from our daily activities.

That is from our soul or from our human spirit. Dreams from the soul realm are more the daily activities of things as well as what I call soul contact. Dreams from our soul can come from our daily activities or from sensitivity to various things around us. One time when I was sharing that in our overnight prayer somebody mistook that and took it in a wrong way. So it is very dangerous sometimes when I share some of these things. Anything you take out of context you can make some heresy out of it. Please take it contextually. If I take somebody's shirt or personal belonging and put it under my pillow and I sleep on it, I would be able to pick up a person's strength, weaknesses and characteristics from that person's shirt or belonging. It has nothing to do with the Holy Spirit or the human spirit in that sense. But it has to do with what I call soul contact. For example if that person is a person full of fear or perhaps that person is an orphan, and insecurity, and loneliness are there. And I take that person's shirt and put it under my pillow and sleep on it, in my dreams under normal circumstances I would pick up loneliness, fear and insecurity. These are things that I may not be involved with directly. How it comes in a dream would be what I call a mirror effect of the soul. Like I would feel myself in a situation in that dream I would be lonely, in despair, which is never a part of my experience at all. How did I pick up from the soul?

To help you understand the scientific application of this, let us take our body odour. The dogs can pick it up in the natural. You sit in your seat and I bring a trained dog and that dog can pick up where you sat. With our nose we cannot pick that up. Now there is a sort of body odour in the soul. If you enter a home the atmosphere of the soul is there in objects and in that person's place. That doesn't mean that when you take second-hand objects you say Oh dear what kind of soul that person has. Thank God for the blood of Jesus it can cleanse all influences. The blood of Jesus can cleanse all soul influences. The reason I say this is because it's a possibility of that affecting dreams. In the dream realm in the soul you could pick that up. Even if somebody comes and stay in my house I could pick up everything from him. Or perhaps I go and stay in your house I could pick up everything in the house. At first I was wondering why I was so sensitive to all these things.

Then you could have dreams that come from your spirit man.

Dreams caused by your spirit are different. Dreams that are caused by your spirit are self-analytical. In other words your spirit man will expose you. You could wear a mask in front of people and hide and put a good front. For example if you have an inner insecurity about something, you will always find it recurring in your dream. It is a self-analytical dream. Your spirit man judges you. Your spirit man points the weaknesses in your own character in order to help you. I won't call those dreams from the Holy Spirit not directly but maybe indirectly. But directly they are not from the Holy Spirit. They are not dreams that are the voice and the Word of God from the Holy Spirit. They are just your human spirit picking things up. In a normal way as in your conscious life your human spirit picks up things and your soul picks up things in your conscious mind. How much more in the sub-conscious life the soul picks up things and our spirit picks up things. So those are what we mean by spirit and soul caused dreams. They are totally different category.

I am talking about dreams from the Holy Spirit. Those are word and a message from God. When God specially give a word or a message usually it is in regard to things to come in the future. Notice that dreams from the human spirit tends to be self-revealing of your present and your past. It gives you a better analysis than your mind no matter how great your I.Q is. Dreams caused from the soul tend to be more exterior stimuli caused from the exterior realm. So dreams directly from the Holy Spirit would still be limited to draw illustrations from your life. If you have been a farmer there is a possibility that He would draw that from your experience to speak about an area in your life in the future. He would possibly and definitely not suddenly draw an illustration from fishing. He draws illustration from your life to speak to you in those areas. If you have been brought up in the city like my children to see a cow is a joy. You are used to buses and noises God will pull it up from your life to make a message out of that in regard to you. He will usually give you dreams from your background.

The other point there is such a thing as a gift of interpretation.

There is such a thing as a sensitivity to the dream realm and the spirit realm. Some people are born with an inherent sensitivity to that. Usually those who are called to be prophets, those who are called to the ministry have a tendency and inborn sensitivity to that kind of realm. So there is such a thing as a gift of dream a dreamer of dreams. And some people have inherent abilities to flow in visions and dreams.

Then on the other hand there is also the gift of the interpretation of dreams. Let's look at the book of Daniel chapter 1:17;

As for these four youths, God gave them learning and skill in all letters and wisdom; and Daniel had understanding in all visions and dreams.

Notice he had a specific gift in that area. It is interesting to note that even Joseph in the book of Genesis had that same gift. It's a gift for the interpretation of dreams. That means that we could pray for God to give us that gift. We have not because we ask not. You could pray and ask God for that special gift to interpret dreams and visions. Not just to receive. It's a gift also to receive it. It is another separate gift to interpret those dreams. Joseph perfected the interpretation of dreams in his life. During his days in prison he could just pick up the interpretation straight away when the butler and the baker called him. And it is because of the gift of the interpretation of dreams that he was brought before Pharaoh. Your gift makes room for you. You have to perfect your gift before your gift makes room for you. So the ability to receive dreams is one. The ability to interpret dreams is another.

And thirdly the ability to apply interpretation is a different category.

You may have the ability to interpret but you may not have the wisdom to apply them. That's a different category altogether. In Genesis chapter 41 after the interpretation of Pharaoh's dream in verse 33 *Now therefore let Pharaoh select a man discreet and wise, and set him over the land of Egypt.* Now this is not part of the interpretation. He had actually completed the interpretation. The interpretation of Pharaoh's dream means seven years of prosperity followed by seven years of famine. He need not have to apply further than the interpretation. But here he moved into what I call application. He says let Pharaoh select a wise man set him over the land of Egypt.

Let Pharaoh proceed to appoint overseers over the land, and take the fifth part of the produce of the land of Egypt during the seven plenteous years. And let them gather all the food of these good years that are coming, and lay up grains under the authority of Pharaoh for food in the cities, and let them keep it. That food shall be a reserve for

Understanding Prophetic Dreams & Visions

the land against the seven years of famine which are to befall the land of Egypt, so that the land may not perish through the famine.

What would you have done if you have a dream? In the dream you see your friend getting into an airplane. And the airplane takes off. Then halfway along its flight the airplane knocks into a high mountain and crashes. You see your friend parachuting down safe and sound. What would have been your interpretation? Secondly, what would have been your application? Most people react to dreams like that with shock and they get in a state of stupor. Most people will take it as the actual type of dream, meaning it will be actually happen.

There are three types of dreams. The first thing you have to do is to determine what classification. Is it parabolic, is it message or is it an actual? Actual means that it will actually happen. Message means that whatever the dream is there is only one key message. Parabolic means everything is in symbols. Most people will come to that friend and ask, "Are you about to fly in an airplane?" If his answer is yes, they will say to him, "Please don't go." They are interpreting it as an actuality, which may not be the case. Or perhaps somebody has a vision and in that vision they see failure all over. Perhaps they see themselves launching into this boat to go fishing. There they are with three fellows. Those three fellows happen to be the exact three fellows in their business relationship. So they see four of them getting into the boat into the Straits of Malacca. He sees the four of them letting out the net. Then as they pull the net halfway here comes a shark. The shark comes and cuts out a big hole in the net. They pull out the net and there was nothing left in the net. Then they say therefore that is saying to them not to go into business together. That's what normally people take. They take the simplified application. That may not be the case. See the yes and no is not there. It is only what will happen.

In a similar way as Acts 21 when Agabus the prophet came and prophesy over Paul, he took his belt tied himself and says this thing will happen to this man. He did not say yes or no to go. All he said was what will happen. But most people take dreams to be simplified yes or no. It is not the way to apply dreams. So you cannot take dreams to be simplified things yes or no. That's not the way to interpret dreams. What about Pharaoh since he saw those things that happened? He saw the seven fat cows and seven lean cows. What does he do? Get into a frenzy and say, "Oh no this is going to happen," and just leave it there? No, it is not the simplified yes-no situation. That's where the application of the interpretation comes in. The interpretation may be for example if a person has a dream about those four fellows going out and pulling out the net and the net got cut off. It is not yes or no. Maybe that God is telling them about dangers that are coming ahead. It may be God wants them to continue. See in the dream they didn't disperse yet. God is warning them about danger that may be coming and that they must be ready to face it. And possibly they could apply in the same way like Pharaoh. Perhaps right now the four partners in their business are doing very well that they got surplus in their bank accounts. Perhaps what God is telling them is a warning, not that they are supposed to call it quits.

A dream is sometimes a vision and prophecy as such that is so easy to misinterpret and misapply the whole thing altogether contrary to what God intended.

A person could take it and say God wants me to get out of this business quickly. Sell all his shares and get out of the business, which God may not want or intended in that dream. That's what I call people who take dreams to be in guesswork, a yes no situation. It is not that way. But what God could be warning regarding a shark that is coming. Who knows it could be a loan shark. God may be just speaking about an area to say not to go into that area. Not to go into an area is different from not going into the business altogether. You have to isolate areas from the whole business altogether.

Let say the dream about this friend of ours who is going on a flight. The most probable person who can have that kind of dream is his wife. It is very unlikely that a stranger would come and say that I had this dream about you. It is different from a person who is in the five-fold office as a prophet. That may be different. Usually they may see vision of that. But then even if they see those visions, God may want them to do something with that person. See there is always a relationship. Let's say there is such a thing as the mountain and the plane. If it is perhaps a symbolic dream, God may be just speaking to him about the impending danger that is coming. Just to be aware of those dangers, that's all.

The first thing when you have a dream classify it as to whether it came from your spirit, soul or Holy Spirit.

After you classified it, if it is in the category of Holy Spirit or human spirit then you can continue to take notice. If it is in the category of the soul you could still use it to your advantage. You could reveal the things that are in the other person. I remember in those days when we started the ministry, I was sleeping on the sae bed with another brother and it happened that somehow in the middle of the night his toes and mine made contact. And I had dreams that were not peculiar to anything I experienced neither in my childhood nor in my present experience. When I woke up in the morning I was wondering what was all these dreams. As I was examining it I found my toes were contacting this person. I found out that I was picking up everything of that person's soul. So I waited till the other brother woke up. I sat him in the chair and say these are all the weaknesses in your life. He says, "Yes how do you know?" That is what I call soul influence. So if you classify correctly you could use all these things to your advantage.

Then after you classified it you could now analyse it. If it were from the Holy Spirit then you would be able to put the laws of interpretation to it. If it is from the Holy Spirit there are the most important. Write down the dreams the Holy Spirit gives to you. If it is dreams from the Holy Spirit apply the laws of interpretation. You realize that whatever it is you will be directly involved with it. So you must write it down. Usually there is a message and then the three areas. Then even after you have the interpretation you need the application, which is a different thing. You got to pray for this area. Sometimes you have the right interpretation but no application. You are still left hanging. Notice that when Joseph applied the dreams that Pharaoh had, he was not asked to do it. But the wisdom of God in his life caused him to apply. If it were a dream from the soul it is more revelation that you know that you picked up something in the soul realm from the other person. But if it is in the realm of the human spirit it is for you to analy

CHAPTER TEN

THE FOUR REALMS OF DREAM

Natural Dreams Versus Spiritual Dreams

In the category of dreams, it is important to note the difference between a natural dream and a spiritual dream. You see, dreams can be caused from your daily activities or they can be caused from the spirit realm. As is mentioned here in the book of Job 33 that God does speaks through dreams. And dreams are one of the most primary easy modes for God to operate and lead and guide our life. My life has been led by dreams all along the way. Dreams play the first category and open way where God communicate to us, even to some unbelievers who have not come to know God yet. This is a general statement in Job 33. It's a general statement that says that God in His mercy, God in His compassion does guide and lead believers and unbelievers through dreams. We can classify dreams as one of the leadings of the Holy Spirit. It's the working of the Holy Spirit. Like Pharaoh king of Egypt was led and guided by a dream. He had a dream that was important but he did not understand what it means.

Many at times there are people who had dreams that they don't understand what it means. And I know that in the world there are some psychological teachings on interpretation of dreams. I am not ignorant of them; I am aware of them. Some of the interpretations are way out and they are not scriptural. If you are an intellectual and you have gone through Sigmund Freud's theories, you will find that he is a psychoanalyst. The problem with Freud is that he only has a natural interpretation of all dreams. In fact he thinks that all dreams flow from mainly the erotic realm. If we put him to the test in Job 33 he would fail the test because he completely excludes the fact that there is a spirit realm. And God communicate in the spirit realm to us. So, that is also another wrong understanding of dreams in this natural.

Understanding Prophetic Dreams & Visions

Dreams can come from the natural realm or the spiritual realm. Now dreams can come from the natural realm tend to be a working of your human spirit and soul. I am excluding dreams that come from the demonic realm. It's not supposed to be a part of the Christian life. If it is ever in our life then it is easily dealt with by confessing to God and a short prayer and meditation on the Word before you sleep will do. Understand your authority as a believer and the power of the blood of Jesus. Jesus promised His beloved sleep. That's in the book of Proverbs. He gave His beloved sleep Proverbs chapter 3. Prov. 3:24 *When you lie down, your sleep will be sweet.* So we rule out the demonic realm if the blood of Jesus covers us. The demonic realm has no interference.

So the only two realms that we have time to deal with is what we call natural dreams and spiritual dreams. Natural dreams come from your daily activities. Every day when you have activity your subconscious mind and your spirit rearranges it. The microprocessor keeps rearranging and putting it into the right slot. That is what I call a natural activity. In the book of Ecclesiastes chapter 5:3 *For a dream comes with much business, and a fool's voice with many words.* Notice that a dream comes through much activity. Verse 7 says *For when dreams increases, empty words grow many; but do you fear God?* This is by Solomon one of the wisest man in the East in his days. He understood the significance of dreams that they come through much activities. This explains that even if you have had dreams, that won't increase your fear of God. Such dreams come from soulish and physical activity and will have little bearing on your spiritual life. They could not be from God since they do not increase the fear of God in you.

There are dreams that come from our subconscious and spirit man aligning together. The language of the spirit man is in visions and dreams, and both are in picture forms. You arrange that in your life every time you go through activities. That form of dream is more for your private edification. It exposes you. For example, you could put up a front in your conscious life, where outwardly you are very outgoing and very sociable and cheerful and you put on a front; in front of people you wear a mask. We all know how to do that. Our conscious mind is very clever to put our image before people. But you have what I call a dual life. Behind inside your conscience and inside your heart you feel lonely, you feel inferior, and you feel dejected and rejected inside your heart and inside your life your true self is hidden from people.

The interesting thing about your dreams is that you cannot hide your true self from yourself. In your dreams who you really are stands out. If outwardly you look like a brave man, in your dreams you are actually afraid. Every single dream you have is one of your inner fears. If outwardly you look like a very upright person with good social life and no apparent weakness in your life but inwardly you know you have. In your dreams you are exposed - it comes out. You cannot hide from yourself in your dream. Who you really are what you really are comes forth and stands out. That's what I call a natural dream. They are useful to a certain extend. They are not used for leading. They are useful to understand your inner self. We must understand our inner self. We must understand what our main weaknesses and strong points are. Your dreams will expose them to you so that you are aware of them and you could deal with them. Each time as you grow and your character develops your dreams also improve. So the dreams come through much activity in your life. Every time when you sleep it has to process the whole thing. What you experienced consciously has to be processed every day. Although some people say they never have dreams, yet they do but they don't remember them. Every person has dreams. And of course unless it is important you would remember them. Otherwise it is not quite so important. So everyone practically has dreams. But there are some who don't remember anything. Those are what I call natural dreams.

Natural dreams are useful for self-analysis. Only the spirit of man will know what is in the man. Even our conscious mind does not know what your true self is. Our conscious mind can be so trained to ignore certain things. But the bible says in I Cor. 2 that the spirit of a man within him knows what is inside the person. So your spirit has the most accurate perception of yourself. Each one of you right now has a perception of yourself in your conscious mind. But the most true and accurate perception is in your spirit man. As we renew our mind what our spirit man perceive is translated into our conscious mind. Then you have a true estimation and judgment of yourself, where you are heading, where you are right now, where you have been. We must live our lives in such a way that what is inside and outside is one and not be a double character.

Understanding Prophetic Dreams & Visions

Having seen what a natural dream and activity is like we want to see what a spiritual dream and activity is like. Those are what we classify as messages from God. The Holy Spirit speaks to us. It's just like in the conscious realm we all have thoughts all the time. Some of our thoughts come from our soul; some of our thoughts come from our spirit man. Other thoughts do some times come from the enemy. But there are some thoughts that are strong and clear with a ring of authority and presence of God which are the thoughts of the Holy Spirit. That's the conscious realm. In the subconscious realm there are dreams that are the result of the activity of the soul and there are dreams that are the result of the activity of the spirit and both are linked together. But there are some dreams that are very authoritative with a measure of God's presence involved. Usually you will remember those dreams. You may even get right immediately after those dreams for no apparent reason. Only those dreams are classified as leadings of the Holy Spirit. Dreams directly instigated by the Holy Spirit with a message. Why does God speak in dreams? There are many things that God could not convey to our conscious mind while we are awake. As a result God has to wait until we are asleep then He speaks to us in a dream. That is one of the major ways that God communicate. Don't neglect that.

Conscious Dreams Versus Subconscious Dreams

For God may speak in one way, or in another; yet man does not perceive it. In a dream, in a vision of the night, when deep sleep falls upon men, while slumbering on their beds, then He opens the ears of men, and seals their instruction. In order to turn man from his deed, and conceal pride from man, He keeps back his soul from the Pit and his life from perishing by the sword (Job 33: 14-18).

Notice here that it says God speaks once then twice. In other words He speaks many times to us. But here he talks about God's system of speaking. I believe we could divide all the various messages into two major areas. One while we are conscious and second while we are sub-conscious. While we are conscious we can hear God speaks through our inward voice of our human spirit, the voice of the Holy Spirit and all supernatural leadings. While we are sub-conscious or while we are asleep God still continue to speak through dreams.

But here the Bible calls it the visions of the night. We have considered different types of dreams.

Here we are looking into greater details. So here it says God speaks once then twice we can divide it into sub-conscious and conscious. When we are neglecting the direction we have received when we are conscious, then He brings to us the secondary line of defence. That will prevent us from going astray. He mentioned three purposes of dreams here: that He is to conceal pride from our life, to keep us from the Pit and to preserve us from perishing by the sword. So, He talks about protecting like the second line of defence. God puts roadblocks to preventing us from falling into evil. The devil's roadblocks and God's roadblocks are different. The devil's roadblocks are to block you from the right way. God's roadblocks are to block you from the wrong way. It's not that easy to fall away from God if you understand God's grace.

Look at the story of Adam and Eve, the story of mankind. Though man has chosen to disobey God yet God's hand keeps reaching down to man. He places road blocks that the moment you go against one there is a signal in the spirit realm and as you keep going against it you will notice that there are many, many warnings along the way before you reached a point when God says that's enough. So, God does place roadblocks and lines of defence to prevent us from going out of His ways. These are the negative aspects of Job 33: 14- 18, which we covered in our earlier messages. Let's take the positive side What happens when you are sensitive in your conscious life to God's direction? We have considered the other aspects when you are disobedient to God's direction while we are awake then the dreams are important. But the opposite side of it is that when we obeying God in our conscious life in the voice of the Holy Spirit. When we are obeying God in all these areas what happens during the dream life? Your dream life takes on a greater dimension. It is almost like that there are two dimensions to our dream life. One when we are disobedient they serve as lines of defence, roadblocks to prevent us from falling deeper into the wrong areas. The other dimension seems to be what I call an avenue of spiritual fellowship and relationship with God when we are obeying God in our conscious life.

Understanding Prophetic Dreams & Visions

Let's first look at the gospel of Matthew. There are three separate incidences that we will consider. The journey of Jesus Christ our Lord is marked by dreams from its very inception:

Now the birth of Jesus Christ took place in this way. When His mother Mary had been betrothed to Joseph, before they came together she was found to be with child of the Holy Spirit; and her husband Joseph, being a just man and unwilling to put her to shame, resolved to send her away quietly. But as he considered this, behold, an angel of the Lord appeared to him in a dream, saying, "Joseph, son of David, do not fear to take Mary your wife, for that which is conceived in her is of the Holy Spirit (Mathew 1:18).

If you remember what we said that it's important to understand the context of the dream: the situations, the circumstances and the situations that precede it in order to have for a proper interpretation. Now here is also an incident where Joseph the night before he slept was thinking about something. And that something which he thought about was affecting his life so much that in a dream God had to speak to him about his last thought before he slept. It is the same with Nebuchadnezzar. Daniel said, "Oh king, you were thinking about what will come to pass after your kingdom before you slept." Then God spoke to him and gave him the marvellous dream about that statue that represents the four Empires and all the other sub-Empires. So the thoughts that we sleep with are important. In case you are first time here we also mentioned about how there are laws of the interpretation of dreams. Symbols that are scriptural must be following their meaning in the bible. Then there is difference in symbols. Symbols that mean something to you will mean something different to me. Then before I interpret I must know what those symbols mean to you. Otherwise if I interpret the symbols what it means to me it may give you a percentage of error.

Now, here is Joseph who is about to sleep. There is a difference here. He was thinking about putting away Mary. I would think that any ordinary righteous man would think about that. I mean who will believe a story like that? But Joseph had a thought over inside him. He loved her. And then suddenly he knew this faint bible prophecy about some Messiah but he would never expect it to come that way. I mean it's not clear to a Hebrew mind that the Messiah would come through a virgin birth. But the truth of the virgin birth was obscure to them. Before he slept he was thinking what to do. One side he was saying that he loves her and wants to keep her. The other side of him was saying that no she could be lying. So he is wrestling within himself. And in that kind of condition he managed to sleep. And in that dream it was not a figurative symbolic dream it was a direct dialog. He saw an angel; the angel just told him this is of God. There was no need for interpretation since this was a direct dialog. That is what I call the other second dimension of dream. It says here in verse 19 *Joseph was a righteous man*. He always sought to obey God in his conscious life. It says he was just, he was righteous, and he always sought to do the right thing. That is the reason why he was thinking of those things.

It's just like the story of Jonah. Some people think that Jonah ran away from God because he did not believe God. It was not so. He believes what God said. And a lot of people are running away from God and they say, "I am like Jonah I am just running away from God." They are frightened of circumstances; they are frightened of this and that. Jonah went away because he believes God. He believes that God was going to send judgment on Nineveh. He ran away because he knew that. He knew that God was going to send judgment. He ran away because he wanted that judgment to happen. Towards the end of the book of Jonah after the judgment didn't come, he got angry with God. So when God says I am going to judge Nineveh, he said, "Good Lord." But then when God says now you go and tell them that judgment is coming and warn them, he said, "No Lord." He believed God that is why he ran away.

So, Joseph was thinking what he was thinking because of the commandments of God's Word. Never before had he had heard such a thing. All the righteous training within him and the just training within him rose up. He would seemingly go against what he is hearing from Mary. And because of his righteous state and in a sense his righteous thought God spoke to him. He was seeking to obey God all he knew how. In his conscious state he was seeking to obey God as much as he knew how to. Therefore the second dimension of dream took place. It is a dimension that I call a direct line with God even in a dream state. The angel appeared to him. The word *appeared* comes from the word that talks about a light that comes to shine so clearly. And in that context the spiritual realm was real to Joseph.

Understanding Prophetic Dreams & Visions

This is not the first time. In chapter 2 verse 13 same angel.

Now when they had departed, behold, an angel of the Lord appeared to Joseph in a dream and said, "Rise take the child and his mother, and flee to Egypt, and remain there till I tell you; for Herod is about to search for the child to destroy him."

Third dream after Herod died in verse 19 *But when Herod died, behold, an angel of the Lord appeared in a dream to Joseph in Egypt, saying, "Rise, take the child and his mother, and go to the land of Israel, for those who sought the child's life are dead.* "Then in verse 22 *And when he heard that Archelaus reigned over Judea in place of his father Herod, he was afraid to go there, and being warned in a dream he withdrew to the district of Galilee.* Fourth dream.

If Joseph had not believe in dreams the whole New Testament story would have been different. In most books on dreams today because of humanism they believe that dreams are just what Ecclesiastes says activity of life. Human beings go through different stages of sleep. The first stage is there are certain sleep patterns that they could measure by electrical activities in the brain. Then there is another stage that is deep sleep. Then there is also another stage called the R.E.M. stage or rapid eye movement stage. And it is at R.E.M. sleep that a person has dreams. And it seems that it is repeated about three or four times during a sleep. And there is a difference in that level of R.E.M. sleep. It reached a stage of brain activity where it's the same brain activity as if you are awake. Just judging by the graph that the brain scan records, they would have judged that the person was awake. But yet that person is asleep. But the brain activity was that much. So their theory is that it is just the brain analysing or going through the motions of experiencing the dream as if it is happening in real life.

These doctors and physiologists know that R.E.M. is more prominent even in unborn child. Before a child is born, before a child even experience human activity, the child in the womb has a high level of R.E.M. higher than adults. Then after a certain stage in the child development, the foetus slowly before birth reaches the normal human stage of R.E.M. But the major development of a foetus is R.E.M. So most of these physiologists could not explained the brain activity of a foetus because they are humanist and their theory was that this R.E.M. sleep comes from your daily activity and the brain is just re-organizing the data that you input every day. But they couldn't explain the little baby because that little baby doesn't have much data input at all but it does so much R.E.M. These so-called brilliant physiologists have this theory from the humanist point of view. This theory was that the R.E.M. sleep is just the brain testing all its circuits. Just like when you build a computer before you market it you test it. So from this point of view they say that as the brain of the foetus is being formed that the body is testing the whole system. As each part is being made so the body goes through all these tests before the child is born.

But from God's Word we have a different understanding. My understanding is there is a certain level that R.E.M. sleep depending on the spiritual state of a person that you relate to the spirit world. Children and babies before the age of accountability are saved. Their spirits are alive. Their spirits have not died yet because they do not know sin. They are innocent. There are enough scripture in the bible to tell us that babies are saved. John the Baptist in the womb was filled with the Spirit. He can't be filled with the Spirit unless he was saved. David when his child died said that he cannot come to me but "I go to him," implying that the child was saved. There are other passages in Psalms too. We know that a foetus and a baby who has not done one single act in life yet is saved. Because the child is saved the spirit of the child is alive. Before a child is born from our Christian viewpoint the R.E.M. sleep relates to the spirit world. A major portion of the R.E.M. sleep relate to the spirit world. But when the child grows into an adult and lives a life of sin and is disobedient to God, the second dimension is restricted and he or she would just have the first dimension of dreams that just warn them all the time. So all the dreams are reduced to what I call the superficial level of just warning. But there is a higher level of dream life that you move into. This is what we call a spiritual dialog, a spiritual fellowship and a spiritual relationship with God where you directly contact the spirit world. Just like the angel contacted Joseph through his dreams four times to protect the life of Jesus. Joseph could never have seen the angel with his eyes.

In fact in the New Testament there are two major Greek words for the word *appear*. One is from the Greek word *optomai* and it means to see with the physical eyes. The other is the word *phaino* where you see it like just a light coming to you. And of course it ties back to spiritual life. It is from the word that is sometimes called *manifest*. It could be a manifestation in the spirit realm. Right now there are angels around but we don't see them. But as we have taught how to be led by the Spirit you can train your conscious state to be conscious of them. In the same way in the dream life there is a stage where in the second dimension you can have a deeper dimension dream that is God's original dimension. This is where you contact the spirit world all the time. In your dream state the higher level of your mind is working. Your conscious mind is only about 5 to 10 percent of your mind. But when you are asleep it goes into deeper levels of your brain.

As we have understood from God's Word the mind of man originally was able with its physical senses to see the spiritual world as the natural world. Before the fall Adam and Eve could see the spirit world and the natural world. If an angel was there they saw the angel. Something happened after the fall. Their physical eyes were still opened but their spiritual eyes were closed. Before the fall, all the time they were physically naked, but they were not conscious of their nakedness. It was because all the time their spiritual eyes were opened and they only saw the spiritual garment over their physical bodies. But when they sinned, their spirit man died and their spiritual eyes were closed; hence they could not see any more spiritual clothing over their bodies, and that was why suddenly they saw themselves naked.

That is why in the fallen state where our bodies are not redeemed yet we naturally cannot see the spirit world. But that is not the way God made man. Our minds were not made to see natural things only. Our minds were originally created to be able to contact the spirit world just as easily as reaching out to touch the one next to you. Somehow that remnant of that mind that God made is still functioning in our dream state. When we are asleep the mind goes into its lower deeper consciousness and there is a point where it is contacting the spirit realm good or evil. For Joseph four times he contacted that angel. These were not the only times in the bible. Let's look at the book of Genesis chapter 15 the life of Abraham. Abraham received a powerful prophecy regarding his descendants; that nations that will arise after him. In Genesis chapter 15 here is an important situation where God cut a covenant with him. But if you study it very deeply you will notice that the whole thing took place while he was asleep. Gen. 15:12 *As the sun was going down, a deep sleep,* interestingly today sleep researchers consider R.E.M. sleep as deep sleep. Abraham was in deep sleep. *And behold horror and great darkness fell upon him.* It looks like a nightmare but it was not because God was showing him the future. And God here was speaking with him and cutting a covenant with him. In verse 13 He said to Abraham,

> *Know of a surety that your descendants will be sojourners in a land that is not theirs, and will be slaves there, and they will be oppressed for four hundred years; but I will bring judgment on the nation which they serve, and afterward they shall come out with great possessions. As for yourself, you shall go to your fathers in peace; you shall be buried in a good old age. And they shall come back here in the fourth generation for the iniquity of the Amorites is not yet complete. When the sun had gone down and was dark, behold, a smoking fire pot and a flaming torch passed between these pieces.*

All these happened when Abraham was sleeping. It's a powerful promise that he received. That is the same category as we classify as second dimension. How did Abraham get into the second dimension? We are beginning to see some of the laws involved. We must be obedient to God as far as we know how in our conscious life. If we are not obedient to God as we know how in our conscious life the second dimension doesn't operate. Your dream stage is in the first dimension, which is covered in the last two teachings. The second dimension does not operate yet if you do not have obedience in the conscious state. What kind of obedience? Obedience to the inward witness of your spirit, obedience to the inward voice of your human spirit, obedience to the voice to the Holy Spirit who instructs you from time to time. When you are obedient in that area then you reach to the second dimension of dreams. And of course you also reject, renounce, and flee from keep away from sin and anything of the devil, even things that may not be categorized as sin but may nurture desires for sin. Apparently Joseph was a righteous man and that would mean he also kept away from appearances of evil.

In our modern culture and civilization today, watching a movie may not be classified as sin but it is one of those things that may lead to sin. In movies there may be tendencies and inclinations towards sin that the average Christian may not consider as sin. But if we occupy our minds with these thoughts and images from these movies, it may prevent us from going to the second dimension of dream. This is why there are few today in our modern world that goes into the second dimension of dream. Of course even in the conscious state we know that not all Christians are led by the Spirit, they move in and out of the Spirit into the flesh realm. Not all Christians are obedient to their inward witness and to the inward voice of the human spirit that is instructing them in the affairs of life. I would say that they are in the minority today. For one thing if you have walked along with God you would have noticed that being led by the Spirit many times means that you do things that you cannot justify, you cannot explain, although you could in the natural but you are not allowed to. And you could be led by God to do things that are contrary to human experience. You would be misunderstood and that is your cross that you will have to carry. Being led by the Spirit is not easy in the natural although it's easy in the spirit. For that reason people rather go the easy way rather than the difficult road. Being led by the Spirit requires faith because we depend on God not on the things that we experience. We don't have to depend on those five senses.

So, here notice Abraham had to chase away the vultures. Now that is the symbol of driving away those things that would come against the sacrifices. There is an effort made in the conscious state. In other words, if God has spoken to you in the conscious level and you are obeying God as best you know how, and yet you are still hitting a wall. Believe me, God will do all He can to get through to you. If there are just a few minor tuning that you need it will come in your conscious state and in your dream state. So, here the background of what we have read was the Lord has spoken to him in verse 8 – 11;

But he said, "O Lord God, how am I to know that I shall possess it?" He said to him. "Bring me a heifer three years old, a she-goat three years old, a ram three years old, a turtledove, and a young pigeon." And he brought him all these, cut them in two and laid each half over against the other; but he did not cut the birds in two. And when birds of prey came down upon the carcasses, Abram drove them away.

I want you to know that that's a lot of work. Don't think that all he has to do is sit down and when vultures came he just drove them away. No those vultures are vicious birds. He would have to take a stick and hit them.

Finally after many hits he was tired. And he fell into deep sleep. Then God spoke. He made a conscious effort to keep those things for God. God told him to get Him the sacrifice. Now if God told him to get these sacrifices ready then Abraham would keep them for God and no vulture is going to get them. They are for God. He won't let anything else touch it. If God says your body is the temple of the Holy Spirit don't let any demon or devil touch it. If God says that something belongs to Him your zeal in protecting it must be demonstrated.

I am sure you remember the story in Moses' time when the Israelites were sinning and the others were crying in repentance and in the midst of the cry then comes one Israelite with his Midanite woman. Phinehas was so filled with zeal that he went straight to the tent and pierced the two of them with a spear and killed them instantly. (Numbers 25) Surprising God said, "Well done Phinehas." God is delighted with people who have zeal. This is not just Old Testament truth. This is also the New Testament in the book of Revelations. God said I rather you be rather hot or cold not in between. If you want to do something for God do it with all your heart. Don't do it half-heartedly.

The second point in getting into the second dimension of dreams is when we have shown zeal in our conscious state. People who are lackadaisical about their Christian life will never get into the second dimension. Why, they are just plain lazy in the things of God. So, why should God give additional revelation and spur them on? God has a way of encouraging us. When you have done all you can and put all that you have into obeying Him the world may be against you, everything in life could be against you and you need some encouragement, and no human come and encourage you God Himself will encourage you.

So, Abraham has zeal in chasing away the wrong things. One of the things that is prophesied about the Lord Jesus in the book of Hebrews 1:9 is *You have loved righteousness and hated lawlessness.* It is not good enough to just turn a blind eye to evil. It's a different thing to feel emotions against sin and evil and to eradicate it. Most people are complacent and in the state of apathy. They have no zeal for God, no anger for the devil and they are just nothing. Today if you want to be a bible-believing Christian who really wants to serve God and live all you know how to please God the world calls you a fanatic. Don't be so serious with God. Don't go that far with God. People want to pull you down when you want to reach further onto God.

There is one more case here we want to consider in the book of I Kings. All these are dreams in the second dimension. I Kings 3:3 *Solomon loved the Lord, walking in the statutes of David his father; only he sacrificed and burnt incense at the high places.* This is not speaking about those sacrifices offered to idols made of stone. Solomon was offering animal sacrifices to God on high places as were the custom of the Jews at that time since the Temple was not built yet. In verse 4 *And the king went to Gibeon to sacrifice there, for that was a great high place;* that confirms it. There were various places where they offer those animals as sacrifices to God. Because the Temple was not built yet only the ark was brought in. After the temple was built all sacrifices was supposed to be centred in Jerusalem. But before that only the ark was brought in. So they have several places that represented like the brazen altar. So here is one place at Gibeon and at Gibeon he sacrificed onto the Lord in verse 4 *Solomon used to offer a thousand burnt offerings upon the altar.* One thousand animals were sacrificed and that's a lot of work. Many people would have to help. A lot of blood was shed. That was a long worship service. Imagine one thousand animals, just to slaughter one takes quite some time. In those days you don't just kill the animals. You have to take out the parts of the animals, separate the fat from the kidney, and then burn only certain parts of each animal and you have to do it one thousand times. It takes a long time. After those sacrifices there was what we will call great effort. Solomon had not fallen away from God yet.

He was No. 1 obedient doing all that he knows how. He did all that he knows how to please God according to the law and according to the standards of those times. The temple was not built yet. It was acceptable to offer in those high places that were there. Secondly there was great effort made. If it says Solomon sacrifice that means Solomon paid for it. When those two things had taken place his obedience was implicit to all that he knew how. And secondly he had a great zeal for God; when he did something he did it well. That was before he grew old. When he was young he sought the Lord. He said when you want to do something for God do it well. If you want to build a temple let's get the best carpenters. Let's get the best wood. That was ingrained when he want to do something he did it well for God. The second point is definitely clear. He had a zeal for God. What's the different between zeal and just plain service? A plain service says as long as it is done its O.K. But it takes zeal is to do it to the best that you can. A normal service may not be your best. You know you could have done it better. But zeal comes when you give your best. Based on that I would reckon that there are very few Christians who have zeal.

Remember zeal is not just attending church service seven days a week. It is also your attitude in life in your work place. To me attending church service is very easy. Just sit, open your eyes, close your mouth and open your ears. Don't misunderstand me I have attended church seven days a week I know what it is like to have seven days of meeting on seven days. And go that way for years and years sometimes never having a break. I know that there is some element of zeal that is necessary too. There are some who only attend church services three times a year: Easter, Christmas and maybe a nephew's wedding. Some Christians may be attending church services seven days a week but when it comes to doing church work they have no zeal. In modern Christianity you could have seminars going on all the time. You could be a Seminar Christian, cruising from one seminar to another but never doing anything for God. If you have an assignment from God you do it and you have to pick your seminars carefully. The most important is be where God wants you to be and do it with all your heart. Zeal is doing your best for God and that's where the second dimension of dream comes.

At Gibeon the Lord appeared to Solomon in a dream by night; and God said, "Ask what I shall give you."

I want you to realize that is a dream. It's a dream where Solomon is relating to the spirit world. It is not just re-arranging data that has been implanted during the day. Solomon didn't receive his wisdom when a prophet laid hands on him. Solomon didn't receive his wisdom through David who laid hands on him although David would naturally have blessed him. Solomon didn't receive his wisdom through an angel appearing in a vision to him like the angel appearing to Mary. He received it in what human being would call the simplest of things in life in a dream. But it was real. That morning when he woke up there was something that was implanted into his life. Imagine going to sleep at night perhaps with an I.Q of 150 and waking up with an I.Q of 400. All because of one dream.

We may receive impartation from God in dreams when we have fulfilled the requirements in our conscious state. As we consider this dream in the second dimension, we realize now that besides interpretation of the first dimension dreams we have certain dreams that are actually of the second dimension. Although they may not be so frequent but they are there and we need to be aware of that. Some dreams are a direct spiritual dialogue. They are not symbolic at all. In no way is the angel symbolic. When Joseph woke up from the dream he did not wonder what that angel symbolize. If Joseph had interpreted Egypt as a symbol of the world and he took it that the dream merely warned him not to be so worldly, he would have stayed back where he was and die at the hands of Herod and his cohorts. It was no symbol. It was a real spiritual dialog with the spirit realm. So understand that there is an aspect of dreams in that category. And when it does occur we need to recognize them. If those things are symbolic and you don't interpret them as symbolic you may get a wrong interpretation. If those things are not symbolic and you interpret them as symbolic you also mess it up.

CHAPTER ELEVEN

UNDERSTANDING PROPHETIC VISIONS

And in the last days it shall be, God declares, that I will pour out my Spirit upon all flesh, and your sons and your daughters shall prophesy, and your young men shall see visions, and your old men shall dream dreams; yes, and on my menservants and my maid servants in those days I will pour out my Spirit; and they shall prophesy. And I will show wonders in the heaven above and signs on the earth beneath, blood and fire, and vapor of smoke; the sun shall be turned into darkness and the moon into blood before the day of the Lord comes, the great and manifest day. And it shall be that whoever calls on the name of the Lord shall be saved. (Acts 2:17).

As depicted in our opening scripture above, the Bible attests to the divine truth that when the Holy Spirit comes, He will cause young men to see *visions*. As aforementioned, a vision is a spiritual perception of supernatural realities that is communicated to a person in the natural realm. It is a supernatural picture or snapshot of what God wants you to see, do or become. We have already established in preceding chapters that the words *sons* and *daughters*, *young men* and *old men* do not just refer to physical age but a level of spiritual maturity. This has nothing to do with physical age because not all fathers are spiritual fathers since some are old when they are born again and they are spiritual babies as far as God is concerned. Taking the leadings from the epistle of John, in 1 John 2:12, the writer uses the words *children*, *young men* and *fathers* to illustrate the different levels of spiritual growth and spiritual maturity. In this context, the definition of *young men* speaks of Christians who are operating at the peak of their spiritual life, moving in the supernatural realm, walking in the depths of revelations of God's word, overcoming spiritual battles and living in the reality of the promises of God.

I am writing to you, young men, because you have overcome the evil one. I write to you, children, because you know the Father. I write to you, fathers, because you know him who is from the beginning. I write to you, young men, because you are strong, and the word of God abides in you, and you have overcome the evil one (1 John 2:12).

In view of the above, it is therefore scripturally evident that the phrase *young men* implies those who are mature in the things of God to a level whereby they are strong in the revelations of God's Word and have overcome the enemy. As we grow in our spiritual life we graduate from the stage of being children through the level of being young men to the level where we become spiritual fathers in the Lord. The other reason why our opening scripture does not refer to physical age is because we all know that its not only old men who dream dreams but young men also dream. In the first chapter of this book, we examined the word *dream* in the book of Acts and we found that it is not the usual word for *dream*. Instead, it's a special word that speaks about the consciousness of the vision of God, that fills your whole life, such that it even rest in the sub-conscious realm. The more you grow in the Lord, the more the vision of God consumes you. By the time you reach the spiritual age of a spiritual father, the vision of God would have saturated your life, even in the subconscious level.

THE THREE TYPES OF VISIONS

Basically, there are *three* types of visions: the *inner vision (spiritual vision)*, the *closed vision (trance)* and the *open vision,* all of which are part of the leadings of the Spirit of God. It is imperative that we know what they are in order that we can flow along with God's manifestation. An *open vision* is a vision where you could see physical things and at the same time see spiritual things and the veil that separates the natural world from the spiritual world is removed such that both realms of existence are visibly open to you. A *closed vision* is a vision in which your physical senses are completely closed up such that if somebody came and shook you while you are having the vision you wouldn't know. An *inner vision* is a vision in which you see inside the corridors of the canvas of your spirit such that when you are consciously awake and somebody touches you, you would be aware of it, as you see an inner picture that is shown to you.

To substantiate this categorization with reference to scriptural evidence, in the Torah account, Moses wrote that Balaam spoke of seeing God while in a closed vision (*trance*). In this context, the word *trance* is not in the original Hebrew text, but was added by the translators for better readability in English. However, both passages speak of Balaam seeing a "vision" with his "eyes open," which is called an *open vision*. An open vision enables the seer to peer beyond the heavenly veil, open a door into the spirit world, and pierce beyond the natural world into the celestial cosmos. When Daniel saw a vision or prophetic symbolism of future events, it occurred by one of two methods—either a *sleeping vision* or an open vision. A sleeping vision emerges when the visionary is fully asleep; yet the imagery they see appears three-dimensional and full of color, with all five senses (seeing, hearing smelling, touching and even tasting) being fully alert, just as though the visionary is fully awake and encountering a literal experience. Daniel spoke of receiving a "night vision" (Daniel 2:19), and a "vision by night" (Daniel 7:2), which was a visitation from God so clear, that the images were burnt into his mind while he was yet sleeping. The first two types of visions are not so common as they come as the Spirit wills, hence there is no training required. You could be a young Christian and yet experience either an open vision or closed vision. There is nothing you can do about it except to understand its interpretation, which we are going to see.

AN OPEN VISION

An open vision is a vision where you could see physical things and at the same time see spiritual things. A vision can become so tangible that at times it becomes difficult to distinguish the vision from real life (Acts 12:9-10). For example, if you were to experience an open vision where the Lord Jesus were to appear and stand in front of you and your eyes could see Him, at the same time you could see people around you. You are wide-awake and conscious yet you could see Him as if He was physically there. The word *open* is used is used in this context to speak about your physical senses being opened to the physical world while at the same time being opened to the spiritual world. An open vision can be so real that the spiritual things look as if they are physical. At times, you could hardly differentiate between the things you see in the spirit realm and those you see in the natural realm.

Understanding Prophetic Dreams & Visions

When the Holy Spirit gives you an open vision, your *dianoia* is more toward your inner realm of your sub-conscious soul. If you were having an open vision right now, you would be able to see the physical world and the spiritual world at the same time. Yet, you are more conscious of the spiritual than the physical. So, God is allowing you to experience the spiritual world and the natural world. You actually are quite close to this veil between the Holy Place and the Most Holy Place. You are conscious of the spirit realm while you are conscious of the natural realm at the same time. You are somewhere in between. That is why an open vision is between the lowest vision (inner vision) and the highest vision (close vision). If I were to tie a rope between the two veils, the rope would touch your consciousness which is somewhere in between. You are more conscious slightly of the spirit realm but you are also conscious of the natural realm. If somebody is running round, you could see the person running. If an angel were flying, you could also see the angel. But you are seeing and experiencing the physical world and the spiritual world at the same time. That is how an open vision operates.

One such controversial figure who had experiences of an open vision in the Bible is Balaam. In Numbers chapter 24, Balaam was identified as an Old Testament prophet who compromised and abused his prophetic gift for personal gain (Jude 11). One day he fell into a *trance* and saw a vision of God:

> *"And Balaam lifted up his eyes, and he saw Israel abiding in his tents according to their tribes; and the spirit of God came upon him. And he took up his parable, and said, Balaam the son of Beor hath said, and the man whose eyes are open hath said: He hath said, which heard the words of God, which saw the vision of the Almighty, falling into a trance, but having his eyes open."* (Numbers 24:2-4). *"And he took up his parable, and said, Balaam the son of Beor hath said, and the man whose eyes are open hath said: He hath said, which heard the words of God, and knew the knowledge of the most High, which saw the vision of the Almighty, falling into a trance, but having his eyes open."* (Numbers 24:15-16).

Do you notice that in the context of the above-mentioned scripture, it talks of Balaam seeing a vision while in a *trance, with his eyes open.* That means he experienced both a *trance (closed vision)* and an *open vision.* Do you notice that it says Balaam saw the vision of the Almighty in a *trance*? In the context of the above scripture, the word *trance* is not in the original Hebrew text, but was added by the translators for better readability in English. Do you also notice that it says Balaam saw the vision of the Almighty in an open vision? Balaam's experience would be classified as an open vision, because he saw a vision with his eyes opened. An open vision enables the seer to pierce beyond the heavenly veil, open a door into the spirit world, and pierce beyond the natural world into the celestial cosmos. For a prophetic seer or prophet to escape out of his visible surroundings, cut through the veil of eternity, and make the invisible visible, there must be a lifting or removing of some form of spiritual scales that cover the human eyes and blind the mind, just as Elisha's servant could not see the invisible army of horses and chariots of fire until Elisha prayed for his servant's eyes to be opened (2 Kings 6:15-17). To see the invisible, some type of blinders must lift from your eyes, and to hear the voice of God, the inner ears of the human spirit must be opened (Revelation 2:7). As for Balaam, he was in tune in all the three areas of vision at the same time: He heard the words of God, meaning his spiritual ears were opened (Numbers 24:15-16) He had knowledge of God, meaning that his spiritual mind was opened (Numbers 24:15-16). And he also saw the vision of God with his eyes opened, meaning his spiritual eyes were opened (Numbers 24:2-4). From birth, some people seem sensitive to spiritual matters and are able to discern activity in the spirit realm, both good and evil. Dreaming dreams that conceal the future or give spiritual instructions and warnings to others can be a gift and even be passed down through the family, as though part of the DNA.

When a prophet like Daniel saw a vision or prophetic symbolism of future events, it occurred by one of two methods—either a sleeping vision or an open vision. Immediately, he was caught up into the heavenly temple and later penned his apocalyptic scroll, revealing the things that are, and that will be in the future (Revelation 1:19). A closed or sleeping vision emerges when the visionary is fully asleep; yet the imagery they see appears three-dimensional and full of color, with all five senses of the seer—seeing, hearing smelling, touching and even tasting—being fully alert, just as though the visionary is fully awake and encountering a literal experience. Daniel spoke of receiving a "night vision" (Daniel 2:19), and a "vision by night" (Daniel 7:2), which was a visitation from God so clear, that the images were burnt into his min while he was yet sleeping. An example of an *open vision* is observed in Daniel 10. On the 24th day of the first month, Daniel and his companions were beside the river Hiddekel (the Tigris), when his eyes turned to see a vision of a man he described, recorded in Daniel 10:

"...behold a certain man clothed in linen, whose waist was girded with gold of Uphaz! His body was like beryl, his face like the appearance of lightning, his eyes like torches of fire, his arms and feet like burnished bronze in color, and the sound of his words like the voice of a multitude." (Daniel 10:5-6 (NKJV).

In the story, Daniel's companions saw nothing, but felt the presence of this angelic messenger as we read: *"...a great terror came over them and they fled to hide themselves"* (Daniel 10:7 (NKJV). Night visions during sleep are common among Biblical prophets, but an open vision, which transports a seer from the present scene to another dimension in an instant, is a unique and rare experience. Ezekiel experienced this, along with the Apostle John when he was a political prisoner surrounded by a watery sea on a desolate, rocky volcanic island called Patmos. John was suddenly "in the Spirit on the Lord's day" (Revelation 1:10).

To substantiate this revelation with reference to scriptural evidence, while Peter was in a prison waiting for trial, he experienced an *open vision*.

And behold, an angel of the Lord appeared, and a light shone in the cell, and he struck Peter on the side and woke him, saying, "Get up quickly." And the chains fell off his hands. And the angel said to him, "Dress yourself and put on your sandals," And he did so. And he said to him, "Wrap your mantle around you and follow me." And he went out and followed him, he did not know that what was done by the angel was real, but thought he was seeing a vision. When they had passed the first and the second guard, they came to the Iron Gate leading into the city. It opened to them of its own accord, and they went out and passed on through one street; and immediately the angel left him. And Peter came to himself, and said, "Now I am sure that the Lord has sent his angel and rescued me from the hand of Herod and from all the Jewish people were expecting." (Acts 12:5).

In the context of the above-mentioned scripture, it is evident that Peter experienced an *open vision*. How do we know it's an open vision? When he woke up first of all an angel touched him. He felt real for somebody shook him up. He was sound asleep. Remember the next day he was supposed to be executed. Only if you have God can you do that. What would you do if you knew that tomorrow you are going to be executed? Most people would be sleepless. It is their last night on earth. But here Peter is sound asleep. Because he knew Jesus, he has no more fear of death. Not only that I believe that he knew that his time has not yet come to go home. He was probably still in his middle age at that time. And the Lord Jesus told him at the end of the gospel of John that when he is old then they would lead you and do something to him. But he was not old yet. So, he knew his time has not come. He slept soundly and the angel shook him up. And he was not sure whether it was a vision that was really happening or not. See, everything was so real. He saw the prison gates. He tells us that he even knew that he passed through the first guard post and the second guard post. And he physically saw the Iron Gate open physically with his eyes. At the same time the angel said, "Follow me." So there he was the angel was walking in front of him and he was following the angel from behind just watching where the angel went. It was an open vision.

An open vision is interesting for when you receive one or you experience one it looks like the spirit realm and the physical realm are just one. It's quite hard to differentiate the two. It all just happened together. It is what you call the fifth dimension happening. Men live in three dimensions. The fourth dimension as described by Albert Einstein is time. Time is one of the dimension scientists discovered in the universe. The fifth dimension is what we call the *spiritual dimension*. Man has not fully discovered the spirit world yet. So here we have the spirit world being experienced as if it's a daily part of life – an open vision.

A CLOSED VISION OR TRANCE

The second type of vision that a person can experience is called the *closed vision*. The closed vision is where you only see the Spirit world. Many times, if you experienced it you would probably not be aware whether you are in the body or in the spirit. Your physical senses are completely closed up. You are not aware of. If somebody came and shook you while you are having a closed vision you wouldn't know. You are in a quote unquote trance like state. You are not aware of your physical surroundings at all (Zechariah (Zechariah 4:1; John (Revelation 1:17). All your total conscious awareness is the spirit world. It was one of these experiences that Paul received when he says he knows not whether it was in the spirit or in the body. That is the experience of a closed vision. The word *closed* is applied to your physical senses. Your physical senses are closed up. And you don't experience them anymore. The full state of it is in a *trance*. The Greek word for trance literally refers to a state in which a man stands outside himself. It is a visionary state wherein the conscious mind and perhaps the body is overridden by divine purposes (Numbers 24:3; 1 Samuel 19:20-24; Acts 11:5; 22-27). When I mention the word *trance*, people think of the wrong kind of trance where a temple deity would possess a person acting as a medium. But the Bible uses the word *trance* so it's all right to use that word. Look at the book of Acts chapter 10 except we must understand that this is the Spirit of God working.

And he became hungry and desire something to eat; but while they were preparing it, he fell into a trance, and the heaven opened and something descending.

And in that vision, he heard a voice, he saw the animals, three times it happened. It was a closed vision. When he came out of it, the vision was gone and he did not fully understand the meaning of that vision. That would be a closed vision. In a close vision, the person's *nous* or consciousness has completely entered into the spirit realm. Your consciousness has gone into the spirit realm. You are completely unaware of the physical world. You are quote unquote caught into the spirit world and caught into the spirit realm of God. Like Revelations 4 John was caught up into the spirit. Acts 10 Peter fell into a trance. He was caught into the spirit realm. Paul in II Cor. 12 says I know a man in Christ who went into the third heaven, he knows not whether in the spirit or in the flesh. There is no more consciousness of the natural realm. You are caught in the spirit realm. And your spirit realm is experiencing all those things and your natural body has lost its consciousness completely.

You notice in the positioning in Moses Tabernacle that laver is placed before the first veil. And the altar of incense is placed before the second veil.

To get through the first veil and the second veil you will have to get to the laver first and then pass the altar of incense into the second veil. What does the laver represents? It represents the Word. In order to experience inner clarity you would need the Word of God to be constantly be upon your *nous*, so that you could clearly receive the signals from the Holy Spirit. For example, it's easier to receive the signal from the Holy Spirit if He is giving some things in the inner vision or spiritual vision where your mind is dwelling upon the Word of God. If your mind is not dwelling on the Word of God but on something else, you cannot receive that signal from God. Your mind must be dwelling on the Word of God and your mind must be flowing with the things of God. Like John 15:3 Jesus said, *"My Word has made you clean."*

To have a close vision, you have to be in the spirit realm or the Most Holy Place. You would notice that the altar of incense is just before the Most Holy Place. Usually you would be deep in prayer to enter into the close vision. Let me take some illustrations from the natural. One of the things that happen before a person fall asleep is that there is rhythmic breathing. Now there is a technique for getting to sleep very fast. There are different stages of sleep. There is the earlier stage then the later stage, which is quite quiet. Then the deepest one is R.E.M. or rapid eye movement sleep. At a certain level of your sleep, you won't be able to hear noises or sounds. But at the lower realm of your sleep, it can wake you up. Some times within one night, you could have a cycle. Let us put it as three phases of sleep: just getting into sleep, quietness and R.E.M. So, you could have stage 1, stage 2 and stage 3. At a certain point in your sleep if a noise is made you could wake up. But at the R.E.M. point when noise is made you won't wake up at all.

Now, there are different levels of moving into the things of the Spirit. There are different levels of vision. Although vision is classified into three main areas spiritual vision, open vision and close vision, yet between them there could be degrees of growth. There could be degrees of levels of consciousness that we develop in God. Through growth a person can develop where they are constantly able to picture the things of the spirit with great clarity almost like an open vision. When you are new to the things of the spirit sometimes, God gives you a vision. Kenneth Hagin calls it a mini vision or flash vision. I call it a fast one. You could be worshiping or doing something and suddenly you saw a picture that came by. And sometimes,

Understanding Prophetic Dreams & Visions

it's blurring and sometimes it's very clear. Sometimes, it's only for a few split seconds. Sometimes, it retains for a long time. What causes the length of time? The level of your consciousness in the realm of the spirit. The further in you are in the realm of the spirit the longer that vision will remain. But when your *nous* is only in the physical realm or Outer Court, the vision can only come and go off very fast. You could miss it. You could miss the direction of God in visions.

Let me give you some scriptures as we close. Let's look at Acts 10. We will take an illustration from the deepest realm of moving into the close vision realm. Acts 10:10 *And he became hungry and desire something to eat; but while they were preparing it, he fell into a trance.* He fell into what I call a close vision. In verse 9 *Peter went up on the housetop to pray, about the sixth hour.* Notice what he was doing. He was praying. That tells you the altar of incense just before he entered into the close vision. Revelations 1: 10 *I was in the Spirit on the Lord's Day, and I heard behind me a loud voice like a trumpet.* What John was experiencing is a close vision. To be in close vision he says, "I was in the Spirit on the Lord's Day." What does he mean when he says "I"? His consciousness, his whole soul was like in the spirit realm.

AN INNER VISION

The third type of vision is called the *inner vision* or some call it the *spiritual vision*. But to make it clearer I like to call it the *inner vision*. The inner vision is a vision that you see inside the corridors of the canvas of your spirit. You are consciously awake and somebody touches you, you would be aware of it. But yet you see an inner picture when you think and it is something akin but quite different to the pictures you see. Now that third type of inner vision is called a spiritual or inner vision. And that is the only type where we can be trained and that is the most common type of vision. This way it's the only kind of vision that we can develop, train and recognize. Let's illustrate with God's voice. God can speak with His audible voice. I heard it only once in my lifetime. God can speak through the voice of the Holy Spirit inside you. That is inside you but its authoritative and loud. Sometimes it sounds like outside but you know it's inside. And then thirdly God can speak through the inward voice of the human spirit. So you can see that we could learn to recognize God's audible voice, the voice of the Holy Spirit and the voice of the human spirit. Most of the time, God will speak to you through your human spirit, less often through the Holy Spirit and thirdly, very infrequently or sometimes none at all through the audible voice of God. Vision also has a relationship to the voice. The most common type of vision that God bring forth is called the spiritual or inner vision. And then less often is what I call the closed vision. And less often still is the open vision. You can't do anything about the first two visions except to be opened to them. But there is a lot you can do about the third type call the spiritual or inner vision.

Of the three types of visions, the highest type of revelation is the third type, the spiritual or inner vision. And the lowest type of vision is the first type of vision, the open vision. This statement is not only made as I discover the things of the Spirit but other men of God have also made the same statement. I believe Kenneth Hagin did say the same thing in his book "I Believe in Visions." He says that the Lord Jesus visited him in the hospital when he went into the permissive will of God and got himself into trouble. It was an open vision. And the Lord taught him about visions. Then the Lord described to him the different types of visions. And the Lord also said the same thing that the lowest type of revelation is an open vision. And the highest type of revelation is the inner or spiritual vision. But the highest type of vision is the open vision. And the lowest type of vision is the inner or spiritual vision. The highest vision that you can reach into the realm of the Spirit is the open vision. Second is the closed vision. Third and the lowest type of vision is the inner or spiritual vision. But when it comes to revelation the highest type of vision is the reverse. And the lowest type of revelation that you can receive is the open vision.

These can be compared to the voice of God. The highest type of revelation that comes through would be not through the audible voice but through sensitivity and development through your inward spirit. Robert Liardon made a statement close to this about what God wants to do in these last days. That God is training His people to the extent that they would know God's thoughts and feelings and that they would just move into it without necessarily hearing from God. He is saying that God's people would reach a point of union with God where they will sort of just move what they want to do. In the past, it has always been man has to hear from

God in an audible voice before they could operate. But the more we move into the end times we have to learn that revelation is progressive and it's going to its fullness. And that is why we had to teach on visions so that we understand what God is doing and what God intends to do and move in our lives. Here is the reason why open vision is the lowest revelation although it is the highest vision. And inner spiritual vision is the highest revelation although it is the lowest vision. If you see an open vision, you don't require much faith. If Jesus were to appear to you right now stand in front of you and say, "I want you to go right now to a house No. 3 Washington Street and you will be a person there whose name is John Smith. You will find his wife lying on the bed. And she has been lying there for 18 months. I want you to go there and raise her up from the bed." You don't require much faith since Jesus just talked with you. He appeared to you in an open vision. You saw Him and you heard His voice ringing in your ears. It doesn't take much faith. All you have to do is just go and obey.

But suppose he received an impression in his spirit that God wants to say something to him and he could not get it quite so clearly. And so, he has to go to God in praise and worship and get into the realm of the Spirit. Get his mind quiet. You have spiritual noises but mental noises sometimes hinder. Then he began to have the very same picture coming. And he sees a house, and he sees a road. And he saw the number there on the house No. 3 Washington Street. He saw a person there in a very faint vision. As he comes out from that inner vision, he wonders whether it is his imagination. See it's easier to doubt an inner vision and impression than it is to doubt an open vision. I know it's easy to doubt what somebody else shares that Jesus just met him in the street. We would look incredulously at him. But if Jesus appears to you, it's not so easy to doubt, when you heard His voice and have seen His face. It's easier to doubt an inner or spiritual vision than it is to doubt an open vision. For that reason it requires more faith to obey an inner vision. Since faith is proportional to pleasing God, things that demand a greater faith are classified under a higher spiritual revelation. The inner or spiritual vision is regarded as the highest form of revelation because it demands more from you. It demands more from your life. It demands more faith from you.

As we see all these things then God in these last days would want to work in our lives to the extend that He began to deal in our lives to show many spiritual and inner visions. And we can walk with God so much that what God thinks and what God sees is automatically channeled into our spirit and we have an inner knowing of flowing with God. Robert Liardon spoke a little about that about the last days where the church would move like it never did before. We will really know God's heart; really know God's mind. We will just move into the things of God. The three ways in which visions can appear to you are similar to the three types of dreams. Vision can appear to you in what I call an *allegorical vision*. Or it can appear to you as a message vision. Or it can appear to you as a clear-cut real life situation vision. You find all those things in the Bible.

The *inner vision* is the lowest type of vision. And in the inner vision, your consciousness is here in the Outer Court (body). So, you are conscious of the physical world but you are also conscious of the spirit world and the things of the spirit and the inner soul. What you received is sometimes like an imagination. God could give you some things that come in thought or it comes in a picture form and sometimes it's not so clear. Your clarity in your inner vision is affected by where your consciousness is. If you happen to be active in the physical realm, your consciousness is not that much of the inner realm of your soul; you are more conscious of the physical realm. And that is why when the Holy Spirit is giving you an inner vision, sometimes you have to quote unquote possibly close up your body realm. You may even need to close your eyes so that you could concentrate to see clearly, what you are receiving in the spirit.

Watching too much of a secular television or reading too many wrong things can affect the inner vision, the Holy Spirit is giving you. As you close your eyes, right now you will see some of those things from your memory echoing through your soul realm. Right now, you could actually see some things in your corridors of your *nous*. Your consciousness is right now at your *nous*. And if you close your eyes right now, don't try to think of anything but let your inner consciousness hang loose. As your inner consciousness hang loose although you may just see a dark screen inside you - if you have been watching too much of secular T.V. a bit of that is coming up. If you have been reading a book recently or whatever things, whatever is your latest impression comes up to the corridors of your screen. If you have been reading the bible much and praying much that comes to your consciousness. That means whatever is your latest experience you see. When you close your eyes, just now whatever was latest in your experience the latest picture came out. The most current picture comes to your mind, whether in the spirit, soul or body realm of your experience comes to your mind.

What you do is that when the Holy Spirit wants to lead you in visions. He can lead you either through the inner vision, open vision or close vision. Most His general leadings function in the inner vision realm. That is why we have to develop a sensitivity to learn how to close off our physical realm so that you could concentrate on what you are receiving from God. In other words, the signals that you are receiving from the Holy Spirit are weak and you need a quiet room in order to concentrate on that. You could turn on the radio and you could find some signals are loud and clear from your local radio station. But some other signals from far off places are a bit weak. They can be received but they are weaker. And sometimes in order to receive it you need to filter it. You need to be in a quieter atmosphere. You will find it very hard to do if you have about one thousand children running all over the place and screaming. You need a quiet place. You may need to create an atmosphere to receive that signal. When you are receiving a signal from the Holy Spirit in leading your life and you are in the *nous* realm, you are awake and it is coming to you, you may need to have a certain quietness to bring about that inner vision. One of easiest way is to close off your physical eyes.

WAYS THROUGH WHICH AN INNER VISION CAN COME OR MANIFEST

It is of paramount significance to highlight the fact that the third type of vision called the spiritual or inner vision, which can come in any of these three ways. It can be allegorical, it could be a message or it could be a direct vision. Whatever it is, the means of receiving them is inside and it can be trained. It's in the corridors and in the canvas of the womb of our spirit.

Allegorical Vision

In Acts 10, Peter had this second type of vision called the trance or close vision. He had the allegorical type of vision. He saw various animals coming down and going up three times and in that cloth that brought the animals down, he saw all kinds of unclean animals. Then God said, "Peter rise kill and eat." And he said, "Lord I have never eaten anything unclean." Then the vision went up and repeated a second time. And again, the voice said, "Peter rise kill and eat." Peter replied the same thing, "I have never eaten anything common or unclean, Lord." It went up and next time it happened a third time. The vision came down and said, "Peter kill and eat." Peter said, "No, Lord I have never eaten anything common or unclean." And then it went up and it stopped. The vision stopped and he came out of it.

The Bible says when Peter was seeing the vision, he was wondering what it meant. This is because allegorical visions are very hard to interpret. The symbols followed the same principles in dreams. The symbols have to be scriptural. That is if a dog represents something bad in the Bible then in your interpretation a dog in your dream or vision should be interpreted as something bad. Your interpretation must be in line with the scriptures. Or if it's an unclean bird then it symbolizes something that is not good. Your interpretations of the symbols in your dreams and visions have to be in line with the bible. If you see a white snake, it is still bad even though it's white and friendly. Your interpretation of the white snake can only be that it is evil, like a wolf in sheepskin. In this case, Peter here was wondering what it meant. And suddenly here come these three Gentiles downstairs and they are looking for Peter. Look at it three Gentiles; they were symbolized by the white cloth coming down three times. Obviously, we need a lot of good interpretations otherwise Peter would think that since God also said, "*Go kill and eat,*" he might think that God was telling him to kill and eat the Gentiles. That would make him a cannibal. What God was saying is go and minister to them. Peter later understood that the vision was telling him to go and minister among the Gentiles. So, that is an allegorical type of vision.

Message Vision

The second type of inner vision can come to people is what I call a message vision. For example, in Acts 16, Paul went to Mysia and then to Bithynia And the Holy Spirit told him not to go to these places and he went in the end to Troas which is a sea-side town. And while he was there he saw a vision in the night in Acts 16. A famous vision we call The Macedonian Man vision. In that vision, he heard a man dressed in Macedonian garment saying, *"Come over here and help us."* Later you read in the book of Acts 16 Paul went into Macedonia and the first place he landed was the capital of that area called Philippi. As he landed in Philippi, he did not look for the man. He just went wherever he found people meeting and he ministered the gospel. In fact, the first people he met in Philippi were women who were praying at the seaside. It's funny he had a vision of a man calling him and he is among women. Then we have these women there. Now Paul understood the vision. The vision is what we call a message vision. It is the same like your message dream. There may be many things in the vision but there is only one main message. And the message was go to Macedonia and minister there but not to go and look for the man. If Paul were to take it as the third type of vision then it would have been different but understood message.

Clear-cut Vision

The third way of experiencing an inner vision is through what I call a clear cut direct vision. A clear-cut vision is one that you don't need interpretation. You take it as it is. An example of this vision is found in Acts 9 where Paul had just been born again on the road to Damascus. Paul was waiting in a house and while he was there fasting three days, Jesus in Acts 9 appeared to Ananias and Jesus told Ananias who Paul was and what his name was, the house he lived in, the Street he stayed in. and part of his future life and ministry. And all Ananias had to do was to go and lay hands on the apostle Paul. Paul was not an apostle at that time yet but he was called to be an apostle. So, the third way a vision can come is a direct vision. A clear-cut vision is just like a clear-cut dream, you don't need interpretation; take it as it is, nothing to interpret.

THE BASIS FOR SPIRITUAL OR INNER VISION

When God made man, He made man a creature that relies very much on visualizing. All of us in essence think in pictures. We can analyse what we think in pictures. For example if I say a dog, you won't have on the screen of your mind the word *a dog*. When I say, *a dog* through your mind comes a picture of some dogs that you know. If you have been dealing with small little dogs, you are thinking about small ones. If you have been with big dogs, you are thinking about big ones. But if I say a black dog, your inner vision changed. See we all think in pictures. If I say a *fierce black dog* or *a fierce big black dog*, our pictures change accordingly.

Scientists have recently discovered that the brain is more than just like computer. Man tries to describe their mind in direct proportion to technology as it is. And so, when men invented the computer they have tried to see the brain function like a computer. In a sense it does. But today they are moving further and beginning to see that the brain is not just a data processing centre. It is but it's not. It is like a hollow graphic processing centre. It stores information in pictures. So the data are actually pictures that are stored. You can recall from your mind a picture of the first house you lived in. Your mind stores information like pictures. When God created man, He made man that way. Why are we touching on this natural area here? Remember this the bible tells us that the things of the natural are made from the spiritual. The patterns of things you see around you tell you about the spiritual realm. We are going at it backwards because we have been trained and brought up in a physically conscious society, sense knowledge society. But actually, God made the spiritual world first and then He made a pattern of it in the natural. Let me give you two scriptures to substantiate this point. In the book of Romans 1: 20;

> *Ever since the creation of the world his invisible nature, namely, his eternal power and deity, has been clearly perceived in the things that have been made. So they are without excuse.*

Understanding Prophetic Dreams & Visions

He is talking about God's creation. That when God created this world He put into His creation the pattern of His attributes that we could recognize. His creative and artistic ability we see in all of creation. His orderliness, all His attributes can be seen in the natural world.

By faith we understand that the worlds were framed by the Word of God so that the things which are seen were not made of things which are visible. (Hebrews 11: 3).

In other words, the world is made of the invisible. Let me go further to say that God made man after a certain spiritual image of man. If you were to die and go to heaven, right now you will find that your spiritual body in heaven having two eyes, two ears, one nose, one mouth, two legs and two hands. There is a pattern. Our spiritual body was the pattern for the physical to be made. There are slight differences. In heaven, our bodies have no physical organs like we have. In Corinthians Paul said that the law is for the body is just as the stomach is for food, then he goes on and say both are done away with. From there, we know that our heavenly body's internal structures are slightly different. There are still two eyes, two ears, one nose, one mouth, two legs, and two hands but we won't have any reproductive organs and no inner organs that we rely on and it is totally different. And so, in that realm of the spirit that was the pattern that God made the human being.

God made us with an inherent ability to visualize and conceive an image inside him. Long ago before Adam fell, man could use a hundred percent of all his intelligence and all his creativity that God has put. Today scientists recognized man is only using 5 or 10 percent of his brain and ability. So we got a lot in reserve that we know not how to use or what to use it for. But there is a lot that we have fallen off from. But just bear this in mind there is a certain tiny little part of our physical body that scientists have been wondering what is it for. A little tiny little hook right the end of your small intestine called your appendix. That is a useless little thing. But there are other biologists who have gone further today. They examine that part of the animal's body where the small intestine join the large intestine to see what is there that is different from us. They came with this fact, that all the herbivorous animals have a structure right there and it's used to specially digest plants and leaves. They stopped there but I took that information and bring this conclusion. Man was once an herbivorous animal and through his development, he has become more of a carnivorous animal. And through time, that organ of his is no more in use and it slowly diminishes until it is a little curved appendix.

We go back to the Bible we found that when God first made man He said of every tree and of every herb you shall eat. Man was originally made a vegetarian. After man fell and after Noah's flood, world conditions were changed. There are four things that we cannot give time to share it. I just give you the four conclusions. Firstly, time changed. The earth that was rotating round the sun at 360 degrees or 360 days a year became 365 days, as we know. Second the earth became tilted and the four seasons started.

Thirdly the covering of water of the earth that was mentioned in Genesis one was dissipated and more sun-light, ultra violet light, infra light, all kinds of radiations that man was protected before started coming through. That was one of the reasons why after Noah's flood you see a sudden change in the life span of man. Where man used to live eight hundred over years suddenly, it became four hundred over years. And now it became one hundred plus. Because there are things that are released after man fell and this earth is not fully what God wanted it to be.

The fourth thing that happened was man's diet was changed. God specially allowed Noah to eat animals. The reason is that because the world has changed. If you were in a cold country, you take a large steak and you can see how warm it can keep you. What we are saying here is that after God made man in His pattern there was a change after the fall. Before the fall man experience tremendous resources, his mind, his soul, his spirit, was perfect. Adam could have lived ten thousand years and would still look the same as the day he was created. There is no way we could fully understand that.

But then when man fell the mind of man became darkened. A part of the life in him was darkened. In Ephesians chapter four speaking about the condition of man this is the description given. Verse 18 *They are darkened in*

Understanding Prophetic Dreams & Visions

their understanding, alienated from the life of God because of the ignorance that is in them, due to their hardness of heart. Here he talks about fallen man in general. Because we are cut off from life the understanding is darkened. Let me take it in a clearer form. Life was cut off therefore the understanding was darkened. Which one was cut off first? Life. When spiritual life was cut off the mind became darkened. So when life was cut off from Adam when he sinned darkness came and man didn't know like he knew before. See before he fell he looked at the animals and straightaway, he would know what it is. He could name them. Do you know today it takes one biologist to study for his whole life about ducks and reach some conclusions about ducks? Thank God that's all going to end in heaven we are going to be restored fully.

In this world right now we have a partial restoration. The reverse is true. If life is removed and darkness come then when life is restored light comes to the understanding. We have testimonies of children who come to church and they make "D" and "E" grades and when spiritual life comes their minds become enlightened and they start making "A" grades. Their understanding became brilliant. Hagin was also one example. The reverse is also true. We have a partial restoration although not a total because this body needs to be changed to have total restoration. So in line with that we look now at Ephesians 1:17-18.

That the God of our Lord Jesus Christ, the Father of glory, may give you a spirit of wisdom and of revelation in the knowledge of Him, the eyes of your understanding being enlightened, (which means to be flooded with light) *that you may know what is the hope of His calling.*

The Greek word that is used here for *eyes of your understanding* is a Greek word that means the eyes of the imagination, the part of man that helps him to visualize. There are two Greek words for the word *mind*. One is the word *dianoia,* which means the imagination. Luke chapter one translates *dianoia* as imagination. Lets turn to Luke 1: 51 *he has shown strength with his arm, he has scattered the proud in the imagination of their hearts.* The word *imagination* comes from the same word as stated *understanding* in Ephesians 1: 17-18.

In studying the bible both in the Greek and in the English, we see that the bible uses two different words for the word *mind* or *understanding*. One is the word *dianoia*, the other is *dialogismos*, and both mean two different things. *Dianoia* means a part of your mind is able to visualize, conceive a picture. *Dialogismos* means the part of your mind that is analytical like one plus one is two. That is not visualizing that is analyzing. It's a part of your mind that can analyze. If A equal B, and B equals C, then A equals C.

The part of our mind that is logical is *dialogismos*. I just give you the scriptures. I just give you the scriptures so that you so that you know what we are bringing forth are scriptural and biblical. For example, the word *dialogismos* is used in Acts 18 verse 4 and verse 19. It speaks about Paul reasoning in the synagogue. Paul was using *dialogismos*. Incidentally, *dialogismos* comes from the Greek word *logis* is where we get our English word *logic*. *Dia* means through seeing through something logically. What Paul was doing was this. He was taking Old Testament scriptures; he was saying this is what the Old Testament said about Jesus, and this is what Jesus did. He was showing from the scriptures that Jesus was fulfilling all the Old Testament scriptures and therefore he was the Messiah. He was reasoning with them from the scriptures.

So, the other part of the word *mind* or *understanding* used in the New Testament is the word *dianoia*, which refers to the ability in our soul that God has given to visualize. Our Western education focuses on logic. We are trained to think scientifically, logically and analytically. Our educational system world relies on one aspect of the mind. Only recently, educators are realizing that there is another part of the mind that is far more powerful, the ability of the mind to visualize. And only today are they beginning to learn to tap on that. Now these are part of our mind that God has created but in its fallen state, it does not function to the fullness that God wants us to function. Here is where we tie up with spiritual and inner vision.

There are three ways you can see one is in the natural with your physical eyes. Second is through your soul. Third is through your spirit. Just as there are three ways you can hear. You can hear in the natural. You can hear in your mind. You can hear in your spirit. There are three ways you can see. You can see with your eyes. You can see with your mind. You can see with your spirit. Spiritual vision is given with the eyes of the spirit. But the eyes of the spirit are connected to the eyes of the mind and they are connected to the eyes of the flesh. Sometimes Satan knowing this has tried through the eyes of the flesh to make an image to the eyes of your soul so that the eyes of your spirit will be blurred. When the serpent was tempting Eve he told Eve about the fruit and what it is supposed to do for them which is all lies anyway. And Eve fell not only because of the reasoning of the serpent in Genesis 3. Eve fell because she saw with her physical eyes. When she saw with her physical eyes, that image got into her soul and it affected the reasoning of her soul and it led her to a decision that caused the spiritual fall.

In the book of Samuel, we read how David was on his rooftop and looked over his neighbour's house and there was a woman bathing. Her name was Bathsheba and what David saw with his physical eyes produced lust in his mind and imagination. And it led him to a decision that cost him dearly. You can see that Satan knows the connection. They are not isolated. God made your physical eyes after the spiritual. The spiritual was there first, followed by the soul and the physical. Now the devil works from outside. He tries to get your eyes to see the wrong thing hoping to impress a wrong image into your soul and lead you into a decision that will cause you to fall in the spirit. He knows the connection.

Now, the key to understanding inner and spiritual vision is to understand the connection between the spirit and the soul, just as Satan understood the connection between the soul and the physical. We must understand the relationship and know how to deal with that area. Lets have some scriptures at this point. Looking at the word *dianoia* and going further from there, turn to the book of Hebrews chapter 8:10-12 here is where I am proving to you that one of the things that God does is to train His people in inner vision based on the study on the Greek word. Remember that the word *mind* in this passage is the word *dianoia*, which is translated as *imagination* in the gospel of Luke chapter one. And in studying the bible, I have come to the conclusion that this word should be translated as *imagination* or *visualizing*.

> *This is the covenant that I will make with the house of Israel after those days, says the Lord; I will put my laws into their minds* (dianoia) *and write them in their hearts, and I will be their God, and they shall be my people.* (Hebrews. 8:10).

The same thing is repeated again in Hebrews 10: 16-17 *"This is the covenant that I will make with them after those days, says the Lord; I will put my laws into their hearts, and write them on their minds."* Then he adds; *"I will remember their sins and their misdeeds no more."*

Did you notice the connection between Luke 1, Hebrews 8 and Hebrews 10? There is something similar in the way the author uses the word *mind*. In case you have not seen it yet this is the similarity. Every time the word *dianoia* or *mind* is used, the word *heart* is mentioned. Why does he says the *mind* and then goes to the *heart. I will write my laws in their minds and in their hearts.* And there in Luke chapter one it says *the imagination of their hearts.* I could give you more than three scriptures. We don't have the time to do that. To show you how every time *dianoia* is used there is a connection to the *heart*.

For the word of God is living and active, sharper than any two-edged sword, piercing to the division of soul and spirit, of joints and marrow, and is a discerner of the thoughts and intents of the heart. (Hebrews 4: 12).

Now look at the words he uses, *soul and spirit, joints and marrow, and is a discerner of the thoughts and intents of the heart.* The bible is giving us a relationship between the soul and the spirit. Many can to a certain extend differentiate the body from their soul. You know that is there a part of you that thinks called the mind. But there is a bodily part called the brain. They are related but you can't quite know how they are related. They could cut you up and not find the soul. They only find your body because the soul is invisible. So, there is a relationship between the soul and the body. There is an inner consciousness in us that is outside of the body, feelings and affection, things that are not necessarily caused by the body. But it's real. It's inside us. Human beings feel hurt, jealousy, envy and other emotions. You don't see the animals feeling all these things. You don't see animals experience the extent of the human experiences. And then human beings know right and wrong to a certain extend. Animals don't know right and wrong. Animals don't have moral laws. Only man has. His soul and his spirit are conscious to a certain extend.

So, we know there are an outer man and an inner man. But the problem is people don't go further than that. There is a difference between the spirit and the soul too. Paul here is saying that your soul and your spirit are related, just as your joints (the Greek word for *joints* talk about all your other bodily parts) and your marrows are related. He is illustrating how the marrow, which is the place where blood is manufactured, is affecting the rest of your body. And then it talks about the relationship between the thoughts and the intents of the heart.

So, having made those relationships this is where we draw our conclusion. The soul has a certain ability to think, to visualize and to see. But the greatest seeing is done from the spirit man. And on the day that you got born again, your spirit man's line with God is restored. Everything that God wants to speak to you, your spirit man automatically receives. There is no breakage, no communication problem, no over flow of data between your spirit man and the Holy Spirit. Everything that God wants to speak to you He speaks through your spirit man.

KEYS TO OPERATING IN THE SPIRIT REALM OF VISIONS

In the spirit realm, there are certain keys to get into the spirit. You have to have what I call rhythmic yielding. There are many ways into that. One could be praying in the Spirit. When you pray in the Spirit, you could put to automatic gear. I would pray very rhythmically and allow my body to flow with the prayer. Out in the world when they play those pop songs in the departmental stores, the worldly people start doing the disco. The tune sets their feet dancing. We all respond to music; there is a rhythm. So likewise, in prayer we realize that we could flow in the rhythmic of the prayer. Imagine keeping that on for hours. It sort of builds your consciousness into the spirit world and you could see the things of God easily. I am showing you practical keys of getting into that realm. When I want to move in the Spirit I have to prepare myself. When I minister, I move into the Spirit. That is why people who minister in the Spirit like music because music helps them to get their consciousness into the spirit realm. Once it get into the spirit realm, it's so easy to take off with visions. So there is a rhythmic pattern of prayer, a rhythmic pattern of worship and a rhythmic pattern of singing. See we are taking illustration for moving from the soul realm into the spirit realm. These are what I call general principles. Outside of that God could any time any place just grant the gift of discerning of spirits and zoom you are in. But I am talking about the normal development of growing our consciousness into the spirit realm.

First Key : Cleansing of the Heart and Mind

Many at times, there is a problem between our spirit man and our soul. The voice of the Spirit is not discerned by the soul that is not trained. Just as our soul can receive impressions from the natural, our souls are subject to impressions from the spiritual realm. And in the area of inner visualizing and spiritual vision what God does is first He cleanses. There has to be a cleansing. You see not every imagination you have is from the Spirit. Some are from the soul, from your eyes. Some memories of what you saw are from the physical realm. We have to clear the channel and let the Spirit flow easily between our heart and mind. Hebrews 8: 11;

And they shall not teach every one his fellow or every one his brother, saying, "Know the Lord." for all shall know Me, from the least of them to the greater."

Then in Hebrews 10: 16 and 17 he says that He will put His laws in their hearts and in their minds and I will write upon them He says in verse 19 *Therefore*. When you see the word therefore there is a conclusion being made by statements that precedes it. So there is a connection in between verses 16-17 where God says He will write His laws in our hearts and minds and verse 19 where we can have the confidence to enter the sanctuary.

Therefore, brethren, since we have confidence to enter the sanctuary by the blood of Jesus, by the new and living way which He opened for us through the curtain, that is, through His flesh, and since we have a great priest over the house of God, let us draw near with a true heart in full assurance of faith, with our heart sprinkled clean from a evil conscience and our bodies washed with pure water. (Hebrew 10: 19).

Now he is saying that there has to be a cleansing that takes place in the area of our hearts where the conscience resides. Let me go into this statement now. The heart is a part of your life that connects intricately with your spirit. And unless a heart is cleansed the channel between the spirit and the soul is affected. Therefore, he says let the heart be cleansed by the blood. So that's the first thing we see here in order to be in a position to really receive an inner spiritual vision. The reason we touch on this area is because seeing pictures is a norm in our life. You see pictures in you all the time. Imagining is something that even children do. In order to dissect and divide what is from God and what is from ourselves and what is from the enemy we need the cleansing by the blood of Jesus. Why the blood? If the intents of your heart are not right, you will not see the right pictures. Your inner man is affected. Let's say you have already made up your mind in certain thing, in the wrong things. Perhaps you are a very lustful person. You have all kinds of wild imaginations because of the things you do and the things you read. If you fill your mind with the wrong things, you will never be able to operate *dianoia* or inner spiritual vision. For Jesus said in Matthew 5: 8:

Blessed are the pure in heart, for they shall see God.

And here is where the first key to break into inner and spiritual vision is to reach a point where our heart is still, cleansed and in union with Jesus. Sometimes, our heart tries to move out of that position. When you worry, your heart is troubled. Or you have sin coming into your life, it will affect your ability to receive in the third kind of vision the spiritual or inner vision. So, the first keys to move into the area of seeing visions is a cleansing of the heart. And it's not something that just applies to being born again. When you are born again, you are cleansed. But we can allow the wrong things to come and we need to confess our sins before God and remain cleansed. For that reason if you have sin in your life and if you try to move into the spirit realm you can receive wrong information. It's dangerous to open yourself to the spirit world if you are not under the blood. Deception will come in. We are talking about a very sacred area. The area of your inner vision and that's the area where God brings tremendous visions to all of us. And everything received through that realm is a picture, is a vision, from the inside coming out. And if your mind is renewed to understand it then the Spirit can lead you in that realm. In the majority of Christians, their inner and spiritual vision is trying to come through but not many are picking it up because of pollution of their mind and of the heart. Only as we cleanse ourselves in the blood can we open ourselves to the realm of the spirit.

Second Key: Focusing on the Vision for Greater Understanding

But the second type of vision is at times more difficult to understand its meaning. Like for example, some of you receive pictures of people coming to you in your prayer. By pictures, I am talking about inner pictures that come. And you are wondering what they are. They need interpretation. Sometimes, it could be asking you to pray for those people or you already were praying for those people. Like for example, some times when I minister and open myself to the spirit realm and it is one of the days that the Spirit operates. So here, as I stand before people to minister and as I stand before a person let's say I have never seen that person before. Suddenly, to my mind comes somebody who has no relationship with this person. I have never met this person before. But to my mind comes a picture of this other person. I am looking at this person but my mind tunes up to my heart and receives the picture. I don't understand it. If I don't understand it, I cannot operate it. And so, I have to seek God for the understanding. Later God showed me that what He was trying to tell me was that this person that I am praying for had the same particular problem that the other guy had. Isn't it marvellous the way He works? So, simple but yet we sometimes missed it. As I was praying for this person, here comes this picture and I don't understand what it was. Later I ask the Lord. The Lord says I am trying to tell you that this person had the same problem. Just tell the person what the problem is. God brings to your mind and heart some pictorial connections. The most important thing is to realize that there is nothing in the natural that causes it. I mean you are not even thinking about this other person. You were concentrating on the Lord Jesus Christ and it just comes in your heart through your mind. And many times when each of you were praying in the realm of the spirit a lot of things go through the corridors of your spirit. It goes through in your heart and in your mind. But we many times don't pay attention to it.

And God says that in the last days His Spirit would be poured out upon all flesh. And young men shall see visions. *Young men* according to our classification are those who come against satanic forces, who overcome the evil one and who are strong in the Word of God. Part of the spiritual battle that you have to fight is learning to let the visions of God lead you in your spiritual weapons. The successful soldier in the army is the one who knows exactly what the commander commands. We have to be in tune and in line with our Chief Commander Jesus Christ. And so He is telling us some things and unless we flow in what He is telling us, we are not waging a good warfare, a powerful warfare that He wants us to fight.

And so, the second thing is to understand those inner visions. A lot of it seems so natural that we miss it. Or it can come in different ways. For some of you this is the way it is coming that you could be opening yourself to allegorical kind of inner vision. As you face a person, you began to open your spirit up and you began to sense a picture coming to you. It could be a basket of fruits. You say what's a basket of fruits related to this guy here. But we need to examine and focus properly on some of our inner visions like binoculars. And you see very carefully and you say it's a particular type of fruit. And you focus it properly and you say the grapes that are there. And you look carefully its all grapes. Then as you examine it more carefully, then you see it's a whole basket full of grapes. And as you focus it, to your mind comes John 15 and then more things come.

Now in this second area here operating things in inner and spiritual visions is slightly different from open and close visions. Open and close visions you received it like the grand slam, like the big bang theory of the universe. The big bang came from God. He spoke, "Let there be light," and there was light. So in the first two types of vision, the visions just come. You could remember the details later. But inner and spiritual vision operates slightly different. And this is a peculiarity. You could focus on it and get clearer details if you are receptive. You could focus on it like a telescope and then you bring it nearer. Then suddenly you could adjust it to go further and you see the background. And it operates in inner and spiritual vision.

You could for example pray for somebody or be in an atmosphere of somebody. Then you suddenly see this person in a field. The picture stays there it doesn't move. If you were not receptive, you did not listen to this kind of message, you are not open to the Spirit, you just let it go and nothing happens. But if you start paying attention to it and opening yourself to it, you began to focus on it and say God is giving something here and you focus on it. As you focus on it, the Holy Spirit may do two things. He may help you zoom on it. And then you go closer and you say this person is dressed in a particular way. Suddenly it can go wide angle and you saw behind that field on the left side there are scorpions there then you see something on the picture. It's interesting when you began to operate in the inner and spiritual vision. The details increase as you flow in them. They are coming out from your heart. The reasons they are different from the other two visions is this is coming out from your heart to your mind. And so there is an information flow that is increasing as you tune to it.

It's just like the data they received through the satellite. As the data comes in you see a picture. More data come in you see a better picture. In the same way, there is a data flow from your heart to your mind. If you close out to the data, it stops. If you open up to it more flow come in. There is where you could focus on zoom or focus on wide angle. We have to let the Holy Spirit guide us. The Holy Spirit is the one who helps you focus on it and you see more details in that realm and operate it. The details will be part of the process to help you to interpret. For example, I am talking about practical thing. Let's say we pray for the church land. Every time I pray all I see is a big map. The more you pray the more the zoom lens focus. Now that we define the land, we will zoom in the details.

Some of you in the business area have been educated in the Western way. You are an analytical, logic, intellectual nut. But you miss out our life's best because you are not trained in *dianoia* in visualizing. The world trained you to visualize in a different way. It depends on the strength of the soul not on the strength of the spirit. The second difference is the world tries to get the vision, tries to let you form the vision and make things go by that vision. Whereas in the spirit realm you don't make the vision, you receive them. God makes them. You can't visualize something that God doesn't want you to have. God makes them we just receive them and co-operate with it. Let it grows within us.

In the business realm, some of you may be praying and you are waiting to hear God's voice. How do you expect God's voice? Through the inner witness, inner voice and the voice of the human spirit. But then way at the corner of your heart is a little picture coming up but you are ignoring it. The more you pray there is a tiny little picture coming out like a little basket of fruit. You say what is this fruit coming into my mind. But the more you pray it keeps bubbling up. Here you are you are trained in analysis but you are not trained about visualizing. And in the end, you are opened to it. You tuned to it. The moment you tune to it, the zoom lens comes out. And you see the basket of fruit and following that fruit, you began to see beyond the fruit. And you see buildings etc. and then God began to speak to you. Then you realize that God was speaking to you to do business in that area. He is telling you I will bear fruit in that area. And He is telling me to go into that field of business. But we missed it because we are not tuned to it.

See a lot of times it is not because God did not speak but it's because we did not hear. Not only that, we look for the wrong areas to hear. God says in the last days He shall give us visions. After this teaching when you pray don't only open your ears, please open your eyes. How would you like to go round the world just with your eyes closed and missed a part of life because you never open your eyes? In the same way, you are trying to receive instructions from God. And all you did is open your spiritual ears when God was trying to bring some things through your eyes. And you missed it because you are not trained in spiritual inner visions.

But the thing that people didn't go further is this. A spiritual and inner vision has focusing ability zoom and wide angle. The details are sometimes in black and white and sometimes in color. The more you zoom on it the clearer. You see the realm of the spirit is exciting. Once you moved into this area of the realm of the spirit, there are so many things in the spirit realm to discover and you don't need the things of the world to entertain you anymore. You have God to entertain you and He will show you things to come.

Let me tell you every man of God and those who walk with God knows the things of the future. Paul knew in Acts 20 he told the people, "I am not going to see you again." And Paul knew when he was going to die. In

2 Timothy, he says assuredly I will be going home. I fought a good fight of faith. Jesus knew when He was going to die. He even knew the exact time they were going to come and betray Him, How did they know? Not only because they opened their ears but because they are opened to the realm of the inner vision. Let me say this, this is very important God speaks more in visions than in voices. Can you see how much you missed if you only got voice? God speaks more in visions than in voices. The whole spiritual realm is a realm of visions. And if you do not train yourself in this area of the inner vision and spiritual vision there is a far lot that you missed. So the second point we talked about is the understanding of the various ways a spiritual vision operates.

Third Key: Learning How to Tell the What, How and When

Thirdly, we learn how to channel the vision. Every vision has its time for fulfilment. Under the third point, remember just three keywords *what, how* and *when*. God will show you what it is the facts. And God will show you how to bring it about. Then that's not good enough God will show you when to start it off. When you operate in the realm of spiritual vision is very important that you move into the realm. And this is what I discover. You move into the realm where time does not count any more. Sometimes, you move into the realm of the spirit and you could see into the realm of the spirit. In the realm of space, there is no time.

If you try to move into the realm of the spirit and try to detect in the life of this person what is it like? The first thing I began to pick up in my spirit is a picture. Not a voice yet. The spirit realm consists primarily of pictures.

I pick up in my spirit a sort of furnace burning with black smoke coming out.

But I must also pick up the time span. Is it something from his past or something from his future? That's why the *when* is important. The *how* is when God tells you to do something and you have to get the details. It's from the past. See I am picking up the *when* and it is from the past. And as I pick up it remains stationery because I am not focusing on it now. Some of you received visions and it remains stationery because you didn't focus on

Understanding Prophetic Dreams & Visions

it. But now I turn and close my eyes and concentrate on what is going on in that spirit realm and see in that spirit realm that furnace.

I begin to see rain coming down and just covering it.

You see more details come as you move into that realm. *And suddenly there was a rainbow over that.* It's a continuous moving picture that flows along.

You are in the covenant of God. In the past your life was dark like a burning furnace something burning to consume. But it seems that there is peace.

It is important for us to see that the realm of the inner vision is continuous and it just moves continuously into that realm. You can focus on it; zoom on it, wide angle. But the third part is very important. What is it exactly, how to go about it and when. Pictures will go with words. As you see the pictures, words start coming and they go together. And the realm of the spirit is such, you hear God's voice but as you see the pictures and you tune to them, the voice and the words go together to form the whole picture.

Let me conclude by giving some principles to guide spiritual vision and its operation. All the three keys essential to operate in the anointing also operate here in receiving and discerning visions. That is in order to flow to the fullness of it we have to receive it first. To receive is very simple. Just to constantly be under the blood, worship and praise the Lord, being in the spiritual atmosphere. It will always keep flowing in your life, richly from your heart. Second, we have to understand it and thirdly we need to interpret it. We have to be in a position to receive them, which when you are born again it starts working in your life. And the reason we teach on this area is because many of you are receiving some spiritual visions but you are not aware that it is spiritual vision. Most of the time, you thought that it was your imagination.

Sometimes when we hear people share how they have seen a vision from the Lord, we get the impression that seeing vision belongs to a few special people. Maybe God speaks to them in vision but God doesn't speak to me in visions. That was my impression when I first knew the Lord as a young

Christian. But as I grew in God and studied the Word, I realize that seeing visions should be a normal part of a Christian life and does not belong to just a few.

Of course, bearing in mind the background that we have already studied and we are not repeating those grounds but I may have to speed it before we go further. That is we should know by now there are three types of vision. One is what we call a close vision. Another is an open vision and the third is spiritual vision. The closed vision is a vision, which you see when you are in a trance. And it's called closed because your five senses are closed up. You do not experience the five senses any more. You are only experiencing the inner spiritual vision. Like for example if right now you have a closed vision, you may see the Lord Jesus and you may see the angels of the Lord but you will be sure whether you are in the spirit or in the flesh. And that was the type of vision that Paul experienced when he said that he knew a man in the Lord who was caught in the spirit whether in the flesh or in the spirit he does not know. Why because he was in a trance. His five senses were temporarily suspended. The vision that Peter saw in Acts 10 of the unclean animals coming down and being taken up three times is a closed vision for he was in a trance.

The second type of vision is what we call an open vision where you are in the vision yet at the same time you see the natural world. For example, you see the Lord Jesus in an open vision you will see the pulpit, you will see the platform, the chairs and the Lord Jesus standing there among the physical and natural things. So, when we say open it means that your natural senses are still opened. An example of an open vision took place in the book of Acts 12 when Peter was being taken out of the prison. An angel was leading him out of that place. Obviously, he had to see the natural place. And he saw the natural doors opened. He saw the angel going through the doors and he also followed the angel. That is an open vision.

The third type of vision is what I call a spiritual vision. That is the vision that you see with the inner eyes of your spirit. That type of vision is sometimes close to what people call the imagination. But it's not imagining it's real. That spiritual vision is what you see with your inner eyes of your spirit.

Understanding Prophetic Dreams & Visions

It's not particularly strong enough for you to say that you have entered in a trance. You are not in a trance. Neither is it an open vision because you cannot see the natural and the spiritual. So, it's just something that you see inside your inner eyes of your spirit. That's called a spiritual vision.

Of the three types of visions, they are classified into the highest vision and the lowest vision. The lowest vision is the spiritual vision. The second is the closed vision and the highest type of vision is the open vision. But the lowest revelation is the highest vision. It's the other way round. The open vision is the highest type of vision. And the spiritual vision is the lowest type of vision. You don't really enter into that spirit realm but you saw a glimpse of it. However, the lowest type of vision is the highest revelation. And the highest type of vision is the lowest revelation. Because when you see an open vision, you don't need much faith. I mean if an angel appear to you and say, "Go to house No. 7, Angel Street and there will be a man named Paul Michaelson. He will have a sickness on his left leg. When you open the door, he will be there." There is no need for you to exercise much faith. All you have to do is just obey. So, that is the lowest type of revelation. The spiritual vision is the lowest type of vision and the highest revelation is what you see with your spirit. And it takes more faith to operate what you see in the spiritual vision. Because of that, it is considered the highest revelation. For you need faith. You will be asking yourself, "Is that from the Lord? Is that from my imagination?" You need more faith to follow. In a prayer meeting, you suddenly have a spiritual vision where you saw this guy Craig Smith in First Avenue.

Then you have to go there to meet him. You are wondering, "Is it from my own imagination? Or, "Is it from the Lord?" To really operate in a spiritual vision you need more faith. What we are going to see here is that it is inherent in each one of us to be able to see visions. Seeing visions is not something that belongs to a few mystical gurus. It is something as common as life itself. To understand the whole concept of seeing vision we need to understand first the makeup of human being that God has created. God made man in His image. When Adam was first created, Adam could relate to the spirit world and the natural world freely. He could touch and reach into the spirit realm as well as the natural realm. There was no blockage of his experience of God. If an angel were there, he would have seen him.

There is no such thing as anything being invisible to Adam's eyes. For the spirit world was as visible and natural as the natural world. It was only after Adam fell that the bible says in Ephesians 4:18 that the understanding of all Gentiles were darkened and alienated from the life of God. When Adam fell his spirit was cut off from the life of God and his understanding was darkened. That is when he could not now see the spiritual realm.

There is a natural light and there is a spiritual light. Let's compare spiritual sight to the sense of sight in the natural realm. In order for us to see in the natural we need light. If suddenly light is removed and we are enclosed in a place where no light comes in it would not be possible for us to see. That is why at night you can't see as clearly as in the daytime for there is less light to see. What do we do in a dark room when we want to see object. You got to feel your way to the switch. Then with light you could see. The sense of natural sight depends on light falling on object, bouncing off an object, and reaching your pupil and your eye. It depends on the perception of light. In the same way, spiritual sight depends on spiritual light. According to the degree of spiritual light that is allowed to enter into our spiritual eyes, we would be able to see visions. It's proportional. Like even if the whole room is bright and your eyes are covered with some objects that prevent light from getting into your eyes you will still not be able to see.

The Bible tells us that in Ephesians 4:18 that the understanding of man has been darkened. There is a shadow that has been cast over the understanding of man. As a result of that, man cannot see into the spirit realm. Let me qualify that. Generally, man cannot see into the spirit realm but we realize that some people are opened to the evil spiritual realm. That is because the demonic powers are at work in their type of imitation light. These demonic powers open such persons to the demonic realm and relate to them. But there is a positive and a good realm of God where God's Spirit works and opens and enlightens the understanding.

They are darkened in their understanding (dianoia) *alienated from the life of God because of the ignorance that is in them, due to their hardness of heart.* (Ephesians 4:18).

Understanding Prophetic Dreams & Visions

See the *dianoia* was darkened. Therefore, they cannot see into that spirit realm. Now the opposite statement where the *dianoia* is flooded with light is over here in Ephesians 1:18;

The eyes of your understanding (dianoia) being enlightened (the Greek actually says flooded with light); that you may know what is the hope of His calling, what are the riches of the glory of His inheritance in the saints, and what is the exceeding greatness of His mighty power toward us who believe, according of His mighty power.

I say that here the believers were having their understanding or their *dianoia* enlightened. Of course, the word *dianoia* has been translated as *imagination* in Luke 1:51 as imagination of their hearts. The *dianoia* is a part of our soul that is able to see into that realm of the spirit. It's a part of us that see pictures. There are two parts to our mind that operates. One part of our mind is a part that reasons and that is the word *dialogismos*. And the word *logis* is where we get the word *logic*. The other part of our mind is a part that sees pictures. Like we say *a dog*, immediately in your mind will come a picture of a dog. When I mention the word *dog* to your mind, right now you recall whatever dog you remember in your life. If you own an Alsatian, you would think of an Alsatian. That is just a part of your mind that just visualizes.

Now our mind at the same time consists of the conscious mind and the subconscious mind. (Illustration) Let's say this person here represents *dialogismos*. And this other person here is *dianoia*. Both of them represent a part of our conscious mind. We could consciously imagine and consciously create a picture. We could consciously reason with facts that are given to us. In that realm, we realize that there is an association and working of the two in our conscious mind. As we look into that, let me give some definitions here. Heb.4: 12;

For the Word of God is living and active, sharper than any two-edged sword, piercing to the division of soul and spirit, of joints and marrow, and discerning the thoughts and intentions of the heart

It tells us that the Word of God is awakening the thoughts and intentions of the heart. It's by the working of God's Word changing and transforming our lives. That working of God here is explained by two Greek words. The word *thoughts* is the Greek word *enthumesis*. And the word *intent* is the word *ennoia,* which has been translated in I Peter 4:1 as the word *mind*. *Enthumesis* has been translated in Acts 10:19 as *thought,* when Peter thought about the vision he saw. The word *ennoia* is a derivation from the word *dianoia* - just knock off the *dia* and put the *en* inside. *Dia* in the Greek means *through* and *en* means inside. The *ennoia* is the inside of your being.

As we look at those two words, we need a little more illustration. So, this brother consists of the conscious mind *dianoia*. And that brother is *dialogismos*. Let take a third brother here to be *ennoia*. And this fourth brother will be *enthumesis*. Now your *dialogismos* and your *dianoia* are the two parts of your conscious mind. One part that reason logically and the other part that imagines and sees pictures creatively. Then you have a sub-conscious mind, which is in the depth of your being. The sub-conscious consists between 90 to 95 percent of our mind. We are only using about 5 percent of our mind in the conscious realm; the sub-conscious is the rest of it. That *ennoia* is the sub-conscious part of your *dianoia*. It's a part of you where the action rises and where the pictures are stored. Right now in your conscious mind, you don't have all the pictures that you have seen from the time you were born until right now. You couldn't because your conscious mind cannot be looking to all those things at one time. So, your conscious mind stores it in the sub-conscious.

Inner healing is the work of the blood of Jesus reaching into your sub-conscious and removing all the bad pictures and the bad reasoning that put bondage in your being. That's what inner healing is. It's the blood of Jesus entering into your subconscious and removing the wrong pictures that are causing your life to be in bondage. Fear can come because of a wrong picture. For example, a person can have fear of water because perhaps at a certain time early in childhood, he or she may have fallen into water and nearly drowned. The picture is locked up inside their *dianoia* and transferred into the *ennoia* even before they have developed their *dialogismos* to reason like an adult. And the rest of their life they are afraid of water. If you ask them why, they cannot explain. But the fear is there. The picture of them drowning is locked up in them. Sometimes it could be other pictures, pictures of hurt. When somebody has hurt you so much that you could remember and picture that hurt, anger, or a crisis that you have gone through, then that picture is still locked in your imagination. Let me tell you the pictures that are locked in your imagination can hold you stronger than prison bars can. You could outwardly be free but that locked picture today motivates you, affects and influences some of your decisions and some of your reactions to people and to circumstances. That is why people need an inner healing for the blood of Jesus to step into that and cleanse it.

Remember Jesus ministers inner healing to people. In the gospel of John, after Peter denied the Lord Jesus, he was trying to keep himself warm while Jesus was on trial. The bible mentioned that the fire that he was warming over was a coal fire. Remember coal fire gives a peculiar smell. It's just like if you fry food with coconut oil, the food has a peculiar taste. Coconut oil gives the food a peculiar taste. And you know that it has been fried with coconut oil and there is no mistake about that. So when you burn something with a coal fire there is a peculiar smell in the house. Now Peter denied Jesus and can you imagine the agony that has entered his life? From that day onwards after he had denied Jesus, the picture of his betraying Jesus has locked in his imagination. And just when the cock crowed Jesus turned and looked at him and he wept and cried. Can you imagine what kind of picture is locked inside his imagination? Later on in the ending of the gospel of John when Peter had gone fishing and Jesus was on the shore, He said, "Children have you any fish?" And Peter realized that it was Jesus and he swam to Jesus and when he came near to Jesus, he smelt the same smell. He smelt the burning of coal fire. Immediately all the memories of that day when he denied the Lord came rushing to his conscious mind. If you had an agonizing crisis and experience at the seaside, I am sure the next time I bring you to the seaside the first thing you do is to remember that bad experience. And it depends on the degree of how it affects your life. If it really has damaged your life, you will never want to go to the seaside again because of that imagination. So, Jesus had to minister inner healing to Peter. Right at the place, Peter remembered everything. Right at that time, Jesus made him confess three times that he love Him to heal the wounds of denying Him three times, "Do you love Me, do you love Me, do you love Me?" In the Greek, Jesus asked Peter, "Do you *agape* Me? Do you *agape* Me? Do you *philo* Me? From that day forward, every time Peter smell coal fire he may at times remember the denial. So, Jesus ministered to him right in that occasion. So, if you have a fear of swimming you need to get into the water to overcome that fear in your life.

So, *dianoia* is the imagining part of you that sees picture. And *ennoia* is the subconscious part of your *dianoia* that locks all those things. And over here we have the *dialogismos* and *enthumesis,* the latter is the sub-conscious part of your *dialogismos*. There is some reasoning that has been locked inside us. Some people store away wrong conclusions in their *enthumesis*. Their opinions are not factual neither are they correct because their reasoning is wrong. But it gets locked into them and today it influences their action, their decisions and everything else because of wrong reasoning. It's just like some people who have the wrong reasoning that God sends sicknesses. See they logically conclude by a superficial reading of the scriptures that God sends sickness. So, in their reasoning they accept it. Or in their reasoning, they accept that the devil is strong and powerful and they accept that they have no authority over the devil. They somehow reason themselves into it. Straightaway, they are put into bondage too. A wrong reasoning can cause us to be in bondage.

It's just like John Osteen's sister. He was sharing how one day he was driving in a certain direction and God spoke to him to go to his sister who was in a mental asylum. When he went there led by the Spirit he asked to see his sister. When his sister came the anointing of God came upon his life. The first word he said was, "Don't tell me God did this." And he commanded the enemy to lose a hold of her life and instantly she was freed. Today she is still all right. And this was the testimony. When John said that statement, "Don't tell me that God did this," she did not hear John's voice. She heard it as if it was a voice of God speaking. And for the first time she started doubting the reasoning, she had earlier. For the first time she did not accept the fact that this problem that she had is from God. And she questions the reasoning that she formerly had. The moment she came to the conclusion somehow was when she heard that voice it was not God who did this to her. Imagine for all those many years she was left up in the asylum she thought that it was God who did that to her. Wrong reasoning can put people into bondage. So there is what I call the reasoning of your conscious mind that after some time it sinks into your sub-conscious. That is why we need the Word of God to renew us, to give us the right principles.

Understanding Prophetic Dreams & Visions

So this part that consist of your sub-conscious mind is made up of the *ennoia* and the *enthumesis*. And the *dianoia* and the *dialogismos* is your conscious mind. There is another part of your mind that is generally called the *nous*. That's the part of your mind that relates to the natural or the spiritual realm. That part of you is the decision maker. Do you realize that your mind can make a decision? You could decide what to think. Right now, we could suddenly decide to think about a buffet lunch and all the food laid on a table and nicely decorated. We could make a decision and say right now imagine that we are in a cold country. There is a part of us that definitely makes a decision whether we tap into *dianoia* and then *ennoia* or we tap into *dialogismos* and then into *enthumesis*. That's your *nous*. Generally, *nous* is just translated as mind or understanding.

Now we are on the topic of growing in visions or developing visions. This is what happens. Every one of us is born with an ability to see into the spirit realm to a certain degree. But what the enemy has done is that man's *dianoia* in his fallen state is darkened (cf Ephesians 4:18). Man's *nous* is also darkened. As a result, man tries to develop his intellect based just on *dialogismos*. The I.Q. test is based on *dialogismos*. It doesn't test you on your ability to visualize. It just merely tests you on your ability to reach a conclusion from hints and facts and statements here and there. This world's education system tries to build a successful life from the logical point of view. The development of logic has become an important aspect of life in this world. But the rest the *dianoia* and *nous* are darkened. But today there is a success-orientated group that teaches how to visualize a successful image and program themselves for success. They are trying to tap into *dianoia*. But that's not in the regular school system.

So realizing that the *dianoia* and the *nous* are darkened, we can understand why men in their fallen state of being today have great difficulty looking into the spirit world and having visions. Some people may have a greater opening in this area than others. Like some scientist may develop on the area of the *dianoia* and the *ennoia* where they could reach a conclusion right on target with the very few facts available that others could not. They could reason deeper. Some artist could develop this part of *dianoia* and *ennoia* more than others. Some people are more akin to lean on their *dianoia* than on their *dialogismos*.

Frequency Revelator

Now the enemy and the devil is attacking the *nous* and through the *nous* preventing people from seeing into the spirit realm. Now let's bring in two extra Greek words. Turn to the book of II Corinthians 3:14 *But their minds (noema) were hardened; for to this day, when they read the old covenant, that same veil remains unlifted, because only through Christ is it taken away.* Then chapter 4:4 *In their case the god of this world has blinded the minds (noema) of the unbelievers, to keep them from seeing the light of the gospel of the glory of Christ, who is the likeness of God.* What is the enemy doing? The enemy is blocking the *noema* from the light of Jesus Christ so that the light of Jesus Christ cannot shine through and touch the person.

There are different degrees of what I call the entrance of spiritual light into our souls and our spirits that is our hearts. According to the degree of the spiritual light, you develop the ability to see visions - some in a small degree and some in a larger degree. We need this understanding in order to move into the realm of developing visions in our life. Remember Ephesians 1:18 Paul prayed that God would give them the spirit of wisdom and revelation that their *dianoia* will be flooded with light. So, on the one hand we see the devil trying to block light from going in and preventing people from moving into that realm of seeing visions.

Now seeing vision is primary in the development of *nous, dianoia* and *ennoia*. The development of the other area of *dialogismos* and *enthumesis* involves the renewal of the mind but we are talking about visualizing here. With that let us go to Luke 24:32 *They said to one another, "Did not our hearts burn within us while He talked to us on the road, while He opened to us the scriptures?"* The word *opened* in verse 32 is the word *dianoigo* - while He *dianoigo* to us the scriptures. That's a powerful word here that Luke chooses to use. In Luke chapter 24:32 he mentioned that He opened the scriptures to them. Then verse 31 *And their eyes were opened (dianoigo) and they recognized Him.* The two disciples were walking with Jesus and they did not know it was Jesus. They saw Him physically but they could not recognize Him. Something was blocking them from seeing Him. But when they were in that room something opened and they saw Him for who He was. They saw in that spirit realm and they recognized it was the Lord and then He disappeared. He is telling us something about how God can open us to the spirit world to see visions.

Two more scriptures in the same chapter. Luke 24:45 *Then He opened (dianoigo) their minds (nous) to understand the scriptures.* He *dianoigo* their *nous*. Remember earlier you read in II Cor. 3 what the devil is doing to your *noema* and *nous*. He is blinding it. He is preventing light from coming to you. But what is the Lord doing? He is opening it. He is opening the *nous* so that the light can go through your *nous* to your *dianoia*. When Paul prayed for their *dianoia* to be flooded with light, it has to flow through the proper channel. The aperture of your spiritual camera is your *nous*.

The aperture is a part of the camera that opens and exposes the film to light. It opens and closes very fast. According to the speed and the length of time it's opened, it allows light to go through. So when there is a very low light, the aperture is opened for a longer period. Our normal camera will find it very difficult to take a picture of a person running. All you see is blur. But what makes some cameras able to take a picture of an object traveling fast like a bullet going through the air is the split second that it allows the light in through the aperture. You can't possibly take a picture of a bullet going through the air with a normal camera. But yet, they have developed cameras that could photograph a bullet moving. How is that possible? There must be sufficient light and then the speed of the opening and closing must be fast and quick so that only the stationery picture of that bullet enters the aperture before it quickly closes up. The rest of the motion of the bullet is not allowed to come in otherwise it blur the whole film. So we see here using illustration from the natural that an important part to visualizing is also in our conscious mind our *nous*. Whether it's blinded or it's opened depends on the great part on our decision too. But it also depends on the Lord. So let's lay some ground work and principles right now with all these conclusions.

Firstly, in order to see and develop the ability to see visions we must increase our openness inside us. That is we need the Lord to open our *nous*. Luke 24:45 you have scripture and verse for it. Apparently, the Lord did something to them. We know of course that ties up to the born again experience. The day you are born again God did something. God did a touch on your life. But remember this, this is only the beginning. What people failed to do is they failed to develop that further. See Jesus did something to them in Luke 24:45 He did something to their *nous*. He made their *nous* a little open. That openness seems to be necessary to see spiritual things and spiritual visions. The word *dianoigo* is the same word that is used in Acts 16:14;

> *One who heard us was a woman named Lydia, from the city of Thyatira, a seller of purple goods, who was a worshipper of God. The Lord opened her heart. I Cor. 2:11 For what person knows a man's thoughts except the spirit of the man which is in him? So also, no one comprehends the thoughts of God except the Spirit of God. Now we have received not the spirit of the world, but the Spirit which is from God, that we might understand the gifts bestowed on us by God.*

So apparently, there is a natural man that is blinded and there is a spiritual man that is enlightened. And your *nous* has an aperture where the light can go in and enlighten and flood your inner most being. So how well and how able you are able to see into the spirit realm depends on your opening of your *nous* by the Lord. That is the first determination. So firstly, it depends on the opening of our *nous* or the opening of our understanding to allow the Spirit to work.

Do you notice you could do that even in a meeting? You could come to a meeting with your heart and spirit closed up and you are not opened to what is taught. Or suppose that you go a meeting and you have heard some wrong things about the minister being a false prophet or false teacher or some wrong ways in him. And you already have a pre-conceived mind to reject his ministry. You have heard some rumour or slander without finding out the facts. By the time you come to his meetings, you are not looking for something to learn. You are looking for something to find fault. There is a part of you that is already closed up instead of being opened up. Now that affects your ability to move into the spirit realm. Now you take that a little further and see how in a meeting let's say in a prayer meeting or in a worship meeting to worship God for long hours. If your mind or *nous* is not trained, you will normally reject any thing that the Lord tries to do. For the natural man does not receive the things of the Spirit of God. And even if God tries to give you a vision, you would have rejected even that because your mind is only trained to receive the *dialogismos* type of ministry. You only allow just a word, line upon line, precept upon precept but you are not opening yourself to the revelation of God's Word through visions. The opening of your *nous* is partly the responsibility of the Lord and partly your decision and your free choice. Or when you come and you just hang loose. The Lord could begin to show things to you in the form of a vision that He never did before.

The second determination of the ability to see vision is the amount of light. You could have a lot of light but the opening of your *nous* will still determine how much light is received. Yet, at the same time you could have very little light around, you could open your *nous* to the fullest possible, and yet not much light gets through. So, the other determination is the amount of light, the intensity and the degree of light that is available. And that would determine the vision that you are able to see. That is why some times in a meeting, in a praise and worship service, in a place where God's presence is strong, do you know it's easier to move into vision than when you are out there doing your accounting work. See there are certain places that you find it easier to develop and see vision than before. If you have developed it any place, any time you will know how to move into that. But if you have not developed it, there are certain places where it's easy to develop it than at other times where there is more intensity of spiritual light. So when we know this teaching the next time you get into a meeting where there is high intensity of light, or high intensity of worship or the Word, you open yourself to it and you learn to develop into that realm and you grow into that vision. And you could see into that realm by the permission of God. Things will begin to come to you even in the spirit realm while you are worshiping. It won't be something that you cook up or imagine. But it is something that is impressed upon your heart from the spirit realm. So, train yourself in that kind of meeting. That's the purpose of meetings like that. So that having trained yourselves then when you get back into the street, into the office or in your normal working life, you could learn to open yourself into the spirit realm and receive things from God. So there is an opening and how important the *nous* is for touching the *dianoia,* and the *ennoia* into that realm. For the opening of our *nous,* we need the Lord to touch us.

Another determination is the cleanliness of the lenses and the cleanliness of the nerves. Sometimes when people develop cataracts the light is still there but there are blockages. That is why we need the Word of God to cleanse us. Or sometimes everything is O.K. but the person lack nerve cells where the light reaches the inner part of the eyes. The nerve cells are missing so they are technically blind. Although the light and the image actually hit the back part of their eyes, they cannot perceive because there are no nerve cells. The wonderful thing is that there are spiritual nerve cells in our *nous* that see and catch pictures from the spirit realm. We are getting input from the spirit realm all the time. There are images that are coming from the spirit realm all the time.

So our ability to receive them depends on whether we are opened or closed. And of course, it also depends on the intensity of light - the greater the intensity of the spirit light the greater we can pick up from the spirit realm. The other third factor is that it depends on whether we have the spiritual nerve cells to pick it up. The wonderful news is that we can develop the spiritual nerve cells. We could grow into the spirit realm and develop our *dianoia* even when we have only developed our *dialogismos* and be a very logical person. I was that way before. I mean I am a very logical person, and I was fastidious about *line upon line, percept upon precept*. I never thought that the day would ever come that I could move into visions. I could never have thought the realm of visions could be my realm. I am not born with the ability to see visions all the time. I have to grow into that area and develop it. Believe me, from the time when I was a young Christian, I literally prayed to God, "Lord, I love to see visions." But it was later on by the grace of God I grew in the Word and God allowed me to see visions. And as I see the development, I realize this is not something that is special. This is a thing that every Christian can develop and grow in. That is why we are teaching on visions so that you could realize that is where it starts.

And the first place where it starts is in your *dianoia*. When the light floods your *dianoia,* you will begin to see pictures. Some of you are seeing pictures but it's blurring. You see the spirit realm and lets says right now close your eyes and visualize Jesus. Some of you will ask how to visualize Jesus? What does He look like? Some of you are having that difficulty. Some of you when you close your eyes all you see is a bright light. Do you realize that for some of us it's very blur? Do you know that in the natural world when a child is born, that little baby cannot focus the eyes very properly yet? But as the baby grows and develop then the eyes begin to focus. So, in the first few weeks of the baby's life, the baby depends a lot on sound. But through time as the baby's eyes develop to focus properly it can go by sight and recognition. In the same way when we all were new Christians, new born babes in Christ, most of us went by hearing. The problem is that many Christians go by hearing all their life. Can you imagine a little baby growing up never seeing the father and mother? Perfect eyes but refuse to develop. And every time he says, "That's the voice of my papa. That's the voice of my mama." If there is a defect that is understandable but if there is a potential to develop and it's not, then something has gone seriously wrong. Think about the spiritual world - we got to grow into that. It's not going to come automatically.

Sometimes we don't grow and develop our *dianoia* because we don't realize that we could do it. When our *dianoia* is slowly developing, we begin to see spiritual things and spiritual visions. What I am teaching has nothing to do with what we call the gift of discerning of spirits, which is a gift. That is a real gift of vision. Remember we differentiate between developing in the gift of prophesying, the ministry of prophesying and the gift of a prophet. In the same way, we got to differentiate between the normal Christian growth in the ability to perceive and see into the spirit world and from the gift of discerning of spirit, which is a gift from God and from a ministry that can develop into that area. If you are going to confuse that then what we teach will not be applicable. You could take it and say that I am teaching that everybody can be a prophet and that is wrong. I am not teaching that. That is the gift and callings of God. We differentiate between the office of a prophet, the ministry of prophesying, the gift of prophecy and the normal ability to learn to prophesy. I Cor. 14 say you all may prophesy one by one that all may learn. So, in the same way there are different categories of visions. There is a realm where some people are born and bred with that gift. If you are called to be a prophet from the time you are born, you may see a vision. That's different and I am not talking about that. Not everybody has that office of a prophet.

Now we are focusing on some areas where the believers can develop in. It's a part and parcel of us since we all have the *dianoia* with its inherent visualizing ability to see the things of God. We can be developed that as we learn to open ourselves and learn to recognize the intensity of light where we could focus on. It's just like if there is darkness right now, it takes a different training to recognize objects. There are different degrees of spiritual light that can affect your inherent ability to see and your spiritual development.

DIFFERENT LEVELS OF VISUALIZING

In order for us to understand the different levels of visualising, we need to first of all define the spirit, soul and body of man. It is in through our being that God is revealing Himself in order for us to see visions. Perhaps there is no better illustration than Moses' Tabernacle that illustrates the spirit, the soul and body of man. Moses Tabernacle if you remember is divided into three major sections, the Outer Court, the Holy Place and then the Most Holy Place. The Outer Court represents the body, the Holy Place represents the soul, and the Most Holy Place represents the human spirit. We would need to see that each piece of furniture that represent Jesus and represent the Christian life. We have touched on that in the study on the Tabernacle. Also, each piece of furniture represents an aspect of our spirit, soul and body. We need to outline it so that we could go deeper into seeing how the visions of God occur in our lives. In the Outer Court, the first piece of furniture is the brazen altar. Then we have the laver. After the Outer Court, there is a veil here. When we enter into the veil into the Holy Place, we will see the candlestick and the table of showbread. When we come right before the second veil separating the Holy Place from the Most Holy Place, there is the altar of incense just outside this veil. When you enter that veil, you have the ark.

We have talked on the Tabernacle from a different perspective on the Christian life and on the end times and many other topics. You can draw a lot of principles on many aspects of the Christian life from the pattern found in the Tabernacle alone. But we are going to teach about the soul and the spirit of man in the area of vision. The Outer Court represents the body. The Holy Place represents your soul; there are three pieces of furniture in the Holy Place. Then you enter into the Most Holy Place and you have the ark. Inside the ark, there are Moses' two tablets, the rod of Aaron and the pot of manna. The brazen altar is Jesus Christ the Lamb of God. The laver: Jesus the Word. The candlestick: Jesus the baptizer and the giver of the Holy Spirit. The table of showbread: Jesus Christ the King of Kings and Lord of Lords. The altar of incense: Jesus Christ our High Priest. The ark: Jesus the glory of God and the fullness of God. Each also represents a part of the Christian life. The brazen altar: the power of the blood. The laver: the power of the Word. The candlestick: the power of the Holy Spirit. The table of showbread: the power of the Name of Jesus. The altar of incense: the power of praise and worship. The ark: the power of the presence and the glory of God. Each one represents an aspect of the Christian life and principle.

In the physical realm, in order for our physical body to begin to be more inclined and be fully sensitized to the things of the Spirit of God, our body (represented by the Outer Court) needs the two realms of the brazen altar and the laver found in the Outer Court. In order for our physical body to be a spiritual sensor or to be sensitive to the things of God and to be used by God, our body has to be in line with the Word and be under the blood of Jesus Christ. Let me give an example here. When the word of knowledge operates through my life God uses my body as a sensor. Somebody else's sicknesses are quote unquote in a sense but not directly transferred for me to experience in my physical body. I sensed a physical sensation. It is not caused naturally. It is not exactly like that person's sickness but there is a quote unquote symptom. If your body is sick there is no way you could be sensitive to that. If your body is not in line with the Word of God, your physical body cannot be used as a sensor for God. For example, you are having your own backache or your own headache then in your ministry's time, you sensed it and you say somebody here has a backache. It's not somebody else's it's yours. But if your body is in good physical health, your body is in line with the Word of God, redeemed from the curse of the law, and you are experiencing that, God can use your body as a sensor. In the physical realm in order for our body to be flowing easily in the things of the spirit, you will need the two realms, the power of the Blood of Jesus and the Word of God. As these two sanctify your body, it becomes sensitive to the things of the spirit.

There are three parts to our soul. One is the will, the second is our emotions and the third area is our intellect. The Holy Spirit wants to flow to all three areas of our soul. The bible says, "Bless the Lord O my soul and all that is within me." We are not only to worship God with our will, that is the starting point, we have to worship God with all our heart, all our mind, all our soul and all our strength. Sometimes, people minister and preach as if your emotion is divorced from you. God wants our emotions to be a part of the spirit realm too. When God created man; spirit, soul and body were to function in the spirit realm and the natural realm simultaneously. So, the three parts of our soul need to be worked on by the Word of God and need to be constantly dealt with in the realm of the spirit.

The three pieces of furniture in the Holy Place symbolize ways in which our soul can be tuned to the things of the Spirit. In other words, they symbolize how the spirit realm works through our intellect, emotions and the will. The candlestick represents the power of the Holy Spirit working. Let me explain that the power of the Holy Spirit will always have to flow through your renewed mind. I Cor. 2: 8 tell us that the natural man does not receive the things of the Spirit. Anyone who has been led by the Spirit to a certain extend will know that the gift of the Spirit operates in proportion to the renewed ness of the mind. God has to deal with your intellect. Your intellect has to be touched and transformed by God, so that the gift of the Spirit can flow through. The limitations of the gift of the Spirit are limited by your thought life.

For the weapons of our warfare are not worldly but have divine power to destroy strongholds. We destroy arguments and every proud obstacles to the knowledge of God, and take every thought captive to obey Christ. (II Cor. 10).

Now in all teaching on the gifts of the Spirit, they will always tell you that the gifts of the Spirit function as spiritual weapons to destroy the works of the devil. So the gifts of the Spirit are the equipment that God gives to us to wage warfare against the enemy. Notice how all our spiritual weapons are not carnal but they are mighty through God. And yet, it has an association with the thought life and the thought realm.

So if you want your intellect to be submissive to God and to flow in the things of God you have to be dealt with by the Word of God in order for the intellect to be a vessel for God to flow through, for God to use. You can talk personally to any person who stands in the prophet office or anybody who operates the gift of prophecy. They will tell you that part of what they receive come also to their mind. They may not describe it as thoroughly but their mind is also used. Of course when we speak a prophecy with our understanding our mind is involved. We are still conscious and our minds do hear the things of the Spirit of God. So the Word has to deal with the mind.

The table of showbread, which represent the power the name of the Lord Jesus Christ and Jesus Christ the King of Kings and Lord of Lords, represents the work of God on your will. This is where the revelation of your position in Christ comes in. Our free will is involved in the realm of our position in Christ. Like for example, you may be affected in the natural realm and be insecure if you do not know your positioning in Christ. But by the power of the Name of Jesus, you can make a choice. You could develop the realm of your freewill. Instead of choosing the doctrines and things of the enemy, you exercise your freewill to go by God's Word and the Name of the Lord Jesus Christ. You choose to go by the Name of Jesus. You go by what Smith Wigglesworth always say, "I am not moved by what I feel; I am not moved by what I see; I am moved only by the Word of God." That is the freewill the free choice. You may have certain things that are in conflict and are contradictory to your normal reasoning but then your freewill chooses God. So, the Name of Jesus strengthens our freewill. And understanding our position in Christ strengthens the area of our choice and deals with the will.

And the altar of incense representing the power of praise, prayers and worship deals with your emotional realm. You notice that when you pray a lot and when you worship God a lot one of the things that is affected is your emotions. There is no way you can really give true worship to God without your emotions being changed and transformed. Worship involves your emotions. Prayer for long period of time involves your emotions. Your emotions are being transformed and changed. The power of praise and worship affects your emotions.

So, we have the will, the emotions and the intellect being instruments of God. The power of the Holy Spirit flows through and affects your intellect.

Frequency Revelator

The name of Jesus the revelation of Jesus Christ affects your will power. Knowledge and truth sets you free. When you know what Jesus had done, you are free. You know you could choose. Sometimes people don't choose because they know not what they have. So, the revelation of your position in Christ and of the Name of Jesus re-enforces your will. If people do not know the things that belong to them, they will never exercise their freewill. But when you know what is yours, your freewill is strengthened because now you know your rights. If somebody comes to your house and say, "This house belongs to me," you know that it belongs to you. You will fight for your rights. You stand on your ground. But if you are not sure yourself, if you don't have any legal document and somebody comes to you and say that house is his, you say, "Is that right?" Your freewill is shaken. You are not sure whether you could stand or not. So the revelation of the Name of Jesus and your position in Christ will strengthen your freewill. Your freewill, your emotions and your intellect are affected. This is your soul area that God wants to deal with.

Of course we come to the ark. In the ark, there are three pieces of instruments there, the manna, the rod and the tablets. Those three represents three realms of your spirit man. The spirit man has three different realms of function. One is the intuition, one is the communion and one is the conscience. Intuition is what we receive from God in a sense of direction. Communion is our union with God and our fellowship and love walk with God. And conscience is our sense of right and wrong. So in those three things the tablets of Moses, the Ten Commandments that are stored in the ark represents your conscience. The manna represents those things that God imparts upon your life. Manna is something that is for partaking. So, that is representative of your communion with God. Manna is something to partake and eat. The rod of Aaron that put forth buds, blossoms and ripe almonds was a sign from God that he was God's chosen priest. His rod was then put back "before the testimony" as a warning against further rebellion (Num. 17: 1-11). Aaron's rod represents the special inner revelation of God or intuition. So these are the three parts of your spirit man.

In the last message, we described the two aspects of the soul. In your soul, you have the *dianoia* and the *dialogismos*. Then in the outer fringes of your soul, you have the *nous* that is your normal consciousness. In your soul realm, you have the *nous,* the *dialogismos* and the *dianoia.* The *nous* represents your conscious mind. The *dianoia* and the *dialogismos* rest more in the realm of your sub-conscious although part of it is in the conscious mind. About 5 percent of our mind is conscious and 95 percent is sub-conscious. That is why the sub-conscious mind is far more powerful than the conscious mind. And it affects and influences the choices of the conscious mind makes. *Dianoia* is a part of your mind that visualizes and sees pictures. The other part of your mind is the *dialogismos* that calculates one plus one equals two. It is the part of your mind that is logical. It brings a logical conclusion in your mind. Now there are two other parts of your mind, the *ennoia* and the *enthumesis.* The *ennoia* is the part of your *dianoia* that resides in the spirit man. Your spirit man has the ability to see pictures also. Of course, the ability to reason is in a higher realm. The *ennoia,* which is related indirectly to *dianoia* and the *enthumesis,* which is indirectly related to *dialogismos* dwell and reside in the realm of your spirit man.

What we have is our consciousness. This is where we relate to visualizing. When you sleep your consciousness transfers into the realm of the sub-conscious. When you are asleep, you are not aware of your physical body at all. Your consciousness resides in the realm of your sub-conscious. There are two veils in Moses' Tabernacle. The *nous* is the conscious part of your mind. The conscious part of your mind relates to the physical world and to the soul realm. The *nous* represents the consciousness of your soul that contacts the physical world and yet it's in contact with the other world inside you, your soul and indirectly the spirit world. There is a consciousness that you will have under normal waking hours. Your consciousness is at the *nous.* You are partly conscious of your conscious mind and you are conscious of the physical world. Your consciousness stands at this veil between the Outer Court (body) and the Holy Place (soul). You are relating to two realms. You are relating to the physical world and the inner realm of your spirit and your soul indirectly. When you are asleep, your consciousness moves out from the conscious realm and goes into the level of your sub-conscious. That is where your *nous* is sort of closed up. The physical world is still there but you are not conscious of the physical world at all. Your consciousness has moved deep

CHAPTER TWELVE

THE PROPHETIC DREAM DICTIONARY

Despite all the dream interpretation books out there, dream symbol meanings are different for each person. Dreams are very personal, and should be interpreted personally. What the dream symbol means to you, what it reminds you of, and how it makes you feel, are all mysterious aspects of dream interpretation that God wants you to unlock. Sometimes, you have to look beyond the obvious, and consider how the dream symbol appears in the dream. For example, in a dream about a bee - what was the bee doing, how and where it was doing it, and how did you feel about it? A dream is often about something other than its obvious meaning. Physical events in the dream commonly represent spiritual, relational, mental, or emotional matters. However, it is important that all dreams be interpreted in line with God's word as it carries all answers humanity might need.

The Meaning Of Dream Symbols:

Dream Symbols About Animals

Bat– witchcraft; unstable; flighty; fear

Bear – judgment; strength; opposition; an evil spirit that wants something you have; economic loss

Bird – symbol of spirits, good or evil

Bull – persecution; spiritual warfare; opposition, accusation; slander, threat

Camel – endurance; long journey; ungainly (not graceful)

Cat – self-willed; untrainable; predator; unclean spirit; bewitching charm; stealthy, sneaky, or deceptive; something precious in the context of a personal pet: Black Cat – witchcraft

Cheetah – swift or fast; predator, danger; play on word for "Cheater"

Chicken – fear, cowardliness; hen can be protection, gossip, motherhood; rooster can be boasting, bragging, proud; chick can be defenceless, innocent

Colt – bearing the burden of others; or stubbornness

Crab – not easy to approach

Crow (raven) – confusion; outspoken; operating in envy or strife; hateful; unclean; God's minister of justice or provision

Cow – subsistence; prosperity

Deer – graceful, swift; sure-footed, agile; timid

Dog – unbelievers; religious hypocrites; loyalty, friendship, or faithfulness: Pit bull Dog – ferocious demonic spirit

Donkey – gentle strength, burden bearer; negative – stubborn

Dove – Holy Spirit

Dragon – Satan

Dinosaur – old stronghold, demonic, danger from the past (generational stronghold)

Eagle – prophetic; prophetic calling

Elephant – invincible or thick skinned; not easily offended; powerful; large; having great impact; storing memory; old memory; long pregnancy

Fish – souls of men

Fox – cunning, evil men; sly, sneaky; something that steals from you

Frog – spirit of lust; demon; curse; witchcraft

Goat – sinner; unbelief; stubborn; argumentative; no discernment; negative person; being blamed for something (as in "scapegoat"); positive – prosperity in some cultures

Hawk – predator; sorcerer; evil spirit; a person who is for war

Hare – fast, hasty, quick

Hen – one who gathers, protects

Horse – power, strength, conquest; spiritual warfare: White Horse – salvation; rescue; redeem; royalty: Black Horse – feminine; bad times; evil (Rev 6:5): Red Horse – persecution; anger; danger; opposition (Rev 6:4)

Leopard – swiftness, sometimes associated with vengeance, predator, danger

Lion – Jesus "Lion of the tribe of Judah"; royalty, kingship, bravery; confidence; Satan seeking to destroy

Mice – something small that bring destruction; devourer, curse, plague, timid

Monkey – foolishness; clinging; mischief; dishonesty; addiction

Mountain Lion – Satan, enemy; predator seeking to destroy

Ox – slow change; subsistence

Pig – ignorance; hypocrisy; religious unbelievers, unclean people; selfish, gluttonous; vicious, vengeful

Ram – sacrifice

Rat – feeds on garbage or impurities; unclean spirit, invader

Raven – evil, Satan

Serpent – Satan & evil spirits

Sheep – the people of God; innocent, vulnerable; humility; submission; sacrifice

Snake – deception, lies; Satan; unforgiveness, bitterness: White Snake – spirit of religion; occult

Sparrow – small value but precious; watched by the Lord

Tiger – danger; powerful minister (both good & evil), soul power, demonic spirit

Tortoise – slow moving; slow change; steady; old; old way of doing something; wise

Turkey – foolish; clumsy; dumb; thanksgiving

Vulture – scavenger; unclean; impure; an evil person; greedy

Weasel – wicked; breaking promises (as in "weaseling out of a deal"); informant or tattletale; traitor

Whale – big impact in the things of the Spirit; going deep in the spirit

Wolf – Satan and evil; false ministries & false teachers; predator

Dream Symbols About People

Baby – new ministry or responsibility that has recently been birthed; new beginning; new idea; dependent, helpless; innocent; sin

Bride – Christ's church; covenant, relationship

Carpenter – Jesus; someone who makes or mends things; building something spiritually or naturally; preacher

Giant – Positive: godly men (as in "a giant of the faith"); strong; conquer; Negative: demons; defilement (as in the Philistine Giant Goliath)

Harlot Or Prostitute – a tempting situation; appealing to your flesh; worldly desire; a demon; spirit of lust; spiritual apostasy

Hijacker – enemy wanting to take control of you or a situation

Husband – Jesus Christ; actual person

Lawyer – Positive: Jesus Christ, our advocate; mediator; Negative: Satan, the accuser of the brethren; legalism

Mob – false accusation

Policemen – authority for good or evil; protector; spiritual authority

Prisoner – a lost soul

Shepherd – Jesus Christ; pastor, leader (good or bad); selfless person; protector

Twins – Positive: double blessing or anointing; Negative: double trouble

Dream Symbols About Transportation

Airplane – (size & type of plane correlates to the interpretation) prophetic ministry; going to heights in the Spirit; new & higher understanding

Armoured Car – protection of God

Automobile – personal ministry or job

Bicycle – individual ministry or calling requiring perseverance

Bus – church or ministry

Chariot – major spiritual encounter

Convertible – open heaven in your personal ministry or job

Fire Truck – rescue; putting out fires of destruction

Helicopter – mobile, flexible, able to get in Spirit quickly

Limousine – Positive: being taken to your destiny in style; Negative: materialism

Understanding Prophetic Dreams & Visions

Mickey Mouse Car – purpose is colourful & entertaining

Motorcycle – fast; powerful; manoeuvrable

Moving Van – transition; change

Riverboat – slow, but impacting many people

Rollercoaster – Positive: a wild ride that God is directing, exciting, but temporary; Negative: a path of destruction that first appears exciting; an emotional trying time with ups and downs

Sailboats – powered by wind of the Spirit

Semi-truck – transporting great quantity of goods

Spaceship – to the outer limits, spiritually speaking

Speedboat – fast, exciting, power in the Spirit

Submarine – undercover and active, but not seen by many; a behind the scenes ministry, hidden ministry

Subway – undercover and active, but not seen by many; a behind the scenes ministry, hidden ministry

Taxi Cab – a shepherd or hireling for someone (driving); paying the price to get where you are going (passenger)

Tow Truck – ministry of helps; gathering the wounded

Tractor – slow power; may speak about a need to plow

Train – a movement of God; denomination

Truck – ability to transport or deliver

Dream Symbols About Clothing

Coat – mantle, anointing

Swimwear – ability to move in the Spirit

Shorts – a walk or calling that is partially fulfilled

Bathrobe – coming out of a place of cleansing

Pajamas – spiritual slumber

Cultural Clothing – missionary calling; prayer calling for a particular country or ethnic group

Wedding Dress – covenant; deep relationship

Shoes – Gospel of peace

Clothing that doesn't fit – walking in something you're not called to

Tattered Clothing – mantle or anointing that's not being taken care of

Dream Symbols About Buildings/Places

Auto Repair Shop – ministry restoration, renewal & repair

Back Porch – history; past

Barn/warehouse – a place of provision & storag

Castle – authority, fortress, royal residence

Country General Store – provision; basics, staples

Elevator – changing position; going up in the spiritual realm, elevated; going down – demotion, trial; backsliding

Farm – place of provision

Foundation – important foundational issues; established; stable or unstable (depending on the context); the gospel; sound doctrine; church government

Garage – place to rest & refresh; place of protection; covering for ministries or people

Understanding Prophetic Dreams & Visions

Garden – a person's heart; love; intimacy; growth

Gas Station – receiving power; refilling or "refueling" of the Spirit; empowering

Hallway – transition that is usually direct or without deviation

High-rise Building – high spiritual calling or high spiritual perspective

Hospital – place of healing, healing anointing

House – person, family; ministry; church

Previous, Old Home – past; inheritance; memory; revisiting old issues

Buying, or living in, the house of a known person in the ministry – God has a similar call on your life.

Two-story House – double anointing

Hotel – transition; temporary; place to relax or receive

Jail or Prison – bondage; rebellion; addiction

Prisoners – lost souls; persecuted saints

Library – learning; knowledge; research

Mall – market place; provision for all your needs in 1 place; Negative – self centeredness; materialism

Mobile Home or Trailer House – temporary place, condition or relationship; movement, easily movable; poverty

Mountain – place of encountering God; obstacle; difficulty; challenge; Kingdom, nation

Office building – getting things accomplished; productivity

Park – rest, peace; leisure; God's blessing; vagrancy

Roof – spiritual covering

School / Classroom – training period; a place of teaching; teaching ministry; teaching anointing

Shack – poverty

Stadium – place of tremendous impact

Staircase – up: promotion; down: demotion, backsliding, failure; heavenly portal; up or down in the spirit and anointing; steps that need to be taken

Swimming Pool – place of spiritual refreshing; a place of God's Spirit; immersed in God; dirty water can indicate spiritual pollution, corruption or backslidden condition

Tent – temporary place of rest; meeting place with God

Theater – on display, visible; going to be shown something; clarity; spiritual sight; fleshly lust

Windows – vision; letting light in, spiritual sight, opportunity (as in an "open window of opportunity")

Zoo – strange; chaos; commotion; very busy place; noisy strife

Dream Symbols About Weather

Earthquake – upheaval; change (by crisis); God's judgment, disaster; trauma, shaking; shock

Fog – clouded issues or thoughts; uncertainty; confusion; temporary

Hail – judgment; destruction; bombardment

Ice/Ice Storm – hard saying; slippery; dangerous

Rain – blessing; cleansing (clear rain); trouble from enemy (dirty rain)

Snow – blessing; refreshing; righteousness; purity; grace (Isaiah 55:10-11a)

Dirty Snow – impure

Snow Drift – barrier; hindrance; opposition

Snow Blizzard – inability to see; storm that blinds you or obstructs your vision

Storms – disturbance; change; spiritual warfare; judgment; sudden calamity or destruction; turbulent times; trial; opposition

White Storm – God's power; revival, outpouring of the Holy Spirit

Tornadoes – destruction, danger; judgment; drastic change; winds of change (negative or positive depending on the color of the tornadoes)

Wind – change (as in "winds of change are blowing"); Positive: Holy Spirit; Negative: adversity

Dream Symbols About Objects

Crown – symbol of authority, to reign; seal of power; Jesus Christ; honor, reward

Television – spiritual sight & understanding; entertainment; fleshly cravings & desires; fleshly spirit; love of the world

Microphone – influence; ministry; authority; being heard

Microwave – impatience; quick work; convenient; sudden

Mirror – God's Word; a person's heart; vanity

Money – gain or loss of favor; power; provision; wealth; spiritual riches; authority; strength of man; covetousness; greed

Check – favour

Credit Card – presumption; lack of trust; attempting to walk in something that you don't have yet; debt

Frequency Revelator

Trees – leaders; mature believers; steady

Fruited Trees – healing

Gate – spiritual authority; entrance point for good or evil

Key – spiritual authority; wisdom; understanding; ability; Jesus

Ladder – ascending or descending; promotion or demotion; going higher into the things of God; portal of heavenly activity (as in Jacobs ladder had angels ascending and descending)

Dream Symbols About Body Parts

Arm – strength; faith

Bald Head – lacking wisdom

Beard – maturity

Hair – wisdom & anointing

Hand – relationship; healing

Immobilized Body Parts – spiritual hindrance; demonic attack

Nakedness – Positive: being transparent; humility; innocence. Negative: lust; temptation; in or of the flesh

Neck – Positive: support or strength. Negative: stiff necked, stubborn

Nose – discernment

Side – relationship; friendship

Teeth – wisdom; comprehension; understanding

Eye Teeth – revelatory understanding

Wisdom Teeth – ability to act in wisdom

Miscellaneous:

Pregnancy – in process of reproducing; preparatory stage; promise of God; Word of God as seed; prophetic word; desire, anticipation, expectancy; purposes of God preparing to come forth

Miscarriage – losing something at the preparatory stage, whether good or bad; plans aborted

Repeating activities – God establishing a matter or issue; repeating because you are not listening

Flying – call or ability of move in the higher things of God; understanding the spirit realm of God

Life seasons – may include former places you have been/lived, and/or former schools, tests, jobs, etc. – Reflect on the significance of that season.

Kiss – coming into agreement; covenant; seductive process; enticement; deception, betrayal; betrayal from a trusted friend

Christmas – gifts; season of rejoicing; spiritual gifts; surprise; good will; benevolence; commercialism

Choking – hindrance; difficulty in accepting something (as in "the news was hard to swallow"); hatred or anger (as in "I could choke her right now"); unfruitful (as in the weeds growing up and **choking the plants)**

Chewing – thinking on something (as in, "I need to chew on that"), meditating; receiving wisdom & understanding

Difficulty Chewing – hard saying; difficulty receiving something

Running – faith; perseverance; working out one's salvation; moving forward with purpose

Swimming – living in the Spirit; moving in the things of the Spirit; operating in the gifts of the Spirit

Dream Symbols About Numbers

God will use numbers as symbols in dreams and visions (Genesis 40 & 41; Daniel 4; and throughout Revelation). Numbers may have a symbolic intent such as the meanings in the chart below. They may also refer to scripture texts. For the cultures of the ancient Near East, numbers had a quantitative (literal) as well as a qualitative (symbolic) value. The practice developed of assigning numerical value to the letters of the Hebrew and Greek alphabets.2. The number value of words is determined by adding the numbers represented by the letters.25. For example, the Greek name for "Jesus" totals 888. A clear example is found at Revelation 13:18, "Here is wisdom. Let him who has understanding calculate the number of the beast, for it is the number of a man: His number is 666." Verse 17 says "the name of the beast, or the number of his name." Thus, the number refers to a specific person. Consider the number "seven." It is used from Genesis to Revelation, ooften with symbolic meaning. Seven is the number of perfection or completion. a) In Genesis chapters one and two, the "seven days of creation" establish the seven day week. "The symbolism of completeness occurs in a wide variety of uses of the number seven. For example, sprinkling the blood of a sacrifice seven times (Lev. 16:14, 19) indicates complete purification. The seven "eyes of the Lord, which range through the whole earth" (Zech. 4:10 NRSV) indicate the completeness of God's sight of everything in His creation."

1 – God

2 – Multiplication, division

3 – Godhead (Triune God)

4 – God's creative works

5 – Grace, redemption

Understanding Prophetic Dreams & Visions

6 – Man

7 – Perfection, completion

8 – New beginnings (Teacher)

9 – Judgment (Evangelist)

10 – Journey, wilderness (Pastor)

11 – Transition (Prophet)

12 – Government (Apostle)

13 – Rebellion

14 – Double anointing

15 – Reprieve, mercy

16 – Established beginnings

17 – Election

25 – Begin ministry training

30 – Begin ministry

111 – My Beloved Son

666 – Full lawlessness

888 – Resurrection

10,000 – Maturity

Dream Symbols About Colours

Red – wisdom, anointing, & power   Negative – anger, war

Blue – revelation, communion   Negative – depression, sorrow, anxiety

Green – growth, prosperity, conscious   Negative – envy, jealousy, pride

Brown – compassion, humility   Negative – compromise, humanism

Gold/amber – purity, glory, holiness   Negative – idolatry, defilement, licentiousness

Purple – authority, royalty   Negative – false authority

Orange – perseverance   Negative – stubbornness

Silver – redemption, grace   Negative – legalism

Yellow – hope, mind   Negative – fear, cowards, intellectual pride

Pink – childlike, love of God   Negative – childishness

Gray – maturity, honor, wisdom   Negative – weakness

White – righteousness, holiness   Negative – religious spirit

Black – death, mystery   Negative – sin, darkness

Dream Symbols About Directions

EAST - Beginning: Law (therefore blessed or cursed); birth; first Genesis 11:2; Job 38:24.

FRONT - Future or Now: (As in FRONT YARD); In the presence of; prophecy; immediate; current. Genesis 6:11; Revelation 1:19.

NORTH - Spiritual: Judgment; heaven; spiritual warfare (as in "taking your inheritance"). Proverbs 25:23; Jeremiah 1:13-14.

LEFT - Spiritual: Weakness (of man), and therefore God's strength or ability; rejected. (Left Turn = spiritual change). Judges 3:20-21; 2 Corinthians

12:9-10.

SOUTH - Natural: Sin; world; temptation; trial; flesh; corruption; deception. Joshua 10:40; Job 37:9)

RIGHT - Natural: Authority; power; the strength of man (flesh) or the power of God revealed through man; accepted. (Right Turn = natural change). Matthew 5:29a, 30a; 1 Peter 3:22.

WEST - End: Grace; death; last; conformed. Exodus 10:19; Luke 12:54.

BACK - Past: As in BACKYARD or BACKDOOR. Previous event or experience (good or evil); that which is behind (in time-for example, past sins or the sins of forefathers); unaware; unsuspecting; hidden; memory. Genesis 22:13; Joshua 8:4.

Dream Symbols About People/Relatives/Trades

BABY - New: Beginning; work; idea; the Church; sin; innocent; dependant; helpless; natural baby. 1 Corinthians 3:1; Isaiah 43:19.

CARPENTER - Builder: Preacher; evangelist; laborer (good or evil); Christ. 2 Kings 22:6; Isaiah 41:7

DOCTOR - Healer: Christ; preacher; authority; medical doctor, when naturally interpreted. Mark 2:17; 2 Chronicles 16:12.

DRUNK - Influenced: Under a spell (i.e., under the influence of the Holy Spirit or a demon's spirit); controlled;fool; stubborn; rebellious; witchcraft. Ephesians 5:18; Proverbs 14:16

EMPLOYER - Servants: pastor, Christ; satan; actual employer, when naturally interpreted. Colossians 3:22; 2 Peter 2:19.

GIANT - Strongman: Stronghold, challenge; obstacle; trouble. Numbers 13:32-33.

INDIAN - First: Flesh (as in "the old man")' firstborn; chief; fierce; savvy;

native. Colossians 3:9; Genesis 49:3.

POLICE - Authority: Natural (civil) or spiritual authority (pastors, etc.), good or evil; protection; angels or demons; an enforcer of a curse of the Law. Romans 13:1; Luke 12:11.

Dream Symbols About Vehicles And Parts

AIRPLANE - Person or work; The Church; ministry; oversight (Soaring=Moved by the Spirit). Habakkuk 1:8; Judges 13:25.

JET - Ministry or Minister: Powerful; fast. (Passenger jet = Church; Fighter = Individual person). Genesis 41:43; 2 Kings 10:16.

AUTOMOBILE - Life: Person; ministry (New car = New ministry or New way of life). Genesis 41:43; 2 Kings 10:16.

AUTO WRECK - Strife: Contention; conflict, calamity; mistake or sin in ministry (as in "failure to maintain right-of-way"). Nahum 2:4. BICYCLE - Works: Works of the flesh (not of faith); self-righteousness; messenger. Galatians 5:4; Galatians 5:19.

BOAT - Church or personal ministry: (Sailboat = moved by the Spirit; Powerboat = powerful or fast progress) Genesis 6:16; 1 Timothy 1:19. BRAKES - Stop: Hindrance; resist; wait. Acts 16:6-7; 2 Peter 2:14.

HELICOPTOR - Ministry: Personal; individual; the Church; versatile; stationary (when unmoving). 2 Timothy 4:2; Romans 8:14.

MOTORCYCLE - Individual: Personal ministry; independent; rebellion; selfish; pride; swift progress. 2 Peter 2:10; 1 Samuel 15:23.

PICKUP TRUCK - Work: Personal ministry or natural work. 1 Chronicles 13:7; Galatians 6:5.

REARVIEW MIRROR - Word: (Driving backward using the rearview mirror = operating by the letter of the Word instead of by God's Spirit); legalistic; looking back; 2 Corinthians 3:6; Genesis 19:26.

RAFT - Adrift: Without direction; aimless; powerless. Ephesians 4:14>

TRACTOR - Powerful work: Slow but powerful ministry. Acts 1:8; Acts 4:33.

TRACTOR-TRAILOR - Large burden: Ministry; powerful and/or large work (truck size is often in proportion to the burden or size of the work).

Miscellaneous

ANKLES - Faith: Weak ankles = weak faith; unsupported; undependable. Ezekiel 47:3.

ARM - Strength or weakness: Savior; deliverer; helper; aid; reaching out. Isaiah 52:10; Psalm 136:12.

BANK - Secure: Church; dependable; safe; saved; sure (as in "you can bank on it"); reserved in Heaven. Luke 19:23; Matthew 6:20.

BINOCULARS - Insight: Understanding; prophetic vision; future event. John 16:13; 2 Corinthians 3:13, 16.

BLEEDING - Wounded: Hurt, naturally or emotionally; dying spiritually; offended; gossip; unclean. Psalm 147:3; Proverbs 18:8.

BLOOD TRANSFUSION - Change: Regeneration; salvation; deliverance. Titus 3:5; Romans 12:2.

BRIDGE- Faith: Trial; way; joined. Genesis 32:22; 1 Corinthians 10:13.

BUTTER - Works: Doing (or not doing) the Word or will of God; deceptive motives; words; smooth. Psalm 55:21; Proverbs 30:33.

CALENDAR - Time: Date: event; appointment. Hosea 6:11.

CARDS - Facts: Honesty (as in "putting all your cards on the table"); truth; expose or reveal; dishonest; cheat; deceitful. Romans 12:17.

CARNIVAL - Worldly: Exhibitionism; divination; competition. Acts 16:16;

Luke 21:34. **CHAIR** - Position: Seat of authority; rest. Esther 3:1; Revelations 13:2.

CHECK - Faith: The currency of the Kingdom of God; provision; trust. Hebrews 11:1; Mark 4:40.

CHOKING - Hinder: Stumbling over something (as in "that's too much to swallow"); hatred or anger (as in "I could choke him!") Mark 4:19.

CHRISTMAS- Gift: Season of rejoicing; spiritual gifts; a surprise; good will. Luke 11:13; 1 Corinthians 14:1.

CLOSET - Private: Personal, prayer; secret sin; hidden. Matthew 6:6; Luke 8:17.

COFFEE - Bitter or Stimulant: Repentance; reaping what one has sown; desire for revenge (bitter envying). Number 9:11; Job 13:26.

DITCH - Habit: Religious tradition; addition; lust; passion. Matthew 15:14; Psalm 7:15.

DOMINOES - Continuous: Chain reaction. Leviticus 26:37.

EARTHQUAKE- Upheaval: change (by crisis), repentance; trial; God's judgment; disaster; trauma. Acts 16:26; Isaiah 29:6.

ECHO- Repetition: Gossip, accusation; voice of many; mocking. Luke 23:21.

EGG - Idea: new thought; plan; promise; potential. Luke 11:12; 1 Timothy 4:15.

FENCE - Barrier: Boundaries; obstacles; religious traditions; doctrines; inhibitions. Genesis 11:6; Jeremiah 15:20.

GARBAGE (DUMP) - Rejected: Hell; evil; vile; corruption. Mark 9:47-48; 1 Corinthians 9:27.

MOWED GRASS - Chastisement: Sickness; financial need or distress; emotional and mental depression or anguish. Amos 7:1-2; 1 Corinthians

11:30-32.

GRAVEYARD - Hidden: Past; curse; evil inheritance; hypocrisy; demon. Matthew 23:27; Luke 11:44.

GRAVEL PIT - Source: The Word of God; abundant supply. Deuteronomy 8:9; 2 Timothy 2:15.

MUDDY ROAD - Flesh: Man's way; lust; passion; temptation; difficulty caused by the weakness of the flesh. Psalm 69:2; Isaiah 57:20.

IRONING - Correction: Change; sanctification; exhorting; teaching righteousness; God's discipline; pressure (from trials). Ephesians 5:27.

LADDER - Ascend or descend: Escape; enable; way; steps. Genesis 28:12-13; John 3:13.

LIPS - Words: Seduction; speech. Proverbs 7:21; Proverbs 10:19.

MAP - Directions: Word of God; correction; advice. Proverbs 6:23.

MICROPHONE - Voice: Authority; ministry; influence. Matthew 10:27.

MIRROR - Word or one's heart: God's Word; looking back; memory, past; vanity; Moses' Law. 1 Corinthians 13:12; Proverbs 27:19.

NEWSPAPER- Announcement: Important event; public exposure; news; gossip. Luke 8:17.

OVEN - Heart: heat of passion; imagination; meditation; judgment. Hosea 7:6; Psalm 21:9.

PAINT BRUSH - Covering: (house painter's brush: regeneration: remodel, renovate; love. Artist's Paint Brush: Illustrative; eloquent; humorous; articulate.) 1 Peter 4:8; Titus 3:5.

PARACHUTING- Leave: Bail out; escape; flee; saved. 2 Corinthians 6:17.

PERFUME - Seduction: Enticement; temptation; persuasion; deception. Proverbs 7:7, 10, 13; Ecclesiastes 10:1.

Frequency Revelator

PIE - Whole: Business endeavors; part of the action. Luke 12:13.

PLAY - Worship: Idolatry; covetousness; true worship; spiritual warfare; strife; competition. Colossians 3:5; 1 Corinthians 9:24.

POSTAGE STAMP - Seal: Authority; authorizations; small or seemingly insignificant, but powerful. Esther 8:8; John 6:27.

RADIO - Unchangeable: Unbelief; unrelenting; contentious; unceasing; tradition. Proverbs 27:15.

RAILROAD TRACK - Tradition: Unchanging; habit; stubborn; gospel. Mark 7:9, 13; Colossians 2:8.

RAPE - Violation: Abuse of authority; hate; desire for revenge; murder. 2 Samuel 13:12, 14-15; Deuteronomy 22:25-26.

REFRIGERATOR - Heart: Motive; attitude; stored in heart; harbor. Matthew 12:35; Mark 7:21-22.

ROCKING CHAIR - Old: Past, memories; medication; retirement; rest. Jeremiah 6:16.

ROLLER COASTER - Unstable: emotional instability; unfaithfulness; wavering; manic-depressive; depression; trials; excitement. Isaiah 40:4; James 1:6-8.

ROLLER SKATES - Speed: Fast; swift advancement or progress. Romans 9:28.

ROUND (shape) - Spiritual: (A round face, ring, building, etc.) Grace; mercy; compassion; forgiveness. Leviticus 19:27.

SEA COAST - Boundary: Flesh (which contains and limits the spirit of man); limitations; weights. Jeremiah 5:22; Jeremiah 47:6-7.

SHOVEL - Tongue: Prayer; confession; slander; dig; search; inquire. 2 Kings 3:16-17; Deuteronomy 23:13

AUTHOR'S PROFILE

Frequency Revelator is an apostle, called by God through His grace to minister the Gospel of the Lord Jesus Christ to all the nations of the world. He is a television minister, lecturer and gifted author, whose writings are Holy Ghost breathings that unveil consistent streams of fresh revelations straight from the Throne Room of Heaven. He is the president, founder and vision bearer of Frequency Revelator Ministries (FRM), a worldwide multiracial ministry that encompasses a myriad of movements with divine visions such as Resurrection Embassy (*The Global Church*), Christ Resurrection Movement (CRM) (*a Global movement for raising the dead*), the Global Apostolic & Prophetic Network (GAP) (a *Network of apostles, prophets and fivefold ministers across the globe*), Revival For Southern Africa (REFOSA) (*a Regional power-packed vision for Southern Africa*) and the Global Destiny Publishing House (GDP) (*the Ministry's publishing company*). The primary vision of this global ministry is to propagate the resurrection power of Christ from the Throne Room of Heaven to the extreme ends of the world and to launch the world into the greater depths of the miraculous. It is for this reason that Frequency Revelator Ministries (FRM) drives divergent apostolic and prophetic ministry visions and spiritual programmes such as the Global School of Resurrection (GSR), Global Resurrection Centre (GRC), the Global Healing Centre (GHC), Global School of Miracles, Signs and Wonders (SMSW), Global School of Kingdom Millionaires (SKM), Global Campus Ministry as well as Resurrection Conferences, Seminars and Training Centers. To fulfil it's global mandate of soul winning, the ministry spearheads the Heavens' Broadcasting Commission (HBC) on television, a strategic ministerial initiative that broadcasts ministry programmes via the Dead Raising Channel *(a.k.a Resurrection TV)* and other Christian Television networks around the world.

Presiding over a global network of apostolic and prophetic visions, Apostle Frequency Revelator considers universities, colleges, high schools and other centers of learning as critical in fulfilling God's purpose and reaching the world for Christ, especially in this end-time season. As a Signs and Wonders Movement, the ministry hosts training sessions at the Global School of Resurrection (GSR) which includes but not limited to, impartation and activation of the gifts of the Spirit, prophetic declaration and ministration, invocations of open visions, angelic encounters and Throne Room visitations, revelational teachings, coaching and mentorship as well as Holy Ghost ministerial training sessions on how to practically raise the dead. This global ministry is therefore characterized by a deep revelation of God's word accompanied by a practical demonstration of God's power through miracles, signs and wonders manifested in raising cripples from wheel chairs, opening the eyes of the blind, unlocking the speech of the dumb, blasting off the ears of the deaf and raising the dead, as a manifestation of the finished works of the cross by the Lord Jesus Christ. The ministry is also punctuated with a plethora of manifestations of the wealth of Heaven through miracle money, coupled with the golden rain of gold dust, silver stones, supernatural oil and a torrent of creative miracles such as the development of the original blue print of body parts on bodily territories where they previously did not exist, germination of hair on bald heads, weight loss and gain, as well as instantaneous healings from HIV/AIDS, cancer, diabetes and every manner of sickness and disease which doctors have declared as incurable.

The author has written a collection of over **50** anointed books, which include *The Realm of Power to Raise the Dead, How to become a Kingdom Millionaire, Deeper Revelations of The Anointing, Practical Demonstrations of The Anointing, How to Operate in the Realm of the Miraculous, The Realm of Glory, Unveiling the Mystery of Miracle Money, New Revelations of Faith, A Divine Revelation of the Supernatural Realm, The Prophetic Move of the Holy Spirit in the Contemporary Global Arena, The Ministry of Angels in the World Today, Kingdom Spiritual Laws and Principles, Divine Rights and Privileges of a Believer, Keys to Unlocking the Supernatural, The Prophetic Dimension, The Dynamics of God's Word, The Practice of God's Presence, Times of Refreshing and Restoration, The Power of Praying in the Throne Room, Understanding Times And Seasons In God's Calendar, How To Defeat The Spirit Of Witchcraft, The Practice Of God's Presence, 21 Ways Of How To Hear God's Voice Clearly, Miracles, Signs And Wonders, Understanding Prophetic Dreams And Visions, Deeper Revelations Of The Glory Realm, The Prophetic Significance Of Gold Dust, Silver Stones, Diamonds And Other Precious Stones, The Power Of The Apostolic Anointing, Deeper Revelations Of The Five-Fold Ministry, The Anatomy And Physiology Of The Anointing, How To Activate And Fully Exercise The Gifts Of The Spirit, Healing Rains, The Realm Of Love, The Revelation Of Jesus, The Second Coming Of Jesus and Rain of Revelations,* which is a daily devotional concordance comprising a yearly record of 365 fresh revelations straight from the Throne Room of God.

Understanding Prophetic Dreams & Visions

Apostle Frequency Revelator resides in South Africa and he is a graduate of Fort Hare University, where his ministry took off. However, as a global minister, his ministry incorporates prophecy, deliverance and miracle healing crusades in the United Kingdom (UK), Southern Africa, India, Australia, USA, Canada and a dense network of ministry visions that covers the rest of the world. As a custodian of God's resurrection power, the apostle has been given a divine mandate from Heaven to raise a new breed of Apostles, Prophets, Pastors, Evangelists, Teachers, Kingdom Millionaires and Miracle Workers (*Dead raisers*) who shall propagate the world with the gospel of the Lord Jesus Christ and practically demonstrate His resurrection power through miracles, signs and wonders manifested in raising people from the dead, thereby launching the world in to the greater depths of the miraculous. To that effect, a conducive platform is therefore enacted for global impartation, mentorship, training and equipping ministers of the gospel for the work of ministry. Notable is the realization that the ministry ushers a new wave of signs and wonders that catapults the Body of Christ into higher realms of glory in which raising the dead is a common occurrence and demonstrating the viscosity of the glory of God in a visible and tangible manner is the order of the day.

AUTHOR'S CONTACT INFORMATION

To know more about the ministry of Apostle Frequency Revelator, his publications, revelational teachings, global seminars, ministry schools, ministry products and Global missions, contact:

Apostle Frequency Revelator

@ Resurrection Embassy

(The Global Church)

Powered by Christ Resurrection Movement (CRM)

(Contact us in South Africa, United Kingdom, USA, Germany, Canada, Australia, India, Holland & Other nations of the world).

As a Global Vision, The Ministry of Apostle Frequency Revelator is present in all the continents of the World. You may contact us from any part of the world so that we can refer you to the Resident Ministry Pastors and Associates in respective nations. Our offices and those of the ministry's publishing company (Global Destiny Publishing House (GDP House), are ready to dispatch any books requested from any part of the world.

Email:
frequency.revelator@gmail.com

Publisher@globaldestinypublishers.com

Cell phone:

+27622436745

+27797921646

Website:
www.globaldestinypublishers.com

Social Media Contacts:

The Author is also accessible on Social media via Facebook, twitter, instagram, YouTube, and other latest forms of social networks, as Apostle Frequency Revelator. For direct communication with the Apostle, you may invite him on Facebook and read his daily posts. You may also watch Apostle Frequency Revelator on the Dead Raising Channel a.k.a Resurrection TV and other Christian Television channels in your area.

Christian products:

You may also purchase DVDs, CDs, MP3s and possibly order all of the 21 anointed books published by Apostle Frequency Revelator, either as hard cover books or e-books. E-books are available on amazon.com, Baines & Nobles, create space, Kalahari.net and other e-book sites. You may also buy them directly from the author@ www.gdphouse.co.za. You may also request a collection of all powerful, revelational teachings by Apostle Frequency Revelator and we will promptly deliver them to you.

Ministry Networks & Partnerships:

If you want to partner with Apostle Frequency Revelator in executing this Global vision, partnership is available through divergent apostolic and prophetic ministry visions and spiritual programmes such as the Global School of Resurrection (GSR), Christ Resurrection Movement (CRM), Resurrection TV (a.k.a The Dead Raising Channel), the Global Apostolic & Prophetic Network (GAP), Global Resurrection Centre (GRC), the Global Healing Centre (GHC), Global School of Miracles, Signs and Wonders (SMSW), School of Kingdom Millionaires (SKM), Global Campus Ministry and other avenues. By partnering with Apostle Frequency Revelator, you are in a way joining hands with God's vision and thus setting yourself up for a life of increase, acceleration and superabundance.

ABOUT THE AUTHOR GLOBAL MISSIONS, PARTNERSHIPS & COLLABORATIONS:

If it happens that you are catapulted into the realm of understanding prophetic dreams and visions following the reading of this book, please share your testimony with Apostle Frequency Revelator at the contacts above, so that you can strengthen other believers' faith in God all around the world. Your testimony will also be included in the next edition of this book.

If you want to invite Apostle Frequency Revelator to your church, city or community to come and spearhead Resurrection Seminars, Conferences, Dead Raising Training Sessions or conduct a Global School of Resurrection (GSR), whether in (Europe, Australia, Canada, USA, South America, Asia or Africa), you are welcome to do so.

If you want to start a Resurrection Centre or establish the Global School of Resurrection (GSR) in your church, city or community under this movement, you are also welcome to do so. We will be more than willing to send Copies of this book to whichever continent you live.

If you want your church or ministry to be part of the Christ Resurrection Movement (CRM) and join the bandwagon of raising the dead all around the world, you are welcome to be part of this Heaven-ordained commission.

If you want more copies of this book so that you can use them in your church for seminars, teachings, conferences, cell groups and global distribution, please don't hesitate to contact Apostle Frequency Revelator so that he can send the copies to whichever continent you are. Upon completion of this book, you may also visit www.amazon.com and under the "Book Review Section," write a brief review, commenting on how this book has impacted your life. This is meant to encourage readership by other believers all around the world.

If you want to donate or give freely to advance this global vision, you may also do so via our ministry website (www.globaldestinypublishers.com) or contact us at the details provided above. If you need a spiritual covering, impartation or mentorship for your Church or ministry as led by the Holy Spirit, you are welcome to contact us and join the league of dead-raising pastors that we are already mentoring in all continents of the world.

If you have a burning message that you would like to share with the whole world and you would want Apostle Frequency Revelator to help you turn your divine ideas and revelations into script and publish your first book, don't hesitate to contact us and submit a draft of your manuscript at the Global Destiny Publishing House (www.globaldestinypublishers.com). We will thoroughly polish your script and turn it into an amazing book filled with Throne Room revelations that will impact millions across the globe, glory to Jesus!

The Lord Jesus Christ is coming back soon!

Made in the USA
Middletown, DE
13 July 2021